CONQUEST OF VIOLENCE

Conquest of Violence
The Gandhian
Philosophy of Conflict

BY JOAN V. BONDURANT

REVISED EDITION

UNIVERSITY OF CALIFORNIA PRESS

BERKELEY, LOS ANGELES, LONDON

1971

AUTHOR'S PREFACE
TO THE REVISED EDITION

———

The technique to which Gandhi gave the name "satyagraha" is at once a mode of action and a method of enquiry. It goes well beyond procedure, or tactic, to define the process for involvement of self and engagement with others in an endeavor essentially creative and necessarily constructive. "Satyagraha is not predominantly civil disobedience, but a quiet and irresistible pursuit of truth," said Gandhi. "On the rarest occasions it becomes civil disobedience. But conscious and willing obedience must . . . precede it."[1]

In the years since this book first appeared, the civil rights movement in the United States has made current the phrases "non-violence" and "civil disobedience," and has revived interest in the methods of Gandhi. It is rarely understood that Gandhi's technique of satyagraha cannot be equated with civil disobedience, and that it goes well beyond the pressure tactics familiar in forms of demonstration and strike.

My purpose in writing this book has been threefold: to define the social and political technique of satyagraha; to formulate its dialectical nature; and to lay the foundation for the fuller development of a philosophy of conflict.

That the suffering and sacrifice of recent years in civil rights movements around the world have made no advance towards a philosophy of conflict, has its own significance. Why, indeed, have civil rights movements given rise to so little reflection upon the nature of the politics of non-violence? Perhaps we are bound by a paralysis born of intensive preoccupation with the pressing issues of the day. We become bruised by the chain of action-reaction and seared by the heat of struggle, both on the line of action and in the debate over policy. We are caught up in a conflict so fundamental that its symptoms are expressed

[1] Quoted from *Young India* in *Teachings of Mahatma Gandhi*, Jag Parvesh Chander, ed. (Lahore: Indian Printing Works, 1945), pp. 498-499.

in the context of alienation when, at the same time, its objectives are held as inalienable rights. It is clear that to some the tactics of non-violence have offered a gratifying mode of action, and that these same tactics raise in the minds of others serious questions about the wisdom of disobedience to law and the implications of extraconstitutional methods.

There was a similar preoccupation with the pressures of the times during the nationalist movement in India, when Gandhi persisted in fashioning the instruments for struggle. But in the 1920's and 30's there had been but little precedent for the new methods, and less time for reflection and analysis of historical event. Today we are presented with perspective. We can analyze and evaluate and discover what, indeed, did happen in India. And what happened — or, more importantly, how it happened — is vastly more complex than is usually supposed. We need to know with precision how the techniques used by an unarmed people functioned, not only to promote their independence, but also to change fundamental social values.

Gandhi was not a philosopher; he was essentially a man of action. But as a man of action, he was acutely aware that reflection was essential not only to the strategic decision as precursor to act, but also to the more subjective understanding of what he, his followers, and his opponents were, and what they could become. When Gandhi sought a word-symbol to distinguish his newly-developing technique from that of passive resistance, he took the word "sadagraha" (firmness in a good cause) and changed it to "satyagraha." "Satya" is derived from the Sanskrit word *sat*, "being," and its meaning is both truth and essence. I have argued (especially in Chapters V and VI) that the key to an understanding of Gandhi's political thought is the technique of satyagraha.

What does it mean to be a satyagrahi? Gandhi repeatedly addressed himself to this question. He not only thought, spoke, and wrote about the continuing exploration of truth, but he fashioned a method of conflict in the exercise of which a man could come to know what he is and what it means to evolve.

In satyagraha, dogma gives way to an open exploration of context. The objective is not to assert propositions, but to create possibilities. In opening up new choices and in confronting an opponent with the demand that he make a choice, the satyagrahi involves himself in acts of "ethical existence." [2] The process forces a continuing examination of one's own motives, an examination undertaken within the context of relationships as they are changed towards a new, restructured, and reintegrated pattern.

Satyagraha goes well beyond the pressure tactics of strike, sit-in, fasting, and other limited efforts characteristic of passive resistance. An analysis of Gandhi's techniques as they operated on the field of action, together with a probing of his reflections, can lead us to fruitful formulations essential for communication. The prospects of contemporary movements can better be evaluated once the creative nature of the Gandhian technique is understood and the complexities of strategy and tactics which distinguish it are explored.

There is a constellation of questions to be asked of movements which profess the use of means ethically superior to violence. These are questions about objectives, procedures, and styles of action. Does the movement seek a genuine solution? When questions of choice are forced upon an opponent, is the stress thereby generated fully recognized? Is the effort one of support and reassurance to the opponent whose change of habit and behavior is so much desired? To what degree has the encounter established (or suppressed) communication? Has the method embraced an adequate process of enquiry? In what way is the force generated through non-violent action directed into creative channels — creative, that is, for all sides and for the total situation?

Questions such as these must be raised in the interest of developing a philosophy of conflict adequate to our times. It is not enough to mouth slogans based upon obscurantist phrases

[2] "Ethical existence" is a familiar concept in existential philosophy. It is used here to suggest the act of becoming, experienced on an ethical plane.

such as "soul-force," or even brotherhood and love. Nor should the jejune contest over who can be the most militant be allowed to derail the individual whose involvement in the process of creative conflict is one dedicated both to a constructive outcome and to a personal realization. Civil disobedience without creative action may, indeed, end in alienation.

Tactics recently put forward as Gandhian may often better be described by the Indian word "duragraha." This is a method characterized by prejudgement and rooted in symbolic violence. The words duragraha and satyagraha are compounds sharing the Sanskrit noun *agraha*, "firm grasping." The prefix *dur* (used in compound for *dus*) denotes "difficult," and one meaning of duragraha is "bias." In the refinement of language for describing techniques of social action, duragraha serves to distinguish those techniques in which the use of harassment obscures or precludes supportive acts aimed at winning over the opponent.[3]

Forms of passive resistance are usually forms of duragraha. They can be contrasted with satyagraha through a series of questions such as those posed above. Duragraha, like satyagraha, deals in pressure. Pressure may be understood to be the action of a force against some opposing force. This mechanical meaning of the term describes only the initial action of satyagraha — a small part in a complex system of dynamics. One who uses satyagraha develops an interacting force with his opponent, and this produces new movement which may change the direction or even the content of the force. The satyagrahi engages his opponent in a manner designed to transform the complexity of relationships so that a new pattern emerges. The subtleties of response from the opponent are channeled back into the satyagrahi's movement and these responding pressures are al-

[3] See pp. 41-45 below for a brief description of how duragraha differs from satyagraha. A fuller treatment comparing these two approaches to conflict is offered in my paper, "Satyagraha vs. Duragraha: The Limits of Symbolic Violence," in: *Gandhi: His Relevance for Our Time*, ed. G. Ramachandran and T. K. Mahadevan (Bombay: Bharatiya Vidya Bhavan, 1964), pp. 67-81.

lowed the maximum opportunity to influence subsequent acts and even to modify the content of the initial claims and objectives. This process has been described more fully in Chapter VI, where I have formulated what I call the Gandhian dialectic.

Like violence itself, acts of symbolic violence, or duragraha, may solve some problems and resolve certain conflicts. But in instances where fundamental change is expected, duragraha is an ineffective method. Those who use it may find themselves the target of reaction and their circumstance reduced to that of rigid opposition. This result can be expected when demands are pressed forward with arrogance or in a spirit of self-righteousness.

There is a further danger in the persistent use of forms of duragraha, and especially of civil disobedience. The experience with democratic institutions in the West has been both extensive and substantial. But repeated challenges thrust forward through direct action may weaken both respect for law and confidence in democratic procedures. The endurance of democratic institutions could be overestimated by those who have never experienced the chaos which issues from large-scale breakdown of law. On the other hand, there is some risk that those who have not experienced the tyranny of authority unmodified by democratic processes may undervalue hard-won devices for effecting change through democratic process. Democracy requires the nurture of each successive generation if it is to be sustained. In those instances where democratic procedures have been damaged through default or design, and where the legal machinery has been turned towards a travesty of justice, civil disobedience may be called into play. The civil rights movement in the United States has developed within just such a context. But if civil disobedience is carried out in the style of duragraha, and not within the framework of satyagraha, it may well lead to widespread indifference to legality and lend itself to those who would use illegal tactics to undermine faith in democratic processes.

To the philosophical anarchist, for whom all forms of government appear to be engines of oppression, satyagraha suggests a quite specific remedy. Was Gandhi himself a philosophical anarchist? This question is examined in Chapter V. An exploration of the dynamic principles at work in satyagraha illuminates the anarchistic ideal and speaks directly to the problem of method.

In the final chapter of this book I have pointed to a central weakness in liberal democratic thought: the failure to provide techniques of action for those critical occasions when the machinery of democratic government no longer functions to resolve large-scale, overt conflict. The argument begins by exploring a basic problem: the relationship between ends and means. Civil disobedience contributes but little to the solution of this problem. In part, this is one result of a protest technique which makes few, albeit rigorous, demands. Its practitioners may become enamored of their means to a degree destructive of sound solutions. Civil disobedience holds small promise unless it is conducted within an approach which gives the ends-means continuum central consideration. I have argued that the effort must be made to design more sophisticated, dynamic, and creative techniques. A careful analysis of the dynamics of satyagraha points the direction in which liberal democratic thought could be advanced.

Is it possible, then, that other alternatives to violence can be fruitfully explored for use in large-scale conflict? Perhaps not — so long as we allow ourselves to be disabled through preoccupation with passive resistance in its several forms of symbolic violence. The limitations of duragraha are so evident in this broader context that those who profess and practice forms of passive resistance consider its use only in instances when civil populations have been overrun by a conqueror. Short of conquest, they offer no more (and no less) than the programs put forward by the several schools of pacifism. However militant they may have become in domestic struggles, they are pacifist in their attitudes towards international conflict. Movements characterized by duragraha become targets for ideologues whose roots can be nourished both from social disruption and from pacifist efforts which would dismantle the apparatus for overt international struggle before alternative methods have been devised. "How fatal it would be, " wrote Karl Jaspers, "for men to yield in good faith, to dispense with force, because they believe in non-violence!"[4] As a single-minded faith and sole commitment, non-violence may serve only to create the vacuum through which those who hold the highest humanistic values can be drawn into tyranny or destruction. If violence is to be replaced with a constructive technique, ideal views of mankind must give way to efforts for devising processes reflecting the psychological needs common to everyman. And in this endeavor, it is also necessary to identify and to limit the use of symbolic violence.

Questions about method in the conduct of conflict have been narrowly conceived, and this may well be one of the results of techniques limited to duress and harassment, and failing in just those practices which distinguish satyagraha. The Gandhian contribution, more directly than any other effort in history, speaks to one of the most fundamental questions of mankind: how can conflict be conducted constructively; how can man engage in conflict without the danger of annihilation?

The years which have passed since this book first appeared have not fulfilled my hope that the experiments which Gandhi began would be extended in a manner which could lead to the development of more sophisticated techniques for the conduct of large-scale conflict. The opportunities are legion, but the efforts have been few in number and weak of conception. The nuclear age has brought its own disabling paralysis, and one of its results is that policy considerations have dominated both practical endeavors and intellectual pursuits.

Gandhi presented us with a remarkable set of experiments, pregnant with meaning for the future. But we cannot expect that Gandhi has given us all the answers. The challenge still

[4] *The Future of Mankind,* trans. E. B. Ashton (Chicago: University of Chicago Press, 1961), p. 39.

remains. How can we use the conflicts of our day to devise the instruments for conducting the struggles of tomorrow? Our present was Gandhi's future. Yet we have selected the less sophisticated tactics of non-violent pressure, oftentimes unaware of our failure to understand the complex techniques developed in the India of earlier decades. It is not, of course, enough to recover the past, or even to cope with the present. For large-scale conflict in the second half of the twentieth century takes on dimensions which threaten annihilation. The alternatives for engaging in conflict constructively can surely be devised. This is the promise which a study of Gandhian satyagraha brings into focus. To reflect upon our contemporary involvement with conflict and to pursue this reflection within the framework of comparison and contrast with the Gandhian experiments is to lay the groundwork. In our time of troubles — well tempered by unprecedented possibility — a philosophy of conflict awaits further delineation. Meanwhile, the immediate and emergent task is to fashion and refine the techniques whereby conflict can be conducted towards creative ends.

JOAN V. BONDURANT

Berkeley, California
February 1965

AUTHOR'S PREFACE

Point not the goal until you plot the course
For ends and means to man are tangled so
That different means quite different aims enforce
*Conceive the means as end in embryo.**

IN times such as ours when conflict is the order of the day and
the potential of technology offers more to fear than to hope,
social and political theory face their gravest challenge. Theoretical political systems have grown increasingly suspect and
intellectual formulations tend less to challenge than repel.
But there is rapidly developing a demand hitherto neglected
by social and political theory. This is the demand for solutions to the problem of conflict—not for theoretical systems of
end-structure aimed at ultimately eliminating conflict, but for
ways of conducting conflict when it arises: ways which are
constructive and not destructive. Such a demand must be met
by a theory of process and of means, and not of further concern for structure, for pattern, and for ends. Basic to such a
theory is a philosophy of action.

In this book I have tried to formulate an approach to a
philosophy of action suggested by the social and political
experiments conducted in our time in India. I have not pre-
sumed to write on Gandhi the man, or his works. Nor have I

* This quatrain was suggested by Arthur Koestler's translation of a
selection from Ferdinand Lassalle's *Franz von Sickingen* in Koestler's
Darkness at Noon (New York: Macmillan, 1941), p. 241. The passage
in the original reads:

> *Das Ziel nicht zeige, zeige auch den Weg*
> *Denn so verwachsen ist hienieden Weg und Ziel,*
> *Dass eines sich stets ändert mit dem andern,*
> *Und andrer Weg auch andres Ziel erzeugt.*

Ferdinand Lassalle, *Franz von Sickingen* (Berlin: Weltgeist-Bücher,
n.d.), p. 89.

written an essay strictly on Gandhian political philosophy. I have tried only to attack a problem inadequately explored in political theory by abstracting from the Gandhian experiments a theoretical key to the problem of social and political conflict. I have further suggested that social and political theory can rise to the challenge of our times only if it grapples with the means whereby end-structures may survive inevitable conflict.

It would not be proper to claim that what I present here is *Gandhi's* philosophy of action, for it is no more than one interpretation of what may be called a *Gandhian* system. My own formulation is suggestive and not definitive. At most, it points the way in which an adequate treatment of the ends-means problem might be undertaken.

Perhaps I should also make explicit what is implied in my interpretation: it is not necessary to subscribe either to the asceticism so characteristic of Gandhi nor to his religious notions in order to understand and to value the central contribution of his technique of non-violent action. The name Gandhi and the word "Gandhism" frequently touch off startling emotional responses. The reservoir of reverence for Gandhi in India is readily understandable. In the West, the response is often of a different order. For the non-Indian is likely either to afford Gandhi the respect due a saint, and thereby to dismiss his significance in the mundane realm of practical politics; or, worried by what appears to him to be a diffuse spirituality, to impute to Gandhi obscurantism and thereby to deny the pertinence of his contribution. Again, fearing that Gandhian notions of political economy necessarily issue in primitive agrarianism, the Westerner tends summarily to reject Gandhi's import as unmeaningful in the current circumstance. Such responses tend to obscure developments which continue to emerge from the Gandhian experience, and to obstruct an understanding of Gandhi's total impact. Even more important, these attitudes serve as a barrier to further exploration of the potentialities of the technique which Gandhi introduced.

In the summer of 1953, I had the rare good fortune to discuss with Jawaharlal Nehru some of the implications of Gandhian *satyagraha*. He spoke with me, not as the Prime Minister of a great State, but as one who had "grown up in this strange complex of ideas and action which Gandhi let loose in India." He went on to express to me the difficulties which Indians have in viewing objectively the Gandhian experiments—Indians have been too close to the greatness of the man to view his works dispassionately. The Westerner who has the temerity to undertake the task of interpreting Gandhian thought can perhaps best do so by searching for its meaning in terms familiar to the West. At least, so it has seemed to this Westerner whose basic predispositions are rationalist and humanist and who shares with some of Gandhi's severest critics an abiding suspicion of religious systems and of obscurantist approaches. It is the unsystematized and often inconsistent jungle of Gandhi's writings that makes it difficult but tempting to others to formulate a "Gandhian Philosophy." With the history of the movements in which Gandhi was involved as evidence from the field of action, it is possible to thread one's way through these extraordinary scraps of writing in search of theme and thesis. In the course of this search one necessarily interprets and abstracts. I hope that in abstracting and interpreting, and finally in formulating one aspect of a philosophy of action, I have not done violence to Gandhi's thought. Inasmuch as Gandhi himself did not formulate his philosophy, the temptation for others to do so lies ever at hand.

The problem of human conflict is perhaps the most fundamental problem of all time. In this age when the physical sciences have outstripped the more slowly advancing social sciences, it is one of undeniable urgency, and one which already attracts social scientists in many disciplines. This essay on satyagraha and political thought is an effort to focus attention on yet another direction in which solutions might be sought. It is hoped that the following pages will raise many questions and suggest certain challenges to students of psychology and sociology and to those working in the intensive areas where two or more such fields of inquiry impinge— such, for example, as communications and propaganda, and politics and anthropology. Indeed, as I have pursued the implications of the Gandhian experiments for political philosophy, suggestions for exploration in many other areas have pressed in upon the mind with great insistence. The further delineation of the Gandhian technique and its adaptation to different levels of conflict in differing cultural settings; the design of a procedure making full use of the latest findings in sociology and psychology; the implication of aspects of satyagraha for a sociology of law; the further sophistication of satyagraha techniques by bringing to bear upon them what can be learned from developing psychoanalytic method—these, and many other areas await exploration by those who would know more of the potential suggested by the Gandhian experience and its significance for formulating an adequate theory for the constructive conduct of conflict.

Those who would explore further may have an interest in the words penned by Jawaharlal Nehru at a time when, truly, he was pressed by the searching, weighty problems which beset the statesman. As he wrote to me a few days after our brief discussion, he had stolen the moments to set down these thoughts because he wished that people might be brought to understand Gandhi's ideas about satyagraha. The following paragraphs were addressed to my original manuscript, "Gandhian Satyagraha and Political Theory: an Interpretation." "To many of us," he wrote, "it is not a new field . . ."

We were hardly in a position to exercise a dispassionate judgment about them, for we ourselves became integral parts of these processes which changed us as individuals and changed the history of India. And yet, in some ways

we are entitled to a hearing and our views may have some
value, though they might not be expressed in the language
of the scholar. We were not only intellectually in touch with
these dynamic ideas but were emotionally aware of many
things, which cannot easily be analysed or put down on
paper. It is nearly three and a half decades now that I first
came in contact with his strange personality and his stranger
ideas. The effect was almost instantaneous, as if an electric
shock went through the system. And yet, the shock was a
soothing and, at the same time, an enlivening one. The
mind struggled with these new ideas often put out without
much method or logic. But the whole system reacted to
them and grew under their impress.

Was it the personality of Gandhi that did this or the force
of the ideas that he represented and that he translated into
action? Was it the rare spectacle of a man whose thought
and word and act were so closely co-related as to form one
integrated whole?

The man has gone, though he lives vividly in the memory
of those who knew him, and innumerable legends have grown
up about him. The story of his deeds has become a part of
the history of India. Many people swear by his name and
exploit it for base purposes. The noble doctrine of Satyagraha is debased and used for wrong ends.

I suppose all this is inevitable. The truth or reality in the
idea that he represented will no doubt survive and, I am
sure, influence men's minds more and more.

In this age of uttermost violence, it is strange to think of
the man who talked always of non-violence. In this age of
consuming fear, this absolutely fearless individual stands
out. He demonstrated to us that there can be a strength far
greater than that of armaments and that a struggle can be
fought, and indeed should be fought, without bitterness
and hatred.

The questions which Jawaharlal Nehru has raised demand

answers from statesman and scholar alike. As the Prime Minister reflected upon Gandhian experiments in which he himself had played so great a part, he saw in them a "new dynamic that Gandhi brought into the political and social field."

That dynamic largely justified itself in India, in spite of the weaknesses and failings of many who call themselves his followers. I do not pretend to understand fully the significance of that technique of action, in which I myself took part. But I feel more and more convinced that it offers us some key to understanding and to the proper resolution of conflict. We see conflict all round us in the world. That is perhaps not surprising. But what is surprising is that the methods adopted to end that conflict have almost always failed miserably and produced greater conflict and more difficult problems. In spite of this patent fact, we pursue the old methods blindly and do not even learn from our own experiences.

Gandhi was never tired of talking about means and ends and of laying stress on the importance of the means. That is the essential difference, I think, between his approach and the normal approach which thinks in terms of ends only, and because means are forgotten, the ends aimed at escape one. It is not realised that the ends must inevitably come out of the means and are governed by those means.

Conflicts are, therefore, seldom resolved. The wrong methods pursued in dealing with them lead to further conflict. The mistaken belief still persists that violence can end a conflict or that war can bring salvation to the world.

Gandhi pointed another way and, what is more, lived it and showed achievement. That surely should at least make us try to understand what this new way was and how far it is possible for us to shape our thoughts and actions in accordance with it.

It is my endeavor in the pages which follow to shed some light upon "this new way."

My interest in the Gandhian impact was first aroused during my residence in India in 1944-1946. Observations made concerning developments in the post-independence period are based both upon my study in India during 1947-1948 and 1952-1953, and upon continuing research in the course of my work as Research Political Scientist with the Indian Press Digests Project (Institute of International Studies), University of California. A fellowship from the Southwestern Region of Soroptimist Clubs supported the writing of the original manuscript. The research conducted in India during 1952-1953 was made possible through a fellowship from the Social Science Research Council.

I am indebted to George Allen & Unwin, Ltd. for permission to quote passages from Clarence Marsh Case, *Non-Violent Coercion: A Study in Methods of Social Pressure*, Halidé Edib, *Inside India*, and S. Radhakrishnan, *Indian Philosophy*, Vol. I; and to Constable and Company Limited for passages from Naomi Mitchison, *The Moral Basis of Politics*. A passage from Jawaharlal Nehru, *The Discovery of India* has been reprinted by permission of The John Day Company. The Macmillan Company has granted permission for the use of material from C. F. Andrews, *Mahatma Gandhi's Ideas*, copyright, 1930; and the *New York Times* has kindly permitted the use of passages from an article by Morris Llewellyn Cooke, "The Quaker Way Wins New Adherents," the New York Times Magazine, June 17, 1951. I am also grateful to the Navajivan Trust for having granted permission to quote passages from Mahadev Desai, *The Gospel of Selfless Action or the Gita According to Gandhi*; Pyarelal, *A Pilgrimage of Peace*; and from the following works by M. K. Gandhi: *An Autobiography or The Story of My Experiments with Truth*, *From Yeravda Mandir: Ashram Observances*, *Non-Violence in Peace and War*. Acknowledgment is made to Oxford University Press, Inc. for passages from Max Weber, *The Theory of Social and Economic Organization*, translated by A. M. Henderson &

Talcott Parsons, edited with an introduction by Talcott Parsons, copyright 1947 by Oxford University Press, New York, Inc., reprinted by permission.

Many friends and colleagues played a part in forwarding the progress of this study and my debt to them is great. I would first mention the many Indian friends who supplied both data and evaluation of the Gandhian movements in India, among them, Professor Nirmal Kumar Bose, The Honorable R. R. Diwakar, Sri R. R. Keithahn, Sri Pyarelal. To Dr. Chandra Uttam Singh belongs the credit for my initial interest in satyagraha. The information, critical comment, and consistent support lent to the work in its early stages by Dr. Satya Prakash Agarwal and Miss Mary L. Allison proved indispensable. Dr. Frances W. Herring read the manuscript at a later stage and made valuable suggestions.

I owe a very special debt of gratitude to my friend and colleague, Dr. Margaret W. Fisher, from whose methods and high standards of scholarship I have learned so much, and upon whose knowledge I have so often drawn. Dr. Fisher's critical reading of the manuscript has allowed me to strengthen and improve the study in many of its aspects. My association with the Indian Press Digests Project together with the research facilities and staff of the Project have enabled me to revise my initial work and to substantiate some of the factual data. I am also indebted to Mrs. Corinne Bennett whose help in preparing the manuscript for the publishers has been invaluable. To these and to many other friends and colleagues I express my keen appreciation—for without them the work would never have been completed if, indeed, it could have been conceived. Sole responsibility for soundness of fact and interpretation rests, of course, with me.

Joan V. Bondurant
Berkeley, California

July 1957

CONTENTS

CONTENTS

CONTENTS

CONQUEST OF VIOLENCE

I

INTRODUCTION

In the West civil disobedience is a familiar, if unpopular, concept. The post-war years in America have witnessed a revival of the debate over the source and meaning of political obligation. The death of Socrates, the dilemma of Antigone, the action of Thoreau—these highlights in the course of man's reflection upon the problem of obligation dignify arguments concerning the conscientious objector's position in the contemporary circumstance, or the refusal of a witness to testify before an American Congressional investigating committee.[1] Civil disobedience has usually been understood to be substantially an individual consideration: it has meant resistance or refusal to obey a given law, usually on grounds that such law offends the individual's conscience or is repugnant to a "higher law" towards which the individual owes prior allegiance. The problem has been one of competing, conflicting moral values, and the solution has appeared to lie—necessarily, but also uneasily—with the individual.

In India, under the leadership of Mohandas K. Gandhi, experiments (as Gandhi called them) which had first been undertaken in South Africa were extended beyond the individual protest. Later experiments conducted during the struggle for Indian independence carried mass action beyond the confining limits of civil disobedience. Out of these emerged a new technique which Gandhi called *satyagraha*. Satyagraha embraced the method and the essential philosophy of civil disobedience, but through its application and refinement it became a technique for social and political change which transcended the substantial limitations of the earlier concept. Satyagraha became something more than a method of resistance to particular legal norms; it became an instrument of

3

struggle for positive objectives and for fundamental change—
a technique more widely used than understood and one which
yet called for testing in the field of social and political action.
When, in 1948, Mahatma Gandhi died by an assassin's bullet,
the "experiments in truth," which he had begun, remained far
from complete.

The most potent legacy Gandhi left to India was the technique of satyagraha. There was in this instrument of action,
power to effect change. "Satyagraha" had become the cry of
all those who felt aggrieved, and popular agitations, however
organized and whatever their objective, were widely described as "satyagraha movements." Informed, responsible, and
concerned Indians today reflect upon the use and meaning of
"satyagraha" with misgivings, yet with hope; with fond memo-
ries, and yet with anxiety for the future. What then, are the
essential characteristics of satyagraha? Is it, as Nehru says, a
tool which when "debased" may be "used for wrong ends"?

The ambivalence which marks the attitude of many former
satyagrahis (those who employ or "offer" satyagraha) is part
of a general and greater confusion which settled in upon inter-
preters of satyagraha once Gandhi was no more leading the
great experiment. To no small extent this confusion follows
upon the failure either to delineate the method in terms of
practical rules of procedure or to formulate the philosophy of
action which informs and conditions the technique. "Satyagraha," the name, has been seized upon to describe many
forms of opposition to government, and to explain almost any
direct social or political action short of organized violence.
Throughout India local "satyagrahas" have been reported almost daily. Partisans readily turn major public issues into
satyagraha objectives; threat and counter-threat are couched
in terms of resort to satyagraha. Those who claim these "satyagrahas" and those who criticize alike appear to accept them
as "satyagraha."

Is, then, satyagraha to be equated with demonstration, with
shouting of slogans, with fasting, with strike and with boycott?

4

Is satyagraha no more than the generic term for all organized efforts in opposition which do not include overt violence? If this were so, the difference between Gandhian satyagraha and mass demonstration for a given political objective would be reduced perhaps to the factor of Gandhi himself. Such an analysis cannot, however, satisfy anyone who has troubled to examine the procedures, and the progress, the assumptions and the behavior involved in satyagraha movements of the Gandhi genre. There are characteristics which clearly mark out one type of action as different from others. Properties peculiar to satyagraha can be described, and it is therefore possible to establish which movements are and which are not to be properly classified as satyagraha. To make this distinction is valuable for those who would interpret the current processes of political and social change in India; and for those who would pursue Gandhi's "experiments with truth" or extend them to other fields of action, to distinguish is essential.

As one threads his way through the Gandhian experiments questions of another sort pose themselves. These questions center upon the role played by Indian tradition, and more specifically, by Hindu tradition. When the evidence is sifted one is struck by the conclusion that the significant contribution of Gandhi lay not in any revival of traditional forms or method, but in a transformation of traditional concepts in such a way that only the symbols remained familiar—for the symbols were made by Gandhi to stand for a quite different set of values.

Gandhi's own use of traditional terms to describe new approaches tends, to be sure, to obscure the essential elements in satyagraha. The problem here—for Indian and Westerner alike—is to probe beyond the traditional garb in which explanations of satyagraha are clothed. Had this technique of action been developed in another cultural matrix, by another leader, it might well have been couched in terms immediately familiar to the rationalist and the humanist. But in the absence of an explicit formulation of satyagraha, there developed an easy and imprecise identification of terms, a habit which persists today. For not only is satyagraha inaccurately equated with non-violence and with passive resistance, but satyagraha is also loosely identified with such further Gandhian concepts as *sarvodaya*.

To clarify the confusion which arises from this faulty identification of Gandhian concepts, it may be helpful to note, in passing, that there are at least three categories into which Gandhian notions may be classed: they are, simply stated, Gandhian objectives, Gandhian principles, and Gandhian means. The overall objectives for Gandhi were these two: swaraj, which, in its broadest political sense, meant independence, and sarvodaya (literally, "uplift of all") which loosely described the ideal society towards which he worked. Following the achievement of political independence, sarvodaya became the primary Gandhian objective, and it is towards this ideal that leading contemporary Gandhian figures of India are still working.[2] Prominent among Gandhian *principles* are non-violence, adherence to truth, and dignity of labor.

Finally, Gandhian *means* include not only satyagraha, which remains the premier technique thus far developed, but also Bhoodan (literally, "land-gift"), a movement for voluntary sacrifice of land inaugurated in 1951 by Vinoba Bhave, as well as Nai Talim, the system of basic education which centers all instruction around a craft and is ideally self-supporting.

Other efforts or objectives given the name Gandhian may be considered ancillary to those here noted. We may call them Gandhian *policies*. Such, for instance, are the subsidiary objectives of prohibition and removal of untouchability, and the program for social and political decentralization. These may be understood as characteristics of sarvodaya, the ideal society. It is such subsidiary objectives as these which make it quite correct to characterize certain of the Directive Principles of State Policy laid down in the Constitution of India as

Gandhi-influenced. In the same way Panchayat Raj legislation, which aims at revitalizing self-government in the villages, and the Bhoodan Yajna legislation, which facilitates the collection and distribution of land, may be said to be influences of Gandhi on contemporary legislation.

We are here concerned with that part of the Gandhian impact which centers upon satyagraha, the premier Gandhian means. An analysis of the function of the concept of satyagraha within and upon Gandhian political thought indicates that satyagraha provides the key to an understanding of Gandhi's political philosophy. One cannot, of course, turn to the writings of Gandhi for a definitive statement in political theory. Gandhi was a political actionist and a practical philosopher; he was not a theorist. His writings abound with inconsistencies—one result of his persistent habit of thinking in public. Whatever philosophical formulations he made were inspired by and directed towards the solving of immediate problems. The unsophisticated explanations which Gandhi offered for his methods, his objectives, his policy, and creed were part of a program of action. They should not be interpreted in terms either of theory or of practical master-planning.

The vast body of Gandhi's writing consists of opinions in the form of short sermons to those who sought his advice, or concise statements in reply to critics. The problems with which he dealt range from experiments in dietary reform to high policy considerations. He wrote only four works of book length.[3] Other books ascribed to Gandhi are collections of articles, pamphlets and speeches organized by subject or by period.[4] One must turn to files of the weekly publications[5] and to collections of his correspondence to follow the evolution in Gandhi's thinking.

From the wealth of material offered in Gandhi's editorials and popular periodical articles one can extract a Gandhian philosophy. In so doing it is possible to emerge with a system of ethics, a way-of-life, a metaphysical formula, or a religion complete with ritual and hagiology. But it is only after a rigorous consideration of the historical realities of specific satyagraha campaigns, together with an analysis of the relationship of Gandhi's teachings to those campaigns, that a valid theory based upon the Gandhian experiment can be formulated.

Satyagraha is a word coined during the movement of Indian resistance in South Africa to the Asiatic Law Amendment Ordinance introduced into the Transvaal Legislative Council in 1906. Gandhi explains that he first called the movement "passive resistance," but as the struggle continued he became aware that "some new principle had come into being." He then announced through the pages of his newspaper, *Indian Opinion*, that a prize would be given for the best name invented to designate the movement. One competitor suggested the word "sadagraha," meaning "firmness in a good cause."

> I liked the word, but it did not fully represent the whole idea I wished it to connote. I therefore corrected it to "Satyagraha." Truth (Satya) implies love and firmness (Agraha) engenders and therefore serves as a synonym for force. I thus began to call the Indian movement "Satyagraha," that is to say, the Force which is born of Truth and Love or non-violence, and gave up the use of the phrase "passive resistance" . . .[6]

From the first use of the word "satyagraha" in South Africa to Gandhi's last days in New Delhi[7] Gandhi not only wrote elucidations of the term, but strove to understand and to explain its implications as the technique evolved. The number of satyagraha efforts undertaken in India during Gandhi's lifetime is impossible to determine. It is well within a conservative estimate to suggest that during the period from 1917 which marks the first large-scale satyagraha led by Gandhi in India (that of the peasants in the indigo fields of Champaran) to the time of Gandhi's death in January 1948, there were hundreds of group satyagraha movements.

In examining satyagraha as it has been applied in historical situations on the Indian scene I shall have occasion to use such words as *force, violence, injury*. A note on definitions may help to clarify the chapters which follow.

Force I take to mean the exercise of physical or intangible power or influence to effect change. *Violence* is the willful application of force in such a way that it is intentionally injurious to the person or group against whom it is applied. *Injury* is understood to include psychological as well as physical harm.[8] *Non-violence* when used in connection with satyagraha means the exercise of power or influence to effect change without injury to the opponent.

In considering the use of non-violent in contradistinction to violent force, the question of coercion arises. *Coercion* has been defined[9] as "the use of either physical or intangible force to compel action contrary to the will or reasoned judgment of the individual or group subjected to such force." Despite the protestations of a few followers of Gandhi that satyagraha is always persuasive and never coercive[10] the method does contain a positive element of coercion. Non-cooperation, boycott, strike—all of these tools which may be used in satyagraha involve an element of compulsion which may effect a change on the part of an opponent which initially was contrary to his will—and he may suffer from the indirect results of these actions. But there remains a significant difference between non-violent and violent coercion.

The difference between violent coercion in which deliberate injury is inflicted upon the opponent and non-violent coercion in which injury indirectly results is a difference of such great degree that it is almost a difference of kind. Certainly this tends to be true in cases of extended and intensive use of violence in the one case and of non-violent coercion in the other. Withholding of services or profits may cause a very real discomfiture to the opponent, and he may interpret this as serious injury—but compared with physical destruction and deliberate undermining of morale, possibly coupled with extreme distortion of truth (as in the use of certain types of psychological warfare), the contrast is significant. Beyond this difference of degree, there are yet other distinguishing elements. In the case of non-violent coercion there is a willingness on the part of the one who would coerce to submit himself to suffering; in contrast, one who uses violence to coerce intentionally causes suffering to his opponent. In one of the few scholarly works published on the problem of non-violent resistance, Clarence Marsh Case contrasts violent and non-violent coercion in these words:

> True non-violent coercion is, and ought to be, a two-edged sword. In other words, it causes, and it is well that it should cause, inconvenience and suffering to those who wield it, as well as to those against whom it is invoked. In this it is exactly contrary to violent methods; for a principal reason accounting for the appalling growth of terrorism in modern times, is the unfortunate fact that the development of fire-arms and high explosives carries no automatic check and penalty for all who use them. As for the methods of non-violent coercion, particularly the strike and the boycott, the public usually stands more or less in position to determine which way the blow shall fall, that is, which party to the controversy shall suffer the greater loss. It is well that this should be so, for it is not in the interest of the general good that any group of men should exert irresponsible power . . . we hold that there is a most vital, salutary, and socially necessary connection between the open, truthful, self-denying spirit of passive resistance and the *constructive* use of non-violent coercion in any of its forms. . . .[11]

The term coercion may carry an odious connotation for those who tend to think in terms of the application of physical force as its primary characterization. But, precisely defined, coercion is the application of either physical or moral force to induce another to do something against his will.[12] Now it may be argued that an appeal to the conscience of an opponent by self-suffering which results in a change of the opponent's behavior is injurious to the extent it means the loss of face or the mental discomfiture of the opponent. Injury of this type, and to this extent, is willingly admitted in the later stages of satyagraha, although it is never initially intended and efforts are made to mitigate it.

Satyagraha allows for several stages of winning over an opponent. The first stage is characterized by persuasion through reason. The subsequent stages enter the realm of persuasion through suffering wherein the satyagrahi attempts to dramatize the issues at stake and to get through to the opponent's unprejudiced judgment so that he may willingly come again onto a level where he may be persuaded through rational argument. Finally, if persuasion by reason or by suffering does not succeed, the satyagrahi may resort to nonviolent coercion characterized by such tools as non-cooperation or civil disobedience. Professor Case denies a contradiction in the term non-violent coercion, and he comments, at the outset of his essay, that the combination of *non-violent* and *coercion* "is not the outcome of a preconceived notion, but represents a working arrangement, to which the writer came naturally during the course of a prolonged effort to find separately the working efficiency of these two principles of human conduct, neither of which was found to function rightly alone."[13] Throughout Gandhi's experiments with satyagraha there appears to be an element of coercion, coercion whose sting is drawn by its non-violent qualification.

By one interpretation it is possible to argue that satyagraha is the heart of every Gandhian pronouncement, that satyagraha is the reagent of every concept with which Gandhi identified himself. For *satya*, derived from the Sanskrit root *sat* means truth, and *agraha*, from the classical Sanskrit root *grah*, means grasp.* Gandhi's description of his life's efforts as "ex-

* More precisely, *satyagraha* is a compound of two Sanskrit nouns, *satya* "truth" (from *sat* "being" with a suffix *-ya*) and *agraha* "firm

periments with truth" and of himself as a persistent satya-grahi (one who practices satyagraha) could lead to the none-too-meaningful conclusion that satyagraha describes every effort at understanding and thereby every reasoned opinion or every intuited belief which takes the undefined name of truth as its motivation and its goal. Such an interpretation leads to the conclusion that a satyagrahi is either merely a "seeker after truth," which is virtually meaningless, or one who has adopted the Gandhian system of morals and values according to which Gandhi himself, as the authority, ordered "the good life." It is the latter construction which commonly leads to the opinion that a satyagrahi must be a vegetarian, must observe *brahmacharya* (continence), must develop *aparigraha* (non-possession) and must manifest other ideal Gandhian at-tributes. But the concept of satyagraha on the one hand is eminently more than an anarchical moral principle and, on the other, it does not make requisite those aspects of Gandhian teaching which specify rules of individual self-living. It is essential rigorously to differentiate satyagraha as technique of action from those specific considerations of right-living with which Gandhi also concerned himself. For satyagraha, as I shall show, is basically an ethic-principle the essence of which is a social technique of action.

In the concluding commentary on the challenge satyagraha poses to Western political theory, I propose the hypothesis that means in political theory have been eclipsed by ends. It may be appropriate here to suggest further that those theories have proved most effective which have most rigorously dealt with the means to achieve their political goals. By most effec-tive I mean most readily adopted and most strictly applied. Contrast the appeal of and the subsequent political action based upon the theory of the French Utopian Socialists with that following upon the theory of Marxist-Leninist Socialism.

---

grasping" (a noun made from the verb *agrah*, which is the root *grah* "seize, grasp" with the verbal prefix *a* "to, towards").

Both had goals of economic and political equity; both were rigorous criticisms of existing political aims and methods. But French Utopian thought restricted itself to the meager consideration of structuring an ideal society and gave but slight attention to the manner in which that ideal could be achieved. The means were far removed from practical actionist techniques; they were expected to follow upon, or automatically to accompany, *a priori* reorganization of the political and social structure. With the Marxists a method was introduced and elaborated for realizing the specified goal.

On the other extreme of political thought, consider the range of degree of effectiveness stretching between the theory of a Thomas Carlyle, based on the aristocratic leader, and a similar theory issuing from Nietzsche into modern Fascism. Despite common goals of a rigid political structure entailing the subservience of the many to the exalted few, the desirability and need for permanence and status, the glory of a hero-dictated society—despite these common goals, the achievement of Fascism in gaining an impressive following and in rigorously conducting the affairs of State eclipses the efforts of Carlyle in the annals of the history of political theory. Whatever may be said by way of explaining the achievement differential in terms of the time and place of appeal, the fact remains that Nietzschean, Fascistic theory glorified the means, whereas Carlyle contented himself with suggestions as to the role and efforts of great men. With Carlyle there was no grand program of war and courage and the letting of blood for the glory of the act itself. The action program, the concentration upon the means, again marks the difference.

Wherever means have been seriously treated in Western political thought, success with theory has tended to be the more pronounced. But as I shall try to show, Western political thought has usually been content with the treatment of means as abstract method, on the one hand, or as social and political machinery, on the other. The Gandhian experiment suggests yet another level on which the treatment of means may function both for theory and in practice. The manner in which satyagraha replaces an end-serving with an end-creating function, and the challenge which such a substitute poses for our present social predicament, is suggested in the chapters which follow.

II

SATYAGRAHA: ITS BASIC PRECEPTS

"I take it, Mr. Gandhi, that you are the author of the satyagraha movement."

"Yes, Sir."

"Will you explain it briefly?"

And so Lord Hunter, as Chairman of the official Committee appointed to inquire into the first nationwide satyagraha movement in India, opened his examination of Mohandas Gandhi.[1] "It is a movement," Gandhi explained, "intended to replace methods of violence and a movement based entirely upon truth. . . ."

It was as a technique of action "intended to replace methods of violence" that satyagraha made its appearance, first in South Africa, and later in India. The philosophy which infused it was not conceived, full-blown, as a logically consistent, systematic statement. But as the technique evolved on the field of social and political action, the philosophical assumptions and the pattern of value fundamental to its operation were laid before those who came to inquire, or to challenge, to adopt or to oppose.

There are a few precepts essential to satyagraha. The degree to which the action technique functions effectively may well be determined by the extent of understanding which the satyagrahi (one engaged in satyagraha) has of these basic elements and the skill with which he applies them in the course of active conflict. The failure to grasp these fundamentals, the failure to discover the manner in which their delicate articulation constitutes the process of satyagraha, may lead to the adoption of outward forms which resemble the Gandhian technique but which are scarcely different from traditional methods of strike, of fasting, or of demonstration.

To explore the Gandhian meanings of the concepts *truth, non-violence, self-suffering*, is to approach the fundamentals of Gandhian philosophy. But the further exploration of the relationship of each of these elements to the others and the understanding of such relationships in terms of the role of the individual as satyagraha's ultimate referent, is essential to an understanding of the technique.

Truth

"Satyagraha is literally holding on to Truth, and it means therefore Truth-force." What is this "truth" which Gandhi incorporated as an essential element of his premier technique? How does it become a "force," and how does it relate to man's action on the field of conflict? "It excludes the use of violence," Gandhi asserted, "because man is not capable of knowing the absolute truth and therefore not competent to punish."[2]

The search for truth has long occupied the minds of men. The concept of the infinite, the absolute, has taken many forms, its role in religion and philosophy issuing at times in disquieting dogma. In India, the Hindu tradition holds out to man the possibility of ultimate realization of the absolute: the consummation of man's strivings is his identification with the Godhead, and such is the meaning of man's self-realization. Gandhi, in defining his personal goal, held with other Hindus that his life's endeavor was ultimately to "see God face to face." His acceptance of the absolute followed the Hindu understanding, and his personal view of God was the Hindu view of the all-pervading Brahma. But Gandhi was fully aware that the absolute cannot be known by the yet unfulfilled human mind. Gandhi never claimed to know truth in any absolute sense, and he repeatedly reminded others that man's inability to know the truth required that he maintain an unceasingly open approach to those who would differ with him. He had discovered, early in his application of satyagraha, "that pursuit of truth did not admit of violence being inflicted on one's opponent but that he must be weaned from error by patience and sympathy." For, he added, "what appears to be truth to the one may appear to be error to the other."[3]

To achieve his own self-realization, Gandhi made his life into "numerous experiments with truth." In "holding on to the truth" he did not suggest that such truth need be or could be a universally valid object of acknowledgement. He said, simply,

> . . . I am but a seeker after Truth. I claim to have found the way to it. I claim to be making a ceaseless effort to find it. But I admit that I have not yet found it. To find Truth completely is to realize oneself and one's destiny, that is, to become perfect. I am painfully conscious of my imperfections, and therein lies all the strength I possess, because it is a rare thing for a man to know his own limitation.[4]

And so, Gandhi, in search of an absolute truth, concerned himself more intensively with the means whereby the realization of such truth might be advanced. The "truth" concept which enters into the technique of satyagraha is clearly not that of the absolute. As he pursued his experiments with satyagraha the relative character of truth as an operative principle became the stronger. Satyagraha, the technique, developed at once as the tool whereby Gandhi dealt with practical social or political problems and the statement of his philosophical beliefs. Commenting on the derivation of the word satyagraha, Gandhi wrote:

> The word 'Satya' (Truth) is derived from 'Sat,' which means being. And nothing is or exists in reality except Truth. That is why 'Sat' or Truth is perhaps the most important name of God. In fact it is more correct to say that Truth is God, than to say that God is Truth . . . . it will be realized that 'Sat' or 'Satya' is the only correct and fully significant name for God.[*]

[*] *Young India*, July 30, 1931, p. 196. For a note on the distinction

Early in his public comments on the truth concept, Gandhi had identified God with Truth. In 1925, in a talk with Christian missionaries in Darjeeling, Gandhi had said that for him "God and Truth are convertible terms."[5] The following year in an address at Wardha he had declared: ["... to me Truth is God and there is no way to find Truth except the way of non-violence."[6]] When he was later (in 1931) asked by a group of conscientious objectors in Switzerland why he regarded God as Truth, Gandhi explained how he had come to believe that the phrase "God is Love" was inadequate and how he had further concluded that God is Truth. He then added that he had found it necessary to go a step further and to say that Truth is God.

> You will see the fine distinction between the two statements, 'God is Truth' and 'Truth is God.' I came to that conclusion after a continuous and relentless search after truth which began fifty years ago. I then found that the nearest approach to truth was through love.[7]

This "fine distinction" has been taken by some commentators to be of substantial significance. N. K. Bose interprets the change as relieving a satyagrahi from the necessity of any theological or at least any specific theological belief.

> With his changed creed, he could easily accommodate as fellow-seekers those who looked on Humanity or any other object as their god, and for which they were prepared to sacrifice their all. By enthroning Truth on the highest pedestal, Gandhi thus truly became a catholic, and lost all trace of separateness from every other honest man who worshipped gods other than his own.[8]

It may have been with Gandhi's deliberate change in the

---

between Knowing and Being in the Hindu truth concept, see J. H. Muirhead, "The Hindu Idea of Truth" in S. Radhakrishnan, ed., *Mahatma Gandhi: Essays and Reflections on His Life and Work* (2nd. ed.; London: Allen & Unwin [1949]), pp. 197-200.

structuring of his theological statements that he consciously allowed for the freer construction of satyagraha. Again, this can be but another example of Gandhi's philosophical formulations following upon his practical experiments and his efforts in applied ethics. In the autobiography he wrote:

> There are innumerable definitions of God, because His manifestations are innumerable. They overwhelm me with wonder and awe and for a moment stun me. But I worship God as Truth only. I have not yet found Him, but I am seeking after Him. I am prepared to sacrifice the things dearest to me in pursuit of this quest. . . . But as long as I have not realized this Absolute Truth so long must I hold by the relative truth as I have conceived it. That relative truth must meanwhile be my beacon, my shield and buckler.[9]

However inadequate Gandhi's philosophical statements may appear to the philosopher, his efforts to explain his understanding of such concepts as truth have direct bearing upon the development of the technique, satyagraha. He concerned himself with such concepts to the degree that they affected human behavior. In elucidating his view of truth he wrote to a friend:

> In "God is Truth," is certainly does not mean "equal to" nor does it merely mean, "is truthful." Truth is not a mere attribute of God, but He is That. He is nothing if He is not That. Truth in Sanskrit means *Sat. Sat* means *Is.* Therefore Truth is implied in *Is.* God is, nothing else is. Therefore the more truthful we are, the nearer we are to God. We *are* only to the extent that we are truthful.[10]

Such fragmentary efforts at ontological or epistemological statement were developed in the course of his action in the field of human interrelationships. As Gandhi pursued his experiments with truth, the concept settled solidly into the sphere of ethical consideration. The emphasis became increasingly centered upon the problem of means. The means became more and more specific, while the end—the individual realization of God, which is Truth—increasingly indeterminate. In 1924 Gandhi had written in *Young India*: "I want to see God face to face. God I *know* is Truth. For me the only certain means of knowing God is non-violence—*ahimsa*—love."[11] As Gandhi's experiments proceeded he evolved the concept of non-violence—a concept of means—and as he did so, his concept of God became the freer. But the relative character of Gandhi's concept of God was made explicit as early as 1919 when Gandhi's examination by the Hunter Committee developed the following exchange between the Committee's counsel and Gandhi:

> Your satyagraha doctrine, so far as I understand it, involves the pursuit of truth and in that pursuit you invite suffering on yourself and do not cause violence to anybody else.
>
> Yes, Sir.
>
> However honestly a man may strive in his search for truth, his notions of truth may be different from the notions of others. Who then is to determine the truth?
>
> The individual himself would determine that.
>
> Different individuals would have different views as to truth. Would that not lead to confusion?
>
> I do not think so.
>
> Honestly striving after truth differs in every case.
>
> That is why the non-violence part was a necessary corollary. Without that there would be confusion and worse.[12]

The role which non-violence plays as an essential element of satyagraha will be examined below. The Gandhian concept of truth, in its non-absolutistic sense, escapes some of the practical difficulties of ethical relativism through its interrelationship with non-violence as an operative principle in satyagraha.

There is an abundance of evidence that Gandhi adopted a social criterion for judging the truth in a given situation. In his *History of Satyagrahashram,* Gandhi writes with reference to doing penance for a wrong:

> The wrong act must be patent, accepted as such by all and spiritually harmful, and the doer must be aware of it. There should be no penance for inferential guilt. To do so might at times result in dangerous consequences. There should be no room for doubt in regard to the fault. Moreover, one should not do penance for an act, which one regards as wrong as his personal faith or opinion. It is possible that what one holds to be wrong today he might regard as innocent tomorrow. So the wrong must be such as is accepted by society to be so. I might regard the non-wearing of *khadi* to be extremely wrong. But my companion might see nothing wrong in it, or might not magnify it as a virtue, and so might wear it indifferently or not wear it at all. If I regard this as a failure and fast for it, it is not penance but coercion. There can also be no penance where the accused person is not conscious of having committed a wrong.*

Here, then, is a suggestion as to how the problem of objectivity is solved in the Gandhian method. While admitting truth to be relative, some objective standard is established. The solution is in terms of "man, the measure." The practical effect of Gandhi's "experiments with truth" is reminiscent of the theoretical solution offered by the German humanistic

---

* Translated from the Gujarati in *Harijan,* July 4, 1948. The passage occurs in the Hindi translation in Mohandas Karamchand Gandhi, *Satyagraha Ashram ka Itihas,* in Hindi, Ramnarayan Chaudhuri, tr. (Ahmedabad: Navajivan Publishing House [1948]), pp. 17-18.

Gandhi would allow for the employment of certain types of satyagraha directed towards an accused person unaware of his wrong if the matter were felt by the satyagrahi to be of fundamental importance.

materialist Feuerbach. The truth which is not absolute—which is not, for Gandhi, God—relates to and partakes of human needs. Individual man searches for truth in terms of the community of which he is a part. "The quest for Truth," said Gandhi, "cannot be prosecuted in a cave."

> When therefore untruth was discovered in the Ashram, I readily pleaded guilty for it myself. That is to say, I have not still attained truth as defined by me. It may be due to ignorance but it is clear that I have not fully understood truth and therefore neither even thought it out nor declared it, still less practised it. But granting all this, was I to leave the Ashram, and resort to some Himalayan cave and impose silence upon myself? That would be sheer cowardice. The quest for truth cannot be prosecuted in a cave. Silence makes no sense where it is necessary to speak. One may live in a cave in certain circumstances, but the common man can be tested only in society.[13]

Gandhi, the social actionist, frequently emphasized those partial manifestations of truth: honesty and integrity.

> Truthfulness is the master-key. Do not lie under any circumstances whatsoever, keep nothing secret, take your teachers and your elders into your confidence and make a clean breast of everything to them. Bear ill-will to none, do not say an evil thing of anyone behind his back, above all "to thine own-self be true," so that you are false to no one else. Truthful dealings even in the least, little things of life is the only secret of a pure life.[14]

These simpler statements—of honesty and integrity—were derived from an implied social epistemology. Gandhi had identified truth with God. Betokening an uneasiness in the realm of theological dogmatism, he expressed the God of his conception in terms relative to limitless individual interpretations. When conflict resulted, he resorted to the dynamics of human interrelationships for criteria to judge the truth, or its approximation, in a given situation. This led him, necessarily, back to the realm of ethics. To an understanding of the ethical implications of his basic metaphysic, and to action based upon them, Gandhi dedicated his life.

Gandhi's writings and teachings had begun when he sought to describe and then to evolve in a rational, communicable manner the technique of action which he had set in motion on the South African political stage. If truth is God, and God is understood in one way by some, in other ways by others how, then, can one "hold on to truth"? Satyagraha is not a dogma. It is neither static nor substantial. Holding on to truth is a dynamic concept and satyagraha a technique of action. How, then, can one proceed to know and to hold to the truth? How can confusion be avoided if striving after truth differs in every case? The answer Gandhi gave lay in the further precept that truth is inseparable from *ahimsa*.

Non-Violence

The word *ahimsa* expresses an ancient Hindu, Jain, and Buddhist ethical precept. The negative prefix "a" plus "himsa," loosely meaning "injury," make up the word which is usually translated as non-violence. Yet *ahimsa* is eminently more than a negative notion. As is characteristic of Hindu and Buddhist terminology, the negative wording implies much which remains unexpressed. The full force of *ahimsa*, explicitly stated, means "action based on the refusal to do harm."[15] Albert Schweitzer, in his short study on Indian thought,[16] calls attention to this further meaning of *ahimsa*. Etymologically, *himsa* is the desiderative form of *han* meaning to kill or to damage, so that *himsa* means to wish to kill.* *Ahimsa*, then, means

---

* *Himsa* is more precisely, derived from the root *hins*, to injure, kill, or destroy, which originally was the desiderative of the root *han*, to slay, kill, or damage. (Monier Monier-Williams, *Sanskrit-English Dictionary, Etymologically and Philologically Arranged*, New ed. enl. and improved [Oxford: Clarendon Press, 1899]).

Cf. Whitney, who notes that the root *hins* is "probably an abbrevi-

renunciation of the will to kill or to damage. Gandhi refined the meaning:

> *Ahimsa* is not the crude thing it has been made to appear. Not to hurt any living thing is no doubt a part of *ahimsa*. But it is its least expression. The principle of *himsa* is hurt by every evil thought, by undue haste, by lying, by hatred, by wishing ill to anybody.[17]

> I accept the interpretation of Ahimsa namely that it is not merely a negative state of harmlessness but it is a positive state of love, of doing good even to the evil-doer. But it does not mean helping the evil-doer to continue the wrong or tolerating it by passive acquiescence. On the contrary, love, the active state of Ahimsa, requires you to resist the wrong-doer by dissociating yourself from him even though it may offend him or injure him physically.[18]

Gandhi here identifies *ahimsa* and love. The proximity of this concept to the Christian charity and to the Greek *agape* is, throughout, apparent. As will be shown in Chapter III, this element in satyagraha has social implications expressed in service and requiring for every satyagraha movement a "constructive program."

The inseparable combination of truth and love in the Gandhian position forms the nucleus of the Gandhian solution to the problem of means.

> . . . without *ahimsa* it is not possible to seek and find Truth. *Ahimsa* and Truth are so intertwined that it is practically impossible to disentangle and separate them. They are like the two sides of a coin, or rather of a smooth unstamped metallic disc. Who can say, which is the obverse, and which is the reverse? Nevertheless *ahimsa* is the means; Truth is the end. Means to be means must

---

ated desiderative . . ." of the root *han*. (William Dwight Whitney, *The Roots, Verb-Forms, and Primary Derivatives of the Sanskrit Language* [Leipzig: Breitkopf and Hartel; London: Trübner and Co., 1885]), p. 205.

always be within our reach, and so *ahimsa* is our supreme duty. If we take care of the means, we are bound to reach the end sooner or later. When once we have grasped this point, final victory is beyond question.[19]

Truth is the end, Love a means thereto. We know what is Love or non-violence, although we find it difficult to follow the law of Love. But as for Truth we know only a fraction of it. Perfect knowledge of Truth is difficult of attainment for man even like the perfect practice of non-violence.[20]

To proceed towards the goal of Truth—truth in the absolute sense—the way must lead through the testing of relative truths as they appear to the individual performer. The testing of truth can be performed only by strict adherence to *ahimsa* —action based upon the refusal to do harm, or, more accurately, upon love. For truth, judged in terms of human needs, would be destroyed, on whichever side it lay, by the use of violence. Non-violence, or *ahimsa*, becomes the supreme value, the one cognizable standard by which true action can be determined.

If there is dogma in the Gandhian philosophy, it centers here: that the only test of truth is action based on the refusal to do harm. Gandhi accepted as his fellow "seekers after truth" persons who espoused various, or no, religions, those who held vastly differing views as to the proper social structuring or constructive programming in a non-violent society. He admitted of error and indecision at many stages of his applied experiment. But the one principle to which he adhered to the end was this theme of *ahimsa*—the supreme and only means to the discovery of social truths. "Those who join the Ashram have to literally accept that meaning," he insisted. And "that meaning" of *ahimsa* took him into a realm much higher than simply non-killing.

Ahimsa really means that you may not offend anybody,

you may not harbor an uncharitable thought even in connection with one who may consider himself to be your enemy. . . . If we resent a friend's action or the so-called enemy's action, we still fall short of this doctrine. . . . If we harbor even this thought, we depart from this doctrine of *ahimsa*. Those who join the Ashram have to literally accept that meaning. That does not mean that we practice that doctrine in its entirety. Far from it. It is an ideal which we have to reach, and it is an ideal to be reached even at this very moment, if we are capable of doing so.[21]

The limitation on human capacity to achieve non-violent action Gandhi recognized. As will be seen in Chapter III, imperfections were expected and, to some extent, tolerated in Gandhian satyagraha movements. When we enquire here into the further meaning of non-violent action, we are brought to the third fundamental element of satyagraha, for

Non-violence in its dynamic condition means conscious suffering. It does not mean meek submission to the will of the evil-doer, but it means the pitting of one's whole soul against the will of the tyrant. Working under this law of our being, it is possible for a single individual to defy the whole might of an unjust empire. . . .[22]

Self-Suffering

Love never claims, it ever gives. Love ever suffers, never resents, never revenges itself.[23]

The test of love is tapasya and tapasya means self-suffering.[24]

The classical Yogic law of self-restraint and self-discipline, and the precept of *tapas* which means penance or austerity are familiar elements in the Indian culture. We shall examine the cultural background in Chapter IV. Here it is enough to understand the meaning of self-suffering, or *tapasya*, as a function of satyagraha.

Self-suffering in the Gandhian ethic has several essential characteristics which clearly mark it off from the practice of *tapas* or asceticism undertaken for its own sake. Self-suffering in satyagraha is directed, first of all, towards the moral persuasion of one because of whom it is undertaken. It is not a substitute for inability to use violent means to achieve victory over an opponent; it is not, that is, a "weapon of the weak." Self-suffering is clearly of a different character from cowardice; nor is it to be exercised indiscriminately. Self-suffering differs from violence in that violence consists of doing injury to another.

> Suffering injury in one's own person is . . . of the essence of non-violence and is the chosen substitute for violence to others. It is not because I value life low that I can countenance with joy thousands voluntarily losing their lives for Satyagraha, but because I know that it results in the long run in the least loss of life, and, what is more, it ennobles those who lose their lives and morally enriches the world for their sacrifice.[25]

The insistence upon self-suffering has, then, an element of expediency in it. The resort to self-sacrifice and voluntary submission to injury is a positive policy and is not merely a matter of last resort. Gandhi was careful to distinguish his method from that of passive resistance, which either suggests lack of capacity to employ violence or tends to be a preliminary step to violence. In his exposition of satyagraha in South Africa,[26] Gandhi reports the comments of a well-wisher in introducing him to a public audience. The speaker observed that the Indians had "had recourse to passive resistance which is a weapon of the weak."[27] Gandhi continued to refer to the "non-violence of the weak" throughout his life whenever he wished to criticize his followers, or when he thought—as he tended to in the last months of his life—that he had failed to instill into others the full meaning of satyagraha as the non-violence of the strong. Satyagraha was at its height when those who practiced it were in a position, as they often were, to use violence effectively but refrained from doing so and invited suffering upon themselves.

Passive resistance may be offered side by side with the use of arms. Satyagraha and brute force, being each a negation of the other, can never go together. In passive resistance there is always present an idea of harassing the other party and there is a simultaneous readiness to undergo any hardships entailed upon us by such activity; while in Satyagraha there is not the remotest idea of injuring the opponent. Satyagraha postulates the conquest of the adversary by suffering in one's own person.[28]

Gandhi guarded against attracting to his satyagraha movement those who feared to take up arms or felt themselves incapable of resistance. "I do believe," he wrote, "that where there is only a choice between cowardice and violence, I would advise violence."[29] Non-violent conduct, Gandhi insisted, is "never demoralizing," whereas cowardice "always is."[30]

Non-violence cannot be taught to a person who fears to die and has no power of resistance. A helpless mouse is not non-violent because he is always eaten by pussy. He would gladly eat the murderess if he could, but he ever tries to flee from her. We do not call him a coward because he is made by nature to behave no better than he does. But a man who, when faced by danger, behaves like a mouse, is rightly called a coward. He harbors violence and hatred in his heart and would kill his enemy if he could without being hurt himself. He is a stranger to non-violence.[31]

Just as *ahimsa* carries in the Gandhian ethic the positive meaning of love and goodwill, self-suffering requires the positive attribute of courage. We shall see (in Chapter III) how the training of satyagrahis sought to develop courage and to inculcate discipline which could overcome fear. For

Just as one must learn the art of killing in the training for violence, so one must learn the art of dying in the training for non-violence. . . . The votary of non-violence has to cultivate the capacity for sacrifice of the highest type in order to be free from fear. . . . He who has not overcome all fear cannot practise *ahimsa* to perfection.[32]

Throughout his teachings on self-suffering Gandhi emphasized the need for discrimination in inviting suffering and sacrifice. Submission was never an element of this concept. Submitting to humiliation should be strictly resisted and, where necessary, the greater self-suffering of the body, even unto death, should be invited. In every case a satyagrahi must refuse to do that which his conscience forbids him to do and must preserve the dignity of the individual though it mean loss of property or even life.[33]

The element of self-suffering in satyagraha is, perhaps, of all three fundamentals, the least acceptable to a Western mind. Yet, such sacrifice may well provide the ultimate means of realizing that characteristic so eminent in Western moral philosophy: the dignity of the individual. In proceeding to consider the role of the individual in the Gandhian ethic, one is reminded of the observation of a contemporary Western thinker:

There are two entirely different types of sacrifice. It is one of the tragic facts of life that the demands of our physical self and the aims of our mental self can conflict; that actually we may have to sacrifice our physical self in order to assert the integrity of our spiritual self. This sacrifice will never lose its tragic quality. Death is never sweet, not even if it is suffered for the highest ideal. It remains unspeakably bitter, and still it can be the utmost assertion of our individuality.[34]

The Role of the Individual

Gandhi's own life is the best practical example of the role

which the individual can play in society. In an age when the place of the individual is being challenged and the specter of total mass-control is raised on every hand, Gandhi has insisted that no power on earth can make a man do a thing against his will. The technique of satyagraha provided the means and suggested the discipline through which resistance could become an active force. The element of self-suffering or sacrifice provided the ultimate alternative. For Gandhi, freedom and preservation of individual integrity were the higher values.

> The bond of the slave is snapped the moment he considers himself to be a free being. He will plainly tell the master: "I was your bondslave till this moment, but I am a slave no longer. You may kill me if you like, but if you keep me alive, I wish to tell you that if you release me from the bondage, of your own accord, I will ask for nothing more from you. You used to feed and clothe me, though I could have provided food and clothing for myself by my labour. . . ."[35]

Gandhi's concern for individual freedom does not seek the elevation of the individual ego. His is not the extreme anarchist position of freedom *per se*.

> If the individual ceases to count, what is left of society? Individual freedom alone can make a man voluntarily surrender himself completely to the service of society. If it is wrested from him, he becomes an automaton and society is ruined. No society can possibly be built on a denial of individual freedom.[36]

Nor is Gandhi's a strictly voluntaristic ethic. The human will may serve as the ultimate protection against an invaded freedom, but the will is not operating alone. However much voluntarism appears to dominate the Gandhian experiment, there are clear indications that Gandhi understood a certain undeniable influence of social institutions on the individual life. "Goondas [ruffians]," he wrote, "do not drop from the sky, nor do they spring from the earth like evil spirits. They are the product of social disorganization, and society is therefore responsible for their existence. In other words, they should be looked upon as a symptom of corruption in our body politic."[37]

The element which leaves no doubt as to the distance of Gandhi's position from that of the determinist is his insistence upon the power of man's will together with his reason to effect change in his society. We have already hinted that Gandhian satyagraha avoids the practical pitfalls of ethical relativism. It does so by establishing an objective standard of judgment in terms of social criteria. Here I am suggesting that his defense of individual freedom and the power of the individual will, though setting him at unbreachable distance from determinism, does not lead to a strictly voluntaristic ethic. For the Gandhian ethic must not only be decided in terms of socially expressed human needs; it must also be tested by non-violence. A brief examination of the relationship which the various elements in satyagraha bear to one another will indicate the practical procedure.

The Relationship of the Three Elements in Satyagraha

The truth concept as it functions in the Gandhian technique of satyagraha has been shown to be that of relative truth. The objective standard by which truth can be judged is a human standard expressed in terms of human needs. The proper means for discovering truth in those terms cannot, then, result in human harm or frustrate rather than fulfill human needs—for in such a procedure truth would become travesty. The discovery of truth, or the resolution of conflict arising out of differences of opinion as to what is truth, must be prosecuted through non-violent action. Action based on the refusal to do harm often requires dealing with violence which may be instigated by the opponent in a conflict. Self-suffering is this further means by which relative truth is tested.

To the three fundamentals of satyagraha may be added

certain corollary elements. Truth in satyagraha leads to an ethical humanism. It follows that *ahimsa* (non-violence), which includes the concept of love, leads in turn to social service. Self-suffering—not for its own sake, but for demonstration of sincerity, and flowing from refusal to injure the opponent while at the same time holding to the truth—implies sacrifice and preparation for sacrifice, even to the death.

Such are the principles which infuse the concept "satyagraha." When these principles are applied to specific political and social action the tools of civil disobedience—non-cooperation, non-violent strike, constructive program—are devised. It is with these specific techniques—or, as Gandhi frequently said, these branches of satyagraha—that Chapter III is concerned.

The Problem of Means in Satyagraha

We shall explore below (in Chapters V and VI) the manner in which Western political thought has treated the ends-means relationship. It is suggested that traditional political theories have failed to deal adequately with the problem of means. Some have admitted defeat by uneasily relying upon techniques of violence as the only alternative in the last resort. Others have made vacant gestures in the direction of a new approach, but have then collapsed of their own weight. Still others have frankly embraced the means of violence, and in approaching an ends-means convertibility based upon violence, have gone down in the ashes of total truth destruction.

The Western relativists have little to offer when the issue is drawn—for they have failed to provide an answer to the "how" which their relativism poses. Because the species is the first criterion of truth for a Feuerbach or a Godwin it was insisted that "that is true in which another agrees with me—agreement is the first criterion of truth. . . ."[38] But on how this agreement is to be achieved once the conflict has arisen, political theorists have been eloquently silent.

In Chapter VI, I shall impose a theoretical construction

upon the Gandhian experiment in an attempt to show how a sort of dialectic may operate in the functioning of satyagraha —a dialectic which closes the breach between theoretical change and practical action, a breach which the Hegelian dialectic was not intended to bridge and which Marxist dialectic filled with the doctrine of economic determinism thereby denying the dynamics of a process which properly is creative.

Here it is enough to comment that the element of non-violence in satyagraha is inseparable from a view of truth which takes as its criterion the needs of man. In the quest for such truth, and in its propagation, it is therefore not possible, in a proper satyagraha, to inflict harm on others. In so behaving, truth itself would lose its meaning. He who claims a different version of truth from the satyagrahi's must be converted by gentleness. Meanwhile, the satyagrahi must re-examine continuously his own position—for his opponent may be closer to the truth than he. Self-suffering, the third element of satyagraha, guarantees the sincerity of the satyagrahi's own opinions, the while it restrains him from propagating uncertain truths. The objective of satyagraha is to win the victory over the conflict situation—to discover further truths and to persuade the opponent, not to triumph over him.

Agreement must, indeed, be achieved. In agreement, the Western relativists insist, lies certain criterion of truth. Agreement achieved through satyagraha implies the carrying of full conviction. Holding to the truth means holding to what the satyagrahi believes to be the truth until he is dissuaded from that position or any part of it. Meanwhile his effort is steadfastly to persuade his opponent. If he suffers, if he dies, in this effort, he has applied the principle of self-suffering, and has asserted the truth, as he sees it—for no power on earth can make a man do a thing against his will.

To avoid possible misinterpretation, it may be well to note here that the effort of satyagraha to reach agreement, and to hold onto truth until agreement is reached, does not imply that two or more persons entertaining contradictory beliefs need become embattled. Gandhi has given much evidence of his willingness to work with others who disagreed strongly with him. So long as there is no serious conflict emerging from such association or contact, there is no need to resort to satyagraha. The satyagraha approach is often that of assuming that those who disagree are each simply holding to a limited view of truth.[39] It is only when beliefs come into serious conflict—when basic needs or impulses or desires are frustrated—that satyagraha becomes appropriate.

Gandhi has referred to non-violence as being both the end and the means. In a prayer speech in New Delhi shortly before his death he commented, once again, that means and ends are convertible terms.[40] This convertibility in the Gandhian doctrine is based upon non-violence.

A more precise statement of the ends-means relationship operating in satyagraha is indicated by Shridharani's phrase describing the means as "the end in process and the ideal in the making."* In the operation of satyagraha, where the protagonist is prepared to revise his opinion and his goal if he is persuaded of their falsity, there is little room for static ends. Perhaps the most characteristic quality of satyagraha is the flexibility in ends which an emphasis on means implies. This is not to suggest that a satyagrahi is a weak or easy opponent. He may persist to the death without relaxing his hold on the original position which he took to be truth. But, significantly, he may easily be won over. His dogma—if such a thing can be alleged of him—lies in adherence to a means, to a technique, which has, as we have seen, specific moral elements at its base. But what action in these terms may mean—what it may lead to as a social, or political, or individual end—is highly unpredictable.

People say that I have changed my view, that I say today

* Krishnalal Shridharani, *War Without Violence* (New York: Harcourt, Brace [1939]), p. 316. I shall explore further the ends-means problem in Chapter VI.

something different from what I said years ago. The fact of the matter is that conditions have changed. I am the same. . . . There has been a gradual evolution in my environment and I react to it as a *Satyagrahi*.[41]

Throughout Gandhi's writings runs the quiet insistence that individual will and reason can effect social and political change. Satyagraha is the technique he developed to point its direction.

III

SATYAGRAHA AS APPLIED SOCIO-
POLITICAL ACTION

Satyagraha is a technique of action. It is characterized by adherence to a stated truth by means of behavior which is not violent but which includes self-suffering. It seeks to effect change and it operates within a conflict situation. As do all techniques of action for effecting change, it employs force. The character and the result of the force of satyagraha are essentially different from those of conventional—violent— techniques of action during conflict.

Satyagraha may use any of several forms of non-violent action. Those which were most commonly employed during the nationalist movement in India are *non-cooperation* and *civil disobedience. Constructive program* is a positive aspect of satyagraha in action, and is the concomitant of resistance-action.

Non-cooperation may include strike, walk-out, *hartal,** and resignation of offices and titles. In principle, non-cooperation is simply the refusal to cooperate with a requirement which is taken to violate fundamental "truths" or refusal to cooperate with those responsible for such violations.

Civil disobedience is the direct contravention of specific laws and may include such activities as non-payment of taxes. Jail-going is a special *non-resistance†* activity undertaken in a

* Voluntary closing of shops and businesses, usually for a twenty-four hour period.

† It must be kept firmly in mind that *non-resistance* does not describe satyagraha. Much confusion of thought on Gandian techniques arises from the failure to distinguish at all times between the active resistance undertaken in satyagraha and the occasional non-resistant effect of such activities as inviting imprisonment. This chapter should make clear the inadequacies of such words as "passive resistance" to express the func-

civil disobedience program. The civil character of satyagraha is maintained by the inviting of and the voluntary submitting to the sanction provided by the law for action contrary to the legal norm.

A special word should be said about fasting and its place in Gandhian satyagraha. Gandhi frequently wrote on the dangers of considering any fast a part of satyagraha. The majority of fasts, he declared, were nothing more than "hunger strikes undertaken without previous preparation and without adequate thought." He repeatedly warned against the indiscriminate use of the fast and was well aware that often "there is violence behind such fasting."[1] Although Gandhi fully believed that fasting could be a most "effective weapon" in the armory of satyagraha,[2] he recognized that its use must be carefully determined.

> Fasting is a fiery weapon. It has its own science. No one, as far as I am aware, has a perfect knowledge of it. Unscientific experimentation with it is bound to be harmful to the one who fasts, and it may even harm the cause espoused. No one who has not earned the right to do so should, therefore, use this weapon. A fast may only be undertaken by him who is associated with the person against whom he fasts. The latter must be directly connected with the purpose for which the fast is being undertaken.[3]

In general, fasting may be used as an adjunct to other forms of satyagraha. It should not be considered a form of satyagraha in the sense of mass action. The development of "representative satyagraha" in which individuals are selected to represent the group in offering* satyagraha may, however, make use of the fast.

---

tioning of satyagraha. It must also be insisted that "non-resistance" in no way characterizes satyagraha and describes only a step in a civil disobedience effort.

* To "offer" satyagraha means to perform an act of satyagraha.

The Essentials of Satyagraha in Action

If one were to lay out a handbook for the conduct of a mass satyagraha campaign based upon the experience with satyagraha in India, the three first chapters might well deal with (1) fundamental rules governing the campaign, (2) the code of discipline, and (3) the steps through which the campaign is to be pursued. Among the points which should enter into such a guide are those outlined below.

FUNDAMENTAL RULES[4]

(1) *Self-reliance at all times.* Outside aid may, in the proper circumstances, be accepted, but should never be counted upon.

(2) *Initiative in the hands of the satyagrahis.* Through continuous assessment of the conflict situation satyagrahis should, by means of constructive efforts where possible, by positive resistance where indicated, or by the tactics of persuasion and adjustment, press the movement ever forward.

(3) *Propagation of the objectives, strategy and tactics of the campaign.* Propaganda must be made an integral part of the movement. Education of the opponent, the public, and participants must continue apace.

(4) *Reduction of demands to a minimum consistent with truth.* Continuing reassessment of the situation and the objectives with a view to possible adjustment of demands is essential.

(5) *Progressive advancement of the movement* through steps and stages determined to be appropriate within the given situation. Decision as to when to proceed to a further phase of the satyagraha must be carefully weighed in the light of the ever-changing circumstance, but a static condition must be avoided. However, direct action is to be launched only after all other efforts to achieve an honorable settlement have been exhausted.

(6) *Examination of weaknesses* within the satyagraha group. The morale and discipline of the satyagrahis must be

maintained through active awareness (by members and leaders alike) of any development of impatience, discouragement, or breakdown of non-violent attitude.

(7) *Persistent search for avenues of cooperation with the adversary on honorable terms.* Every effort should be made to win over the opponent by helping him (where this is consistent with the satyagrahi's true objectives) thereby demonstrating sincerity to achieve an agreement with, rather than a triumph over, the adversary.

(8) *Refusal to surrender essentials in negotiation.* Satyagraha excludes all compromise which affects basic principles or essential portions of valid objectives. Care must be exercised not to engage in bargaining or barter.

(9) *Insistence upon full agreement* on fundamentals before accepting a settlement.

CODE OF DISCIPLINE

The following points were laid down by Gandhi as a code for volunteers in the 1930 movement:[5]

(1) Harbor no anger but suffer the anger of the opponent. Refuse to return the assaults of the opponent.

(2) Do not submit to any order given in anger, even though severe punishment is threatened for disobeying.

(3) Refrain from insults and swearing.

(4) Protect opponents from insult or attack, even at the risk of life.

(5) Do not resist arrest nor the attachment of property, unless holding property as a trustee.

(6) Refuse to surrender any property held in trust at the risk of life.

(7) If taken prisoner, behave in an exemplary manner.

(8) As a member of a satyagraha unit, obey the orders of satyagraha leaders, and resign from the unit in the event of serious disagreement.

(9) Do not expect guarantees for maintenance of dependents.

STEPS IN A SATYAGRAHA CAMPAIGN[6]

The outline below is applicable to a movement growing out of grievances against an established political order. These steps could be adapted to other conflict situations.

(1) *Negotiation and arbitration.* Every effort to resolve the conflict or redress the grievance through established channels must be exhausted before the further steps are undertaken.

(2) *Preparation of the group for direct action.* Immediately upon recognizing the existence of a conflict situation which might lead to direct action, motives are to be carefully examined, exercises in self-discipline initiated, and the fullest discussion launched within the group regarding issues at stake, appropriate procedures to be undertaken, the circumstance of the opponents, the climate of public opinion, etc. This step often included, for Indian satyagrahis, purificatory fasting.

(3) *Agitation.* This step includes an active propaganda campaign together with such demonstrations as mass-meetings, parades, slogan-shouting.

(4) *Issuing of an ultimatum.* A final strong appeal to the opponent should be made explaining what further steps will be taken if no agreement can be reached. The wording and manner of presentation of the ultimatum should offer the widest scope for agreement, allowing for face-saving on the part of the opponent, and should present a constructive solution to the problem.

(5) *Economic boycott and forms of strike.* Picketing may be widely employed, together with continued demonstrations and education of the public. Sitting *dharna* (a form of sit-down strike) may be employed, as well as non-violent labor strike, and attempts to organize a general strike.

(6) *Non-cooperation.* Depending upon the nature of the issues at stake, such action as non-payment of taxes, boycott

of schools and other public institutions, ostracism, or even voluntary exile may be initiated.

(7) *Civil disobedience.* Great care should be exercised in the selection of laws to be contravened. Such laws should be either central to the grievance, or symbolic.

(8) *Usurping of the functions of government.* Shridharani calls this "assertive satyagraha." Fullest preparations are necessary to make this step effective.

(9) *Parallel government.* The establishment of parallel functions should grow out of step (8), and these should be strengthened in such a way that the greatest possible cooperation from the public can be obtained.

The specific action which is to be undertaken in a given satyagraha movement will, of course, be determined by the nature of the circumstance itself. As in the extensive and intensive preparations for violent combat, much depends upon discipline, leadership, preparation, steadfast purpose, and the adaptation of basic principles and procedures to specific circumstances. An analysis of historic satyagraha campaigns in India indicates directions in which preparation for satyagraha might be developed to strengthen such movements and to avoid potential weaknesses. Gandhi and other Indian leaders accepted all who would join their campaigns. They developed tactics and rules as they moved to meet well-advanced situations of conflict. Had they been able to select their crusaders and to train them for their respective roles in the satyagraha operation, the movements might well have been even more dramatic. Even so, the degree of success with which they met is especially striking when one considers that they worked on an *ad hoc* basis, and that they dealt with a mass populace which had no prior understanding of the techniques involved and very few of whom had any consistent discipline in the application of these techniques.

Satyagraha or Duragraha?

Before introducing an outline of several representative

movements which occurred in India during Gandhi's lifetime, it may be well to call to mind that there are movements which in some respects resemble satyagraha but which do not measure up in essentials to the genuine Gandhian technique. How, then, is one to judge whether or not a movement is indeed satyagraha?

At the outset, let us recognize that no movement can be expected to achieve perfection in its procedure or effect. Violent combat, as is well-known, has a strikingly low efficiency rating. The constructive program aspect of satyagraha lends to such a campaign a distinct initial advantage. Nevertheless, no combat procedure, non-violent or violent, will operate with complete efficiency either in effecting discipline or in advancing according to plan and tactic. Persisting satyagraha campaigns have met with a high degree of success, and many have achieved the complete elimination of physical violence, but perhaps none has remained perfectly non-violent throughout its many aspects. In raising the question as to how a satyagraha movement is to be distinguished, we are not concerned with the degree of success of that movement either in its approach to the ideal or in winning the objectives set before its participants. The question is not one of degree, but of kind (allowing, of course, for the ever-present possibility of a difference of degree so great as to approach a difference in kind). The question of distinguishing between satyagraha and what Indians call *duragraha* (stubborn persistence) centers upon some eminently characteristic qualities.

Perhaps the most evident of the distinguishing characteristics of a true satyagraha lie within its program of action. The first question to ask about a given movement to determine its true character, is one which would test the extent to which it has followed the steps leading from the initial insistence upon exhausting available channels for settling the dispute, through the further steps, especially those involving persistent efforts to achieve agreement without the humiliation of the opponent. A proper satyagraha effort through mass action would show evidence of having proceeded, in general, through such steps as outlined above. The fullest publicity regarding the intentions of those involved in the campaign would necessarily have been made available. Efforts to minimize hardship for the opponent would also be in evidence. The constructive program of a movement is yet another earmark of proper Gandhian satyagraha. Has the movement undertaken positive, constructive steps with a view to providing services to its own members and to the public, and even in some cases, to the opponent? Readiness to accept the penalties provided by the law is, again, typical of satyagraha, just as resort to legal defense is uncharacteristic. A genuine satyagraha campaign is, throughout, active and constructive, aggressive and synthesizing. Insistence upon arriving at the truths of the situation, together with persistence in exploring new and creative approaches, are fundamental.

At once one can eliminate simple fasting or simple demonstration or strike, for they clearly do not fulfill the essentials for a movement qualifying as satyagraha. At most, fasting or demonstration or strike may be used during some stage of a satyagraha campaign; in themselves they are nothing more than the action which each respective name signifies and so should not be called satyagraha.

Upon examining movements which have recently taken place in India under the name satyagraha, it is possible to classify many as hunger-strikes, sit-down strikes, boycott, or *duragraha.* Many of the teachers' strikes of recent years in India thus failed to justify themselves as Gandhian satyagraha; the agitation on the part of orthodox Hindu groups for seizure of Kashmir could scarcely be called a Gandhian satyagraha movement; the demonstrations undertaken prior to 1953 in the Telugu-speaking area of South India for a separate Andhra State did not constitute genuine Gandhian satyagraha. (This is not to suggest, of course, that participants in those movements could not have been Gandhi-like in character, nor do I intend in any way to detract from their devotion to or to pass any judgment on the justice of their respective causes.) Some of these actions succeeded, for *duragraha*, like violence, may well succeed in achieving limited objectives. But it is essential, I believe, to understand that not every movement is *ipso facto* satyagraha merely because it avoids physically violent resistance.

A review of the contemporary history of political events in India suggests that *duragraha* and demonstration, strike and fasting—under the name of satyagraha—are the techniques of the day. Certainly they are more easily organized, less demanding in terms of leadership and control, than Gandhian satyagraha. Oftentimes they are quite spontaneous in development and are readily assigned the name satyagraha. An examination of these movements on the basis of criteria suggested here would bring substantial doubt to bear upon the genuineness, in terms of satyagraha, of many recent resistance campaigns. However, there have been several remarkable, genuine, and instructive satyagraha campaigns in the post-Gandhian period in India. Of these, perhaps the two most notable occurred in widely separated parts of India: in Manbhum district, Bihar, and in Surat district, Bombay. During the early stages of the Manbhum movement, satyagraha, pursued against great odds, displayed manifest adherence to basic principles, and proceeded step by step even to the point of maintaining a system of local government (through the creation of popular panchayats) which came into conflict with state authority. The Pardi satyagraha in Bombay State, a much better publicized movement, was organized and led by Praja Socialists against the State government of Bombay.[7] This movement was pressed through the several steps of a proper satyagraha campaign and finally succeeded in winning government action on the satyagraha's objective of return of grasslands to cultivation. A study of these and other movements in contemporary India would serve further to illuminate the processes involved in applied Gandhian satyagraha. In the following pages I have attempted brief analyses of five satyagraha campaigns during the Gandhian era and have tried to demonstrate how and why they are satyagraha, not *duragraha,* even though none was one hundred percent non-violent or successful and one failed in a very important respect.

An Analysis of Five Satyagraha Campaigns*

The five examples of satyagraha outlined below have been selected to illustrate the use of the technique for widely divergent objectives in different social or political situations and by different social groups against various types of opposition. The selection was, indeed, a difficult one, for recent Indian history provides hundreds of satyagraha movements within many environments. My choice has at times been influenced by the availability of evidence, although some important and better-documented movements have here been omitted in favor of others which illustrate the operation of the technique within particular circumstances. Two of the campaigns included were not led by Gandhi, a factor which influenced their selection inasmuch as my purpose is to describe the technique rather than Gandhi's role as a leader. One of the campaigns outlined illustrates the use of satyagraha in behalf of untouchables against an entrenched Brahman group; another describes a peasant movement against local and state government; a third deals with a campaign launched by laborers against mill-owners. Two of the movements were all-India campaigns conducted for political objectives and directed against the central government.

To introduce some consistency into the treatment of these satyagraha movements—and the better to test them for their genuineness as true satyagraha—I have outlined each according to the following ten points:

1. Dates, duration, and locale
2. Objectives
3. Satyagraha participants and leadership
4. Participants and leadership of the opposition

* The reader whose primary interest centers upon political philosophy may wish to skip the outlines which follow and to rejoin the text on p. 102.

5. Organization and constructive program
6. Preparation for action
7. Preliminary action
8. Action
9. Reaction of opponents
10. Results

Summary analyses, which follow the outlines of the five movements, consider how closely the respective campaigns approached the satyagraha ideal and wherein they failed, and illustrate how these movements were true satyagraha in the sense in which we have used the term.

THE VYKOM TEMPLE ROAD SATYAGRAHA[8]

Dates, duration, and locale

(1) Spring 1924 to autumn 1925.
(2) Pursued over sixteen months.
(3) The village Vykom, State of Travancore, at the southern tip of India.

Objectives

(1) *Immediate*: To remove the prohibition upon the use by untouchables of roadways passing the temple. This was a serious disability inasmuch as it required untouchables to take a long, circuitous route to reach their dwellings.
(2) *Long-range*: A step towards ridding Hinduism of the "blot" of untouchability.

Satyagraha participants and leadership

(1) *Character of leadership*: Among the initiators of the movement was a Syrian Christian. However, opinion favored Hindu leaders because of the reform objective. Local Hindus took up the prominent leadership roles. Gandhi, who kept in touch with the campaign from the beginning, was not its leader and was not

in Travancore until late in the movement, when he was instrumental in securing a concession from the State government.

(2) *Character of participants*: Hindus, both untouchables and caste (including orthodox) Hindus provided the majority of participants. Sikhs from the Punjab offered direct support by opening a kitchen to feed satyagrahis, but upon Gandhi's recommendation, they were replaced by local Hindus so that orthodox Hindu opponents might not be offended.

(3) *Number of participants*: Active satyagrahis residing in the camp established for the volunteers was about 50. Many others cooperated, with estimates of total participants varying from 600 to "thousands."

Participants and leadership of the opposition

(1) *Orthodox Hindus*. An occasional untouchable was numbered among the opposition, but the majority were high caste Hindus, especially Brahmans. An orthodox Hindu society, the Savarna Mahajana Sabha, supported the Brahman position throughout the struggle.

(2) *Police* of the State of Travancore.

(3) *Members of the Travancore Legislative Council*. The majority on the Council supported the orthodox position.

Organization and constructive program

(1) *Camp headquarters*: A satyagraha ashram (camp) was established early in the campaign.

(2) *Constructive activity*: Daily maintenance and camp routine were made an integral part of the movement, with satyagrahis assigned either maintenance duties or direct action duties. A high degree of self-sufficiency was attained. Hand-spinning, building of

47

a school, and other constructive efforts were continued during the movement.

Preparation for action

(1) *Prayer*: A religious tone was given the movement, with prayer meetings an important part of ashram life.

(2) *Instruction in satyagraha*: Participants in the campaign engaged in discussion of the principles underlying satyagraha. Emphasis was laid upon understanding the viewpoint of their orthodox opponents, and upon winning them over through persuasion.

Preliminary action

(1) *Negotiation*: Among the efforts made to negotiate a settlement was a deputation to State authorities.

(2) *Agitation*: Efforts were made to attract public attention to the disabilities of the Vykom untouchables.

Action

First phase:

(1) Procession of untouchables and caste Hindus taken along the forbidden road. Refusal to retaliate when attacked and beaten by Brahmans.

(2) Submission to arrest. A second procession along the road led to the arrest of satyagrahi leaders.

(3) Replacement of leaders. Upon the arrest of satyagrahis, others came forward to fill their places.

(4) Submission of secondary leadership to arrest.

Second phase:

(1) Opposition to police barricade. Upon the erection by police of a barricade on the road, caste Hindus alongside untouchables took up positions opposite the police and held them day after day.

(2) Action during monsoon. When the monsoon flooded the road and the police occupied their positions in boats, satyagrahis continued to stand three-hour shifts, in some instances even up to shoulders in water.

Third phase:

(1) Persuasion of State authorities. Gandhi, visiting Travancore for the first time during the movement in April 1925, persuaded the authorities to remove the barricade.

(2) Announcement of intention not to take advantage of removal of barricade. Satyagrahis refrained from entering the road even though the barricade and police cordon had been removed. They announced they would not enter upon the road until the Brahmans were fully persuaded, and the government declared acceptance of untouchable use of the road.

(3) Persuasion of Brahman opponents. Through persistent reasoning supported by prayer, the opposition was won over.

Reaction of opponents

(1) *Violence* against satyagrahis by personal physical attack.

(2) *Imprisonment* of satyagrahis following arrest.

(3) *Cessation of arrests* when prisons became overcrowded.

(4) *Erection of barricade.* Police built and manned barricade on the roadway upon an order to prevent entry.

(5) *Support by State Legislative Council.* Majority of the State Council upheld police action.

(6) *Social ostracism* of satyagraha organizers. Ostracism, accompanied by threats of depriving participants of

family property and barring them from other family privileges, was especially serious.

(7) *Removal of barricades.* Following Gandhi's talks (in April 1925) with State authorities, police were ordered to remove the barricades which they had manned daily.

(8) *Confusion over satyagraha reaction.* Brahmans, who had expected them to re-enter the roadway as soon as police cordon and barricade were removed, were thrown off balance when satyagrahis refrained from entering the road.

(9) *Capitulation.* In the autumn of 1925, the Brahmans declared: "We cannot any longer resist the prayers that have been made to us, and we are ready to receive the untouchables."

Results

(1) *Roads opened to all comers.* The immediate objective of the satyagraha had been fully achieved.

(2) *Brahman areas elsewhere opened.* In other parts of India this campaign had repercussions, with the opening to untouchables of areas and temples formerly closed to them.

(3) *Conditions of untouchables improved.* Through an extension of the constructive program, the general condition of untouchables was improved.

(4) *Long-range results:* The campaign constituted a major turning point in the fight against untouchability.

SUMMARY ANALYSIS OF THE VYKOM TEMPLE ROAD SATYAGRAHA

The Vykom satyagraha measures up to the greater part of the satyagraha ideal. The position of "truth" to which the participants clung was the right of every human individual to pass along a public road[9] without discrimination on the basis of caste. The method employed in asserting this "truth" was that of non-violent demonstration and contravention of the custom which they took to be unjust. The action appears to have been scrupulously non-violent although there were times when questionable action such as scaling the police barricades was urged on the part of supporters.

Self-suffering was characteristic of the attitude of the satyagrahis. They persisted in courageous offering of satyagraha throughout the sixteen months, suffering physically both from attacks of their orthodox opponents and from the inclemency of the weather which, during the monsoon, forced them to stand waist-deep in water. After the police cordon had been withdrawn, they persisted in peaceful satyagraha to bring about the persuasion of their opponents before entering upon the road in dispute.

The constructive character of the effort and the exemplary conduct of the participants were at all times in evidence. Members of the satyagraha camp not only maintained their own services, but by daily spinning contributed to the Congress *khadi* fund and to the All-India Deshabandhu Memorial Fund.[10] In this way they identified the Vykom movement with the independence struggle. They retained a flexible leadership and adapted their program to accord with the opinion of those who criticized the acceptance of support from non-Hindu communities, conceding the desirability of preserving the campaign's character of "reform from within."

The emphasis on persuasion was never lost sight of. Religious sensitivity of the opposition was scrupulously considered. It was this consideration which Gandhi expressed in *Young India,* May 1, 1924:

> Satyagraha is a process of conversion. The reformers, I am sure, do not seek to force their views upon the community; they strive to touch its heart. Outside pecuniary help must interfere with the love process if I may so describe the method of Satyagraha. Thus viewed the pro-

posed Sikh free kitchen, I can only regard, as a menace
to the frightened Hindus of Vykom.

There is no doubt in my mind about it that the orthodox Hindus who still think that worship of God is inconsistent with touching a portion of their own co-religionists
and that a religious life is summed up in ablutions and
avoidance of physical pollutions merely are alarmed at
the developments of the movement at Vykom. They believe that their religion is in danger. It behooves the or-
ganisers therefore, to set even the most orthodox and the
most bigoted at ease and to assure them that they do not
seek to bring about the reform by compulsion. . . .

Propaganda attending the struggle was perhaps less an integral part of the campaign than is desired in ideal satyagraha.
It was incidentally supplied by the publicity given the movement by Gandhi's statements in *Young India* and by the interest of the national press in the controversy. The satyagrahis
themselves did not publish literature on the struggle.

Contravention of the religious customary rule (comparable
to civil disobedience in campaigns of resistance to government) went hand-in-hand with negotiations and talks with
State officials and with the orthodox opposition.

The initiative was only occasionally lost by the satyagrahis.
Perhaps the most difficult stage began after the police cordon
had been removed. Satyagrahis, without losing equilibrium in
the action, continued their demonstration in efforts to persuade the Brahmans.

At no time were the satyagrahi demands excessive. The
issue was clear and at no point did the satyagrahis compromise
their immediate objective of opening the road to all comers.
There was, however, an attitude of understanding towards the
adversary. Before terminating their action, satyagrahis insisted upon and secured full agreement with the opponent.

THE BARDOLI CAMPAIGN OF PEASANTS AGAINST THE GOVERNMENT
OF BOMBAY[11]

Dates, Duration, and Locale

(1) Officially began 12 February, 1928; concluded 4
August 1928.

(2) Movement continued for six months.

(3) Action took place in Bardoli *taluka* in Surat district,
Bombay Presidency.

Objectives

(1) The *immediate*, single objective of the direct action:
To persuade the government to launch an impartial
enquiry into the enhancement of the land revenue
assessment in Bardoli.

(2) *Nature of the basic grievance*: Through arbitrary
machinery of the Revenue Department, the Bombay
government had, in 1927, enhanced the assessment
in Bardoli *taluka* by a nominal 22 per cent which,
when applied, amounted in some cases to as much as
60 per cent enhancement. (Jurisdiction of the civil
courts in matters of revenue assessment had been
excluded by a special Act of the Legislature.)

(3) *Claims of the Bardoli peasants*:

(a) The rate of enhancement was unjust.

(b) The rate had been established without full
and appropriate investigation.

(c) The tax official's report was inaccurate.

(d) An increase in the tax was unwarranted.

(4) *Further implications of the movement*: Though this
campaign was limited to the local objective, it was
explained by Gandhi that similar conditions existed
in other parts of India and that the Bardoli experience would exercise a wide influence. The duty to
resist arbitrary unjust levies was a universal duty.
"Whatever awakens people to a sense of their

53

wrongs," Gandhi wrote in *Young India* (8 March 1928), "and whatever gives them strength for disciplined and peaceful resistance and habituates them to corporate suffering brings us nearer Swaraj."

Satyagraha participants and leadership

(1) *Commander of the campaign*: Sardar Vallabhbhai Patel, who was invited by the people to come to Bardoli to lead them in a struggle for redress of their grievances.

(2) *Secondary leadership*: Constructive workers including two Muslims who had worked with Gandhi in South Africa. From outside the district also came several women including a Parsi from Bombay City.

(3) *The role of Gandhi*: Gandhi supported the campaign through his writings in *Young India*. He visited Bardoli six months after satyagraha had been launched and then placed himself under Sardar Patel's command.

(4) *Active satyagrahis* ("volunteers"): Numbered about 250 and included Hindus of all and no castes, Muslims, a few Parsis. Several thousand *Kaliparaj* (aboriginals) cooperated with the movement. Women freely participated and led some of the central action.

(5) *Sympathizers and cooperators*: Most of the people of the *taluka* (total population was 87,000) ultimately cooperated. Initial reluctance on the part of moneylenders, village headmen, subordinate officials, but later many of these joined the campaign, the officials resigning their positions.

Participants and leadership of the opposition

(1) *Officials* of the Revenue Department.

(2) *Police* of the district re-enforced by contingents of Pathans (Muslims of the North West Frontier

Province) brought from Bombay City (described as "strong-arm" men).

(3) *The Governor of Bombay* who declared the issue to be: "whether the writ of His Majesty the King-Emperor is to run in a portion of His Majesty's dominions, or whether the edict of some unofficial body of individuals is to be obeyed. That issue . . . is one which Government is prepared to meet with all the power which Government possesses."

Organization and constructive program

(1) *Nucleus organization*: The four centers of constructive work already established in the *taluka*.

(2) *Expanded organization*: With Bardoli village as headquarters, a total of 16 satyagraha camps were established at various villages within the *taluka*.

(3) *Publicity Office*: From headquarters, a daily news bulletin was issued, as were occasional pamphlets and speeches of Sardar Patel. Initially 5,000 copies were printed at Surat (center of the district) and distributed through the satyagraha organization free of charge to peasants of Bardoli. Later an increase in copies to 14,000 made possible circulation of this publicity to other villages and towns in the province. Paid subscriptions were received from outside the district.

(4) *Direction of the campaign*: Instructions to volunteers emanated from headquarters and were carried by satyagrahi messengers.

(5) *Constructive work*: Spinning and social welfare activities were continued throughout the campaign, with an emphasis upon the entire khadi program. The wearing of *khadi* was required of satyagrahis and it served as a sort of uniform.

Preparation for action

(1) *Educating the people* in the meaning of the struggle: Speeches by leaders emphasized the need for discipline and preparation to undergo hardship and austerity. Government reaction was expected to be harsh and to include imprisonment and land confiscation.

(2) *Using mass media of communication:* Songs about the satyagraha were composed and taught. Mass meetings were held where prayers were recited, satyagraha songs sung, and excerpts from Gandhi's autobiography read.

(3) *Eliciting response from villagers:* Signatures were collected to the satyagraha pledge. Efforts were made to convert headmen to the cause by persuading them they should become spokesmen for their respective villages, rather than agents of the government. News bulletins from neighboring *talukas* expressing sympathy and encouragement were circulated.

(4) *Anticipating opposition:* Protests were recorded from those refusing to sign the satyagraha pledge. (Later, those who had refused were subjected to social boycott, but care was taken not to deprive them of necessities.) Peasants were prepared to refuse to cultivate lands for any outside purchasers of land which might be forfeited.

Preliminary action

(1) *Opposition to the Revenue Department report* for the *taluka* was expressed from mid-1926. The local Congress Party organization published a critical report to show that peasants could not sustain the enhanced assessments.

(2) *Petitioning:* A Committee organized by the Congress waited upon the Revenue Member of the State government early in 1927.

(3) *Conference held* in Bardoli, September 1927, unanimously resolved to withhold payment of the enhanced portion of the assessment.

(4) *Patel invited to lead satyagraha* following a government order (5 January 1928) to collectors to proceed with collections. Patel examined the entire situation, then accepted presidency of the conference of peasants which met 4 February.

(5) *Patel initiated correspondence with the government.* Upon the reply that the government was "not prepared to make any concession," a resolution was adopted (12 February) setting forth the demand for an enquiry and the refusal of the peasants to pay the assessment until the government either accepted the amount of the old assessment as full payment or until an impartial tribunal was appointed to investigate the entire situation.

Action

(1) *Non-cooperation*: Peasants met revenue collectors with closed doors, or, receiving them, read extracts aloud from Patel's speeches and tried by argument to persuade them that they could not collect the revenue. When police re-enforcements broke down doors and carried away equipment, peasants began to dismantle carts and other equipment, hiding the parts in different places.

(2) *Technical trespass*: Women volunteers built huts and camped on attached lands. Peasants continued regular sowing despite the change in legal status of land.

(3) *Submission to arrest*: Volunteers followed officials everywhere, camping on roads outside official bungalows. When arrested, they were replaced by others "until authorities tired of the process."

(4) *Resignation of offices*: Petty village officials were

persuaded to resign in protest. Several elected members of the Bombay Legislative Council resigned seats in sympathy.

(5) *Protest at the national level*: The President of the Central Legislative Assembly placed the facts before the Viceroy and contributed heavily to satyagraha funds, pledging monthly financial support.

(6) *Treatment of the opponents*: Collectors were supplied all needs "at market rates." Continued emphasis upon non-violence and lack of resentment was urged by Patel, who explained that they could "melt even the stony heart of an autocratic Commissioner." The quit-rent, which was not subject to enhancement, was paid in full. Leaders urged that the Pathan "strong-arm" police and Muslim officials especially be treated as friends.

(7) *Social boycott*: Exercised with restraint. Those discovered seceding from the group were urged to pay "sooner rather than later," whereupon some, instead of paying the revenue, contributed to the satyagraha fund.

(8) *Rejection of violent tactics*: Suggestions of erecting barricades along the roads or of puncturing tires were firmly rejected.

(9) *Non-possession used as a tool*: All conveniences were discarded, even brass vessels, with the objective ". . . we will see that Government will have nothing on which they can lay their hands."

(10) *Revision of demands*: In July Patel was invited to confer with the Governor. The government insisted upon full payment before agreeing to an enquiry, which might then be conducted by a Revenue officer, possibly together with a Judicial officer. Patel accepted the principle of an official enquiry provided it be judicial in nature and that representatives of

the people be invited to give evidence. Additional demands were presented:

(a) Satyagrahi prisoners to be discharged.
(b) Restoration of all forfeited lands.
(c) Payment at market price for confiscated movable property.
(d) Remission of all dismissals and other punishments arising from the struggle.

Patel reasserted the intention of the satyagrahis to arrive at a solution honorable both to the government and people.

(11) *Agreement reached*: On 4 August, a formula was agreed upon which would meet the satyagrahis' full basic demands yet save face for the government.

Reaction of opponents

(1) *Land seizure*: Widescale attachment of land in payment of revenue. Forfeiture notices reported well above 1,500.

(2) *Attachment of movable property*: Police, supported by Pathan re-enforcements, forcibly seized personal property, including utensils, cots, carts, buffaloes.

(3) *Arrests*: Widescale arrest for obstructing performance of official duties and for criminal trespass.

(4) *Violence*: Repeated instances of police violence resulting in personal injury.

(5) *Misrepresentation of facts*: Attempts to cajole peasants into paying assessment by saying that a prominent citizen of the village had paid. One case reported of Collector paying the amount himself and pressing the receipt upon a villager in order to use him as an example.

(6) *Propaganda against organizers of satyagraha*: Accounts circulated that villagers were terrorized by outside organizers into withholding payment.

(7) *Announcement of exemption from delay penalty*: Attempt to obtain payment during later months of campaign by promising exemption from fine if paid within given time.

(8) *Issue of counter-propaganda*: The State Information Bureau supplied leaflets, which were distributed under the direction of the District Collector.

(9) *Use of minority groups*: Introduction of Muslims as officials and police to split peasants on the basis of religious community; pressure on Parsis and Banias (moneylenders). Banias advised to keep currency notes on hand so that they might be attached, which would, in effect, amount to full payment.

(10) *Concessions*: As the campaign proceeded, Pathans were removed from the police forces. Some villages were regrouped with the effect that rates of enhancement were reduced. The demand for an enquiry was finally agreed to upon the undertaking by satyagrahis that conditions of payment would be fulfilled. The wording of the agreement allowed the government to save face.

Results

(1) *Enquiry Committee* (known as the Broomfield Committee) was appointed, thus fulfilling the initial single demand of the satyagraha. This Committee investigated conditions in Bardoli and the neighboring *taluka*, Chorasi, from November 1928 to March 1929. Representatives of the villagers were freely heard. The Committee reported that the people "though naturally not lacking in complaints, were entirely lacking in hostility. . . ."

(2) *Forfeited lands restored* to their original owners. The District Collector, who had declared that sold lands would never be restored, was replaced by a

new Collector who accomplished the restoration of lands.

(3) *All satyagrahis taken prisoner were released.*

(4) *Subordinate officials who had resigned during the movement were reinstated.*

(5) *Assessment revised:* The Enquiry Committee finally recommended an enhancement not to exceed 6¼ per cent. In the final assessment settlement, factors which the Committee had declared itself incompetent to rule upon were taken into consideration at the insistence of the peasants with the result that virtually no enhancement of revenue was assessed in Bardoli.

(6) *Closer cooperation was established between Hindus and Muslims,* moneylenders and peasants, and between other sections of the community. Indeed, the effect extended well beyond Bardoli. As Nehru observed, "the real success of their campaign . . . lay in the effect it produced amongst the peasantry all over India. Bardoli became a sign and a symbol of hope and strength and victory to the Indian peasant."

SUMMARY ANALYSIS OF THE BARDOLI CAMPAIGN

The Bardoli campaign exemplifies a full satyagraha movement which proceeded through very nearly all the steps and abided by the fundamental rules outlined for Gandhian satyagraha.

The "truth" objective in Bardoli was taken to be the granting of an impartial enquiry into the enhanced assessment of land tax. To this objective the satyagrahis clung without compromise. They demonstrated sincerity and determination through enduring the penalties of arrest and attachment of land—penalties which followed, according to law, from the refusal to pay the land tax.

Non-violent action characterized the campaign. Persuasive tactics were employed, including the coercive element of social boycott. (The government claimed that threats of ex-communication were made by satyagrahis.) However, vindictiveness appears to have been kept to a minimum and satyagraha leaders demonstrated their willingness to accept fully any person who wished to join the movement, at whatever stage, and also those who rejoined after having once seceded from it. Action towards the opponent was kept on a high level of non-violent non-cooperation. Necessities were provided to government officials, and all suggestions for resorting to material injury (such as the puncturing of tires) were rejected.

Direct action was developed only at the point persistent efforts at negotiation, petition, and other constitutional methods had failed to achieve redress of serious grievances.

Preparation for the direct action campaign included extensive education of participants in their duties as satyagrahis. There is no evidence of the use of fasting as a purificatory measure. Through prayers, readings, and community singing the preparation was put on a high moral plane.

During the agitational stage of the movement, mass meetings were widely organized. There was little use made of procession and other public demonstration, for in the case of Bardoli, the majority of the population could safely be assumed to be in favor of the satyagrahi's objectives. The February 12th resolution constituted the ultimatum of the Bardoli satyagraha, for it announced determination not to pay revenue until the government should appoint an impartial tribunal or, as an alternative, accept as full payment the amount of the earlier, unrevised, revenue assessment.

Economic boycott played only a minor role in the campaign and took the form of refusing to supply officials and other members of the opposition with non-essential goods and services.

The satyagraha was predominantly in the form of non-co-operation. The one notable element of civil disobedience was the insistent plowing and planting of lands which had been attached as though their legal status had not changed. Technical trespass was also extended—especially by women volunteers—through the building of huts and the camping upon forfeited land.

The final step in the movement directed against government, that of usurping the functions of government, was only partially present in the Bardoli campaign. The satyagraha committee without doubt was directing much of the life of the villagers throughout the *taluka*, especially during the latter months of the campaign. For an official to receive any services in the *taluka*, he had to have the permission of the satyagraha headquarters. This aspect of the campaign was especially alarming to the government in opposition. The question which the Governor raised as to whether "the writ of His Majesty the King-Emperor" or "the edict of some unofficial body" was to constitute the effective order was, indeed, a question of substance.

As for the guiding rules of satyagraha, the Bardoli movement followed them with a high degree of consistency. The movement was sustained largely by the efforts of those directly involved. Initiative was kept by the satyagrahis right up to the point of the final agreement. The government's reaction often followed upon a successful move of the satyagraha. This was demonstrated by the government's counter-propaganda measures. Specific acts of non-cooperation require, of course, the government to make the first move. The government issued final notices to pay the assessment or suffer forfeiture of land. Non-cooperation with the notice followed. This frequently involved sending letters of refusal, coupled with persuasive arguments, to individual officials urging them to resign their positions rather than press attachment action.

The demands were kept at a minimum and, in the course of the movement they were revised—in this case, upwards—to include remission of penalties resulting from the movement itself.

Propaganda was certainly an integral part of this campaign (as it was not in the Vykom struggle). Not only did this publicity function to strengthen the confidence of the peasants of Bardoli and to control mass action, but it also secured significant aid in funds and moral support from neighboring districts and, finally, from the country at large.

A continuing assessment of the situation and an examination of internal weaknesses were undertaken by the skilled leaders of the movement, and especially by Sardar Patel, who was a master at organization. New tactics were developed to meet specific situations as they arose. There was at no time an attempt to obscure the inner weaknesses of the satyagraha movement. The delicate problem of maintaining unity of action from the several religious, caste, and occupational communities within the Bardoli populace was never minimized. The opposition efforts to emphasize these divisions required skilled counter-measures. The progressive character of the satyagraha was evidenced in the change from an emphasis upon "fearlessness" in the early stages of the movement to "peace" and unity in the later stages. The strength of the peasant participants was persistently increased by cooperative activities.

Sardar Patel, as leader of the movement, repeatedly announced the desire to come to terms with the government. Yet, he at no time was willing to surrender the essential demand. When the settlement was finally achieved, Patel conceded the letter of the government counter-demand that the original tax be paid before the enquiry could be granted. The wording of the agreement, that "the conditions will be fulfilled," allowed the government to save face and yet met the full demands of the satyagrahis for an impartial enquiry. Finally, there was full agreement between the satyagraha leaders and the government on the fundamental position of the peasants' demand for an enquiry.

THE AHMEDABAD LABOR SATYAGRAHA[12]

Dates, duration, and locale

(1) February-March 1918.

(2) Duration of the actual satyagraha movement was 25 days.

(3) The dispute developed between the textile laborers and the mill-owners of Ahmedabad in Bombay Presidency.

Objectives

(1) *Background*: The dispute over the amount of "dearness" (cost of living) allowance to be paid to textile workers began with the withdrawal of a special bonus which had been granted to workers (in August 1917) to persuade them to continue work during a plague epidemic. The "plague bonus" in some cases was as high as 70 to 80 per cent of the workers' wages, and had been continued after danger from the plague had subsided. When (in January 1918) mill-owners made known their intention of withdrawing the bonus, workers made an appeal for at least a 50 per cent increase on the July salaries as a continuing cost of living allowance. They pointed to the sharp rise in prices, amounting to as much as two to four times the old prices.

Gandhi was informed of the situation first by one of the mill-owners, who asked that he intervene. He went to Ahmedabad and began his own investigation. Both sides agreed to submit the dispute to an arbitration board to consist of three representatives from each side. Gandhi was one of those appointed on behalf of the workers.

The arbitration had scarcely got underway (and Gandhi had temporarily left Ahmedabad) when laborers in some of the mills, acting upon fear of threatened lockout, struck work. Thereupon the arbitration broke down, the mill-owners declaring that they would not abide by the arbitration and would dismiss all the workers who were not willing to accept a 20 per cent increase as the living allowance.

Upon Gandhi's further investigation into details of costs and workers' conditions, he concluded that a 35 per cent increase was a just demand. He thereupon advised the workers to demand no more and no less than 35 per cent. When the mill-owners rejected this demand, conflict followed. Gandhi, who had entered the earlier situation as a conciliator, became the leader of the workers, and introduced satyagraha as the technique whereby a constructive solution could be achieved.

(2) *Immediate objective*: A 35 per cent increase in cost of living allowance or submission of the dispute to arbitration.

Satyagraha participants and leadership

(1) *Gandhi*: Peculiar to the Ahmedabad satyagraha was the close personal relationship between the leaders on opposing sides. Gandhi was a close friend both of the strikers and of the mill-owners.

(2) *Secondary leadership*: Anasuya Sarabhai, an effective labor organizer, was in the vanguard of the satyagraha strikers. Her brother, Ambalal Sarabhai, led the struggle on behalf of management. Other satyagraha leaders included Vallabhbhai Patel, Chhaganlal Gandhi, and Shankarlal Banker.

(3) *Participants* included thousands (between five and ten thousand) of laborers in the textile mills of Ahmedabad.

Participants and leadership of the opposition

    (1) *Management*: Represented by the Mill Agents' Group.

    (2) *Chief leader*: Ambalal Sarabhai, whom Gandhi described as the man "at the back of the mill-owners' unbending attitude towards the strike." Gandhi paid him this tribute: "His resolute will and transparent sincerity were wonderful and captured my heart. It was a pleasure to be pitched against him."

Organization and constructive program

    (1) *Self-sufficiency principle*: Gandhi insisted that during the strike period, the laborers earn a living by undertaking other labor. Many were employed in building a weaving school at the Gandhi ashram.

    (2) *Welfare activities*: Gandhi and other leaders instructed laborers in sanitation, rendered medical and other assistance, and organized the collection of information with regard to living conditions among laborers. Out of the experience of this struggle emerged the Ahmedabad Textile Labour Association with its extensive program of welfare benefits to members.

    (3) *Daily information bulletins* were issued.

    (4) *Organized daily meetings* tackled emerging problems.

Preparation for action

    (1) *Injunctions laid upon the satyagrahis*:

        (a) No violence.

        (b) No molestation of "blacklegs."

        (c) No dependence upon alms, but self-support through other labor.

        (d) No surrender, however long the strike.

    (2) *Satyagraha pledge* repeated daily at meetings:

        (a) Not to resume work until the 35 per cent increase was secured (based on wages of the previous July).

(b) Not to indulge in mischief, quarrelling, robbing, plundering, or abusive language or cause damage to mill-owners' property, but to behave peacefully during the period of lockout.

Action

(1) *Demonstrations*: Daily parades were taken through the streets of Ahmedabad with banners reading *"Ek tek!"* (united resolve).

(2) *Response to end of lockout*: Following the mill-owners announcement that the mills would be open to all who would accept a 20 per cent increase, some workers wavered in the strike resolve. Gandhi intensified his appeal to the laborers to remain firm, insisting upon the justice of a 35 per cent increase.

(3) *Fasting*: Upon signs of weakness within the laborers' ranks (including menacing attitudes towards blacklegs) Gandhi declared: "Unless the strikers rally and continue the strike till a settlement is reached, or till they leave the mills altogether, I will not touch any food." Gandhi acted upon this resolve. He dissuaded laborers from fasting with him, but many shared the first day of his fast.

(4) *Rejection of first offer*: On the third evening of the fast, Ambalal Sarabhai, leader of the mill-owners, offered immediately to concede 35 per cent if Gandhi would keep away from the laborers "for all time in future." Gandhi rejected this "exorbitant" demand, and at the same time acknowledged the coercive element in his fast.

(5) *Agreement*: In response to the representation that the mill-owners also had their own "pledge" to keep (of not granting more than 20 per cent increase), Gandhi agreed to settle the dispute by arbitration

and to compromise on details of the settlement. The following formula, suggested by Gandhi, was accepted by the mill-owners:

    (a) Workers were to resume work the following day (20 March) and on that day they would get a 35 per cent increase; on the second day of work (21 March) they would receive a 20 per cent increase.

    (b) From the third day (22 March) they would receive an increase in the amount decided by the arbitrator (but not to exceed 35 per cent).

    (c) Professor Anandshanker Dhruva, Vice-Principal of Gujarat College, was to be the Arbitrator.

    (d) During the period before the announcement of the award, workers were to be paid an increase of 27½ per cent.

    (e) The amount of increase decided upon by the Arbitrator was to be adjusted against the 27½ per cent, i.e., if the arbitration award was in excess of 27½, then employers would pay the additional amount, retroactively; if the award was less than 27½ per cent, the workers would refund the difference.

(6) *Acceptance of the settlement by workers*: Gandhi broke his fast upon the announcement of the settlement. Leaders from different sections of labor made speeches expressing gratitude and accepted the distribution of sweets by the employers. (This is a traditional manner of celebration and the expression of satisfaction.)

Reaction of opponents

    (1) *Lockout*: Imposed by the mill-owners on 22 February.

(2) *End of lockout*: All workers invited to return to work on the basis of a 20 per cent increase. (12 March.)

(3) *Counter-propaganda*: Leaflets were issued in an attempt to refute the case of the satyagrahis. Data on living costs presented by the satyagrahis challenged. Mill-owners' statement advised workers that they could earn more by "attending more carefully to their work" and suggested that mills were not run "out of love for humanity."

(4) *Circulation of rumors*: Rumors intended to weaken the stand of the strikers were reported to have been circulated by the mill-owners.

(5) *Negotiations with Gandhi*: Leader of the mill-owners (Ambalal Sarabhai) offered to concede the increase to induce Gandhi to terminate his fast. Asked Gandhi to keep away from laborers "for all time in future and leave matters between us and the workers entirely to us."

(6) *Capitulation*: Agreed to Gandhi's formula for submitting the dispute to arbitration.

Results

(1) *Arbitration of dispute*.

(2) *Decision*: Full 35 per cent increase on July pay granted to all mill-hands, together with the 7½ per cent additional increase for the period elapsed between the time of resumption of work and the announcement of the award. Decision was announced 8 October 1918.

(3) *Public reassured* by peaceful behavior of strikers: A British officer summed up Ahmedabad reaction by reporting that he had never seen or heard of such a peaceful struggle.

(4) *Long-term effects*: The development of the Ahmedabad Textile Labour Association with a constitution pledging members to truth and non-violence, and a

program including medical aid, maternity benefits, education, physical culture, recreation, and social reform activities—a pioneer in labor union organization in India.

SUMMARY ANALYSIS OF THE AHMEDABAD
LABOR SATYAGRAHA

A primary characteristic of the Ahmedabad labor satyagraha was the use of the fast as an instrument of non-violent force. Gandhi admitted the coercive character of this fast, and in his autobiography declared that it "was not free from a grave defect." For, he explained, his close and cordial relations with the mill-owners made it certain that his fast "could not but affect their decision." He had undertaken the fast because of the lapse on the part of the laborers and to stiffen their determination to keep the no-work pledge. He recognized "as a satyagrahi" that he should not fast against the mill-owners but "ought to leave them free to be influenced by the mill-hands' strike alone." Upon his insistence that they not let his fast influence them, Gandhi tells us that the mill-owners "received my words coldly and even flung keen, delicate bits of sarcasm at me, as indeed they had a perfect right to do."[13] It is clear, then, by Gandhi's own judgment, that the Ahmedabad movement did not measure up to ideal satyagraha. But that the movement does qualify as satyagraha, in the sense in which I have described the technique, can be seen by examining its further characteristics and the steps followed throughout its procedure.

The social justice underlying the demand for increased allowance constituted for this movement the "truth" factor. Arbitration of the dispute was a possible alternative. Non-violence was observed with slight transgressions into "menacing" attitudes towards blacklegs. The element of self-suffering was present both in the workers' forfeiture of pay and in the fasting of Gandhi. The preparation of the workers to undertake work unfamiliar to them, and especially work which oftentimes they considered beneath them, was a new departure in labor action. Skilled workers were persuaded by satyagraha leaders to do such work as carrying heavy loads of brick for a building project at the ashram. Other constructive elements of satyagraha (such as sanitation drives) were also present even though the duration of the strike was brief.

The propaganda program was an integral part of this labor satyagraha, both in the form of the series of leaflets issued by satyagraha leaders and the shouting of slogans during processions through the streets of Ahmedabad. Efforts were made to effect a settlement before resorting to direct action. Throughout the struggle, the initiative remained with the satyagrahis although there was very little positive non-violent aggressive action. The inner weaknesses of the laborers were evident, and Gandhi's decision to fast was an admission of those weaknesses.

The Ahmedabad movement illustrates the role which arbitration may play in the course of satyagraha. The conviction that the demand had been kept as low as was consistent with "truth" was subject to the constant readiness incumbent upon a satyagrahi to concede that he may have been in error, and his preparation to be so persuaded. Satyagrahis in this case had neither been dissuaded from their initial demand of the 35 per cent increase, nor had they persuaded their opponents to concede the demand. At any stage in a satyagraha movement, arbitration may enter as a tool for settling the dispute provided the satyagrahis are satisfied that the climate has improved to a point where arbitration will be fair and effective. In Ahmedabad it had been the breakdown of arbitration in the first instance which had precipitated the struggle. The satyagraha succeeded in changing the situation to the point where arbitration could again be undertaken. Satyagrahis had nothing to lose, Gandhi was convinced, from submitting the dispute to a third party insofar as the satyagraha demand had been kept as low as possible. He was fully prepared to press the case before the arbitrator and to expect a favorable decision. This confidence was, in fact, justified, for the full 35 per cent was in the end awarded. Clearly, satyagrahis take some risk in submitting their demands to arbitration, for they agree to abide by the judgment of a third party's view of the "truth." Nevertheless, a satyagrahi is bound to seek a solution through some form of negotiation or arbitration early in his efforts and, in every case, before resorting to direct action. If these efforts have failed (as they had in this case), one of the purposes of direct action is to establish a situation which will allow for arbitration. Depending upon the character of a given conflict situation, a final solution through arbitration may bring about the conclusion of a given satyagraha movement.

The further significance of the Ahmedabad satyagraha is reflected in the development of the Ahmedabad Textile Labour Association which grew out of the work done among the laborers in this and subsequent labor actions. Writing in 1946, G. N. Dhawan commented that the Ahmedabad Textile Labour Association was "the most powerful labour union in the country with a membership of 55,000" and that it was recognized as outstanding for its "indigenous character . . . and its system of joint arbitration and conciliation fostered by the influence of Gandhiji."[14] The union's devotion to principles of non-violence and to constructive welfare work is notable. The Association also has, since 1937, trained its members in supplementary occupations so that in case of a lockout or strike or, of course, loss of employment, they could be self-sustaining. Such a training program follows from the fundamentals of satyagraha.

NATIONWIDE SATYAGRAHA AGAINST THE ROWLATT BILLS[15]

Dates, duration, and locale

(1) 1 March 1919 to 18 April 1919.

(2) Seven weeks.

(3) This campaign was the first nationwide satyagraha

movement to be launched in India. Plan of action originated in Ahmedabad; headquarters were established in Bombay. The most vigorous action developed in Bombay Presidency and in Northern India, with Madras City and Calcutta also prominent centers of struggle.

Objectives

(1) *Background*:

(a) Provisions of the Rowlatt Bills: As an outcome of the recommendations made by the Sedition Committee presided over by Sir Sidney Rowlatt in 1918, legislation was drafted to strengthen the hand of the government in the control of crime, including sedition. The so-called Rowlatt Act (Government of India Act No. XI of 1919) "was framed to enable anarchical offences to be tried expeditiously before a strong court consisting of three High Court judges, with no right of appeal." It also provided for powers of preventive detention— the arrest and confinement of persons suspected of acts threatening public safety—as well as power to order a person suspected of subversive activities to furnish security, to reside in a particular place, or to abstain from any specified act. The Act further provided that "dangerous" persons could be continuously detained.

A second Bill, which was "intended to make a permanent change in the ordinary criminal law of the land," was never brought before the Indian Legislative Council. It included provisions such as: ". . . possession of a seditious document with the intention to publish or to circulate the same . . . to be punishable with imprisonment."

(b) The Government argument: The defenders of the Rowlatt Bills emphasized their safeguards. The procedure was to be brought into operation only when the Governor-General was satisfied that in any particular part of British India offenses of a revolutionary character were prevalent. An investigating authority was also established which was to examine the material upon which orders against any persons were framed. This authority was to include one judicial officer and one non-official Indian.

(c) The opposition argument: To Indians, the Bills were "unjust, subversive of the principles of liberty and justice, destructive of the elementary rights of an individual on which the safety of India as a whole and of the State itself is based." The Bills appeared to embody a denial of promises made by British statesmen during the war and to confirm suspicion that Britain intended to deprive India of progress towards independence. They also represented an "encroachment on the ordinary rights of free citizens," including the withdrawal of trial by jury and right of appeal in cases of sedition, the authorization of trials *in camera* and admission of evidence not subjected to cross-examination, the reserving to the Executive the right to restrict liberty of an individual, and curbs on freedom of speech, press, and assembly. Popular resentment of the Bills was extreme and widespread.

(2) *The immediate objective* of this satyagraha was the withdrawal of the enacted Bill, "An Act to Cope with

Anarchical and Revolutionary Crime," and preven-
tion of the passage of the second Bill.

(3) *Long-range objectives*: In mobilizing popular support and intensifying political awareness, the movement was part of the continuing nationalist struggle.

Satyagraha participants and leadership

(1) *Gandhi* initiated the movement together with asso-
ciates at his ashram in Ahmedabad.

(2) *Secondary leadership*: Members of Gandhi's ashram
at Ahmedabad and nationalist leaders throughout
India.

(3) *Number of participants*: The over-all program of
satyagraha is said to have involved "millions" in all
parts of India. Response from the South was unex-
pectedly good. In Bombay City the number of special
volunteers (active satyagrahis) was reported to have
been 600.

(4) *Characteristics of participants*: The official British
report noted the "unprecedented fraternization" between Hindus and Muslims, even those of the lower
classes. Women and children also participated in the
direct action.

Participants and leadership of the opposition

(1) *Officials* of the Government of India.

(2) *Indian police* led by *British police officers*.

Organization and constructive program

(1) A *Satyagraha Sabha* was established in Bombay as
headquarters for the movement.

(2) *Selection of laws*: Following the decision to engage
in civil disobedience, a Satyagraha Committee was
appointed to select the laws which were to be civilly
disobeyed.

(3) *Local Committees established* in other parts of India to educate the people in the principles and technique of satyagraha.

(4) *Constructive work methods* were introduced at the Satyagraha Sabha.

Preparation for action

(1) *The Satyagraha Pledge*: The publication of the following pledge carried not only the statement of the objective, but also emphasized principles of truth and non-violence:

Being conscientiously of opinion that the Bill known as the Indian Criminal Law Amendment Bill No. 1 of 1919 and the Criminal Law Emergency Powers Bill No. 2 of 1919 are unjust, subversive of the principles of liberty and justice, and destructive of the elementary rights of an individual on which the safety of India as a whole and the State itself is based, we solemnly affirm that in the event of these Bills becoming law and until they are withdrawn, we shall refuse civilly to obey these laws and such other laws as the committee to be hereafter appointed may think fit and we further affirm that in the struggle we will faithfully follow truth and refrain from violence to life, person or property.

(2) *Discussion* of the issues at popular meetings and signing of the satyagraha pledge.

(3) *Purification*: Mass participation was signalized by a day of "humiliation and prayer." Every satyagrahi was required to observe a 24-hour fast as discipline to fit him to offer civil disobedience. Signing of the satyagraha pledge was also required of all civil resisters. Those who did not sign the pledge and fast for 24 hours were not to engage in civil disobedience, but could non-cooperate with the government in oth-

er ways. They could take another vow "to follow Truth at all costs and to refrain from violence."

(4) *Preparation described by an official*: The opposition agreed that Gandhi had "expressly condemned any resort to material force," and that "there was nothing in Mr. Gandhi's attitude or pronouncements which could have justified Government in taking any steps against him before the inception of the movement."

(5) *Criticism of Rowlatt legislation in the Council*: Non-official members of the Indian Legislative Council vehemently attacked the Rowlatt Bills. An official government source noted that this denunciation, together with the publication of the satyagraha pledge "laid the foundation of an agitation so intensive as to be without parallel in recent years."

Preliminary action

(1) *Appeal to the Viceroy*: Upon the passage of the first Rowlatt Bill, Gandhi urged the Viceroy (through both private and public letters) not to give it his assent. Should the Bill become law, Gandhi warned, no other course was open but direct mass action.

(2) *Plan for civil disobedience*: Satyagrahis were pledged to disobey the Rowlatt Act if applied to them. It was also decided to place the movement on a broader basis by selecting other laws to contravene. This decision reflected the further implications of the movement as part of the nationalist struggle, and it alienated some of the national leaders. Motilal Nehru, who opposed the decision, indicated later (in his Presidential address to the 1919 Congress Session) his belief in the revolutionary potential of satyagraha.

(3) *Widescale publicity*: During the entire month of March the press was filled with reports of protest

meetings, articles and letters opposing the Rowlatt legislation.

Action

(1) *Hartal*: The closing of shops took place throughout the country. The date, originally set for 30 March, was later changed to 6 April. Hartal began in Delhi on 30 March because leaders of the movement there had not received the announcement of postponement. Hartal elsewhere occurred on the 6th and was very nearly complete.

(2) *Demonstration*: Processions were taken through the streets of the major cities. Initial adherence to strict non-violence.

(3) *Contravention of selected laws*: The Committee decided to disobey only such laws as lent themselves to mass disobedience:

(a) Preparation of salt from sea-water—a contravention of the salt tax law.

(b) Sale of proscribed literature: Prohibited literature was sold in the open (the seller was to be easily traceable). Portions of prohibited books were read to the public. The intention to sell literature was publicly announced by the Satyagraha Sabha. If enough copies were not available others were to be made by hand. Books selected for circulation were: *Hind Swaraj*, by Gandhi; the Gujarati adaptation of Ruskin's *Unto this Last*, translated by Gandhi (entitled *Sarvodaya*); *The Story of a Satyagrahi*, a paraphrase of the *Defence and Death of Socrates*. All these titles had been proscribed by the government.

(c) Publication and circulation of an unregistered newspaper: Gandhi published a newspaper called *Satyagrahi*. This paper published in-

structions on behavior in prison, reaction to
fine, attachment of property, and urged no
evasion or defense. Large sums were collected
from the sale of prohibited literature, the
proceeds going into the general fund for support of civil disobedience.

(4) *Outbreak of violence:* In response to violent retal-
iation by police, and later to the arrest of leaders,
non-violence broke down in many places after the
first day of mass demonstration. Stone-throwing was
reported in Delhi, and elsewhere buildings were
burned, telegraph lines cut, and both English and
Indian officers killed.

(5) *Gandhi suspended movement* and went on "peni-
tential fast" for three days.

(6) *Gandhi's advice to other satyagrahis:* Acknowledg-
ing the deviation from true satyagraha, Gandhi urged
others to fast and to "confess" their guilt. "I was
firmly of opinion," he wrote, "that those who wanted
to lead the people to Satyagraha ought to be able to
keep the people within the limited non-violence expected of them."

Reaction of the opponents

(1) *Determination to pass the Rowlatt Bills into law:*
The first Bill was forced into Select Committee by
the use of the official majority. There it was modified
in an effort to conciliate the public by limiting its
effectiveness to a three-year period.

(2) *Violent repression:* Police firings were reported from
the first day of *hartal* and processions, which opened
30 March in Delhi. *Lathi* charges occurred wherever
satyagraha entered the active phase (a *lathi* is a
metal-capped staff commonly carried by policemen).

(3) *Response to the sale of proscribed literature:* The
government chose to avoid further complications by

refraining from making arrests for breach of the proscription laws. Officials rationalized by taking the view that the books had not, in fact, been sold, and those which had were new editions and did not come under proscription regulations.

(4) *Restraint of Gandhi*: As Gandhi tried to proceed from Bombay to the Punjab, he was served with a notice prohibiting his entry into the Punjab. He was arrested upon his refusal to obey this order and was escorted by police back to Bombay.

(5) *Martial law* imposed in Ahmedabad, Lahore, and Amritsar. It was out of the martial law rule under General Dyer that the infamous Jallianwala Bagh massacre emerged in Amritsar. Police, under the direction of British officers, fired upon a crowd gathered within a confined area, killing hundreds of helpless persons. This period also saw degrading punishments, such as public flogging and the hated "crawling order" which forced Indians to crawl upon their bellies when passing a certain lane where an Englishwoman had been assaulted.

Results

(1) *Immediate result*: The objective of the campaign was not immediately realized (and the campaign was broken off before it reached its natural conclusion). However, the second Rowlatt Bill was never brought before the Legislative Council, and the Act which had precipitated the campaign was never invoked by the government.

(2) *Gandhi's revision of prerequisites for satyagraha*: It was with reference to the Rowlatt Bills satyagraha and his failure to anticipate the character of the response that Gandhi used the phrase "Himalayan miscalculation." Upon learning of the breakdown of the

action into violence, he realized that the people had not been properly prepared for offering satyagraha. "I realized that before a people could be fit for offering civil disobedience, they should thoroughly understand its deeper implications," he wrote. He determined that before he would again lead such a movement "it would be necessary to create a band of well-tried, pure-hearted volunteers who thoroughly understood the strict conditions of Satyagraha. They could explain these to the people, and by sleepless vigilance keep them on the right path."

(3) *Organization of a corps of satyagrahis*: Through the Satyagraha Sabha, Gandhi raised a corps of volunteers and commenced the work of educating the public with regard to the meaning and practice of satyagraha.

(4) *Cooperation with authorities*: In the belief that "before one can be fit for the practice of civil disobedience one must have rendered a willing and respectful obedience to the state laws," Gandhi announced that satyagrahis must "ceaselessly" help the authorities "in all the ways available to us as Satyagrahis" in order "to restore order and curb lawlessness." They must, he said, "fearlessly spread the doctrine of Satya and Ahimsa and then and not till then shall we be able to undertake mass Satyagraha."

SUMMARY ANALYSIS OF THE SATYAGRAHA AGAINST THE ROWLATT BILLS

The Rowlatt satyagraha was, in terms of Gandhian satyagraha, a failure. It was characterized by the outbreak of violence. Forces had been released which Gandhi and his workers could not control. The weaknesses in the campaign which issued in this result will be examined presently. Does the Rowlatt satyagraha disprove Gandhi's claims for the efficacy of non-violent action? Or was this movement more accurately *duragraha* rather than *satyagraha*?

An analysis of the procedure of the campaign indicates that most of the steps in a proper satyagraha were present and that most of the rules were operative. It is correct, I believe, to describe this movement as true Gandhian satyagraha. The immediate objective was clearly the removal of a law taken to be unjust. The "truth" goal of the campaign was the abolition of laws believed to violate the individual's civil rights, and for politically aware Indians, the Rowlatt Bills symbolized the further injustice of India's subjugation by the British. Plans for action against the government adhered to non-violent principles. Laws were to be quietly contravened, and their selection was such as to assure the easiest possible contravention with the least possible provocation to violence from the police. Self-suffering was invited wherever opposition from police was encountered. The mode of behavior for active resisters was elaborated in the publication *Satyagrahi*, which was sold in contravention of the law requiring publications to be registered. The satyagraha was launched with a fast intended to forge unity among satyagrahis and to instill determination tempered by objectivity.

Basic rules for the prosecution of satyagraha are also to be found in the Rowlatt movement:

(1) The attitude of self-reliance was characteristic of the satyagraha organization. Financial support was achieved through the publication and sale of literature.

(2) The initiative was, in the early stages of the satyagraha, retained in satyagrahi hands. Once violence had broken out, the satyagrahis were overwhelmed with the task of controlling the populace, and the initiative passed to the opposition, which imposed severe repressive measures resulting in further violence.

(3) Propaganda was certainly made an integral part of the campaign. The press detailed the case against the Rowlatt Act

and carried daily reports of the agitation. The Satyagraha Sabha issued bulletins and instructions to participants in the campaign.

(4) Demands for fundamental civil rights were clearly stated.

(5) The resort to civil disobedience came after other attempts at honorable settlement had been made. Gandhi had entered into correspondence with the government urging the abandonment of the objectionable Act. Unofficial members in the Legislative Council attempted to have the Bill killed in the Legislature. The Government was apprised of the intention of the satyagrahis to launch civil disobedience, and of all other steps in the organized movement.

(6) Morale and discipline within satyagraha ranks were not strong enough to restrain violence on the part of the public. The results of this campaign indicated the necessity for greater awareness of internal weaknesses and more thorough preparation of all satyagrahis for their responsibilities.

(7) Attempts were made throughout the preliminary action to establish a climate of opinion which would allow for maximum cooperation with the government in suppressing "anarchical crimes" without resort to the objectionable Rowlatt legislation. In the later stages, Gandhi waited upon government authorities and finally sought their permission to address the meeting in Ahmedabad, where he announced suspension of the campaign.

(8) At no time was there a suggestion on the part of the satyagrahis that the essential demand (withdrawal of the Act and abandonment of the second Bill) could be compromised.

(9) The movement was suspended before an explicit settlement could be achieved.

Again, an examination of the steps through which the satyagraha against the Rowlatt Bills proceeded, reveals that this movement qualified as true Gandhian satyagraha:

(1) Negotiation was fully attempted.

(2) Preparation of satyagrahis was undertaken through self-purificatory fasting and instruction in non-violent action. However, in the light of the results, it may be said that this stage of preparation should have been extended, both in breadth and in intensity. Fasting, it should be noted, was used only for the purpose of self-discipline and later by Gandhi as a penance for the outbreak of violence; but fasting as coercion was no part of the campaign.

(3) Agitation was fully conducted and was nationwide.

(4) The ultimatum in the form of the satyagraha pledge was unequivocal, as was Gandhi's statement to the Viceroy.

(5) Economic boycott did not play a part in the movement; the hartal which opened the campaign functioned as symbolic strike.

(6) Non-cooperation was not the central activity in this movement. However, it was used by individuals. (No less a person than the poet Rabindranath Tagore surrendered his knighthood in a gesture of non-cooperation as a result of this satyagraha.)

(7) Civil disobedience characterized the campaign. The further step of selecting laws other than the one against which the movement was directed, was a feature of the movement. Contravention of laws regulating publication and distribution of literature was highly organized.

(8) The campaign did not extend to the point of usurping the functions of government, although in Bombay the Satyagraha Sabha appears to have supplanted the government temporarily in securing allegiance from the populace.

The campaign against the Rowlatt Bills did, then, contain the essential factors which mark a proper satyagraha movement. But why did the movement result in widespread disorder and disintegrate into violence which necessitated its suspension?

The foremost reason for the failure of the campaign to remain non-violent lies in the inadequate preparation of those who participated, especially those on the periphery of the campaign. The code of discipline, which was understood and adhered to by some of the central figures in the campaign, was not sufficiently ingrained in enough of the volunteers to assure strict adherence to satyagraha. Leadership was not extensive enough to control a suddenly activated mass following. As Gandhi was to point out to the Hunter Committee, which investigated the disturbance, the masses of India had formerly remained completely inert. Indian leaders had never before attracted them into political action. They were completely undisciplined. The Rowlatt movement tapped, for the first time, resources which had long lain dormant. Motilal Nehru described the change which this satyagraha effected:

> A new force was suddenly introduced into our politics, a force with the most tremendous potentialities. India's masses were suddenly awakened and the message of Satyagraha entered the humblest home. Some of us did not entirely agree with the wording of the Satyagraha pledge, many were of opinion that the time had not come for civil disobedience. But few, I imagine, can disagree with the essentials of the doctrine. These, as I conceive them, are truth, fearlessness and non-violence.[16]

Gandhi's "Himalayan miscalculation," as he called it, lay largely in his failure to anticipate the overwhelming response among the masses which his appeal invoked. "They had found a new force," he explained, "but they did not know what it was and how to use it." Whereas a group of the leading satyagrahis may have understood the character and implications of non-violent action, the masses had had virtually no indoctrination in the meaning of satyagraha.

Because of the stature which Gandhi had attained as a social leader, he was able to control this newly released force in places where he could personally direct operations. The results in other places, however, clearly indicated the need for the development of strength and depth in secondary leadership.

The departure from satyagraha principles was most marked in places where Gandhi was prevented by authorities from proceeding. A direct appeal by Gandhi was never directly made in Delhi or in the Punjab. Upon Gandhi's arrest, those who had had little knowledge and experience with the more difficult techniques of non-violent action turned to the expression of their resentment through violence—the one well-understood method of relieving immediate tensions. Once the leaders in non-violence had been removed—or, when false rumors were spread that they had been arrested—the reaction tended to be one of violence to procure their release. Such was the case in Ahmedabad, where Anasuya Sarabhai (who had shared in the leadership of the 1918 satyagraha of the textile workers) was reported to have been arrested. There was, then, a failure to establish a chain of succession in leadership as well as a failure in thorough-going discipline. That violence was not the outcome of civil disobedience, itself, appeared quite clear from the fact that where violence reached its peak —notably in the Punjab—there had been no civil disobedience, and that, conversely, satyagraha in the form of civil disobedience flourished in other parts of India where there was virtually no outbreak of violence. (Motilal Nehru, who had initially rejected Gandhi's methods, acknowledged this significant fact in his comments on the movement later that year.[17])

There were, of course, many sympathizers and participants in the general movement against the Rowlatt Act who had no intention of following the lead in non-violence. This factor is undoubtedly to be expected in any mass satyagraha of extensive nationwide character. The evidence which was brought before the Hunter Committee showed that the violence which occurred in Ahmedabad was effected in an "organized manner." The satyagraha plan had not provided for the countering of organized violence on the part of those who claimed to belong to the movement. Non-violent strategy in a campaign of such proportions should allow for tactical operations in several directions. There was a failure on the part of the Satyagraha Sabha to anticipate the extent to which violence might have been employed, and to prepare oblique non-violent counter-movements.

In sum, the Rowlatt satyagraha's disintegration into violence was the result of an appeal to the masses before they had been adequately prepared to offer satyagraha. It was a failure to communicate the meaning, the philosophy, and the implications of the all-important technique to its mass participants, and finally the failure to plan for a non-violent resistance to elements within its own ranks which had turned to violent means.

The failure of the Rowlatt satyagraha was, then, not a failure in terms of the efficacy of the technique of satyagraha; it was the failure of those who planned and executed the movement adequately to train participants in the technique and to apply the technique, where necessary, to counter within their own ranks departures from fundamental principles.

THE SALT SATYAGRAHA[18]

Note: The Salt Satyagraha was part of the year-long Civil Disobedience movement of 1930-31. The following outline touches upon the entire movement, although many of the details of that extensive struggle have been omitted.

Dates, duration, and locale

(1) March 1930-March 1931.
(2) In its extended form, civil disobedience continued for about one year.
(3) A national movement, with headquarters in Bombay. Satyagraha activities were launched in every province.

Objectives

(1) *Immediate*: Removal of the Salt Acts. These statutes provided for a government monopoly of salt. Revenue realized from the Salt Tax amounted at this time to $25,000,000 out of a total revenue of about $800,000,000. These laws were held to work a hardship on the people, especially the poor, and to constitute the taxation of a necessity.

(2) *Long-range*: The Salt Acts were chosen by Gandhi for contravention in a general civil disobedience movement because they not only appeared to be basically unjust in themselves, but also because they symbolized an unpopular, unrepresentative, and alien government. British official sources described the object of the satyagraha as "nothing less than to cause a complete paralysis of the administrative machinery. . . ." The ultimate objective of civil disobedience was complete independence.

Satyagraha participants and leadership

(1) *Gandhi* and other leaders of the Indian National Congress.

(2) *Secondary leadership*: In the opening phase, direct participation was limited to disciplined members of Gandhi's ashram at Ahmedabad, selected by Gandhi to make the march to the sea. They were described as "soldiers who had been steeled to the disciplines and hardships which a two hundred mile march on foot would necessarily entail on them."

Prominent Congressmen served as organizers in other parts of India. Among these were Rajagopalachariar in Tamilnad, Vallabhbhai Patel for the whole of Gujarat, Jawaharlal Nehru in the United Provinces, Satish Chandra Das Gupta in Bengal, Konda Venkatappaya in Andhra, and Gopabandhu Chowdhury in Utkal (Orissa).

(3) *Participants*: After the initial breach of the salt laws, Indians throughout the country participated.

(4) *Characteristics of participants*: The official government report indicated that the majority of participants were Hindus, but that Muslims did take part, especially on the Frontier. Officials expressed concern that the "Hindu mercantile and industrial community showed active sympathy" and financially supported the movement. Another "unexpected" element among satyagrahis was a large number of Indian women. "Thousands of them—many being of good family and high educational attainments—suddenly emerged from the seclusion of their homes and in some instances actually from *purdah*, in order to join Congress demonstrations and assist in picketing. . . ."

Participants and leadership of the opposition

(1) *Officials* of the Government of India.

(2) *Police*, both British and Indian.

(3) *Units of the army.*

Organization and constructive program

(1) *Role of the Indian National Congress*: This campaign was conducted as part of an over-all political movement for independence. It was a program adopted by the largest political opposition party in India and so was planned in the light of the organization and constitutional make-up of the Party. The Congress Party delegated to Gandhi full power and responsibility for organizing and leading the campaign (by resolution, 21 March 1930).

(2) *Succession of leadership*: Extensive powers were given to the president of the Congress (then Jawaharlal Nehru) to act on behalf of the executive committee in case it could not meet. The president was empowered to nominate a successor in the event of

his removal from action, the successor, in turn, was to have the same power of appointment of a successor. Similar powers were given to provincial and local Congress chiefs.

(3) *Khadi*: The wearing of hand-spun cloth was imperative for all satyagrahis—it became the uniform of the Congress and the movement.

(4) *Other aspects of constructive work*: Welfare and self-sufficiency work was considered one of the ways in which the cause could be promoted. A satyagrahi should "find himself in one of the following states," Gandhi instructed: "1. In prison or in an analogous state, or 2. Engaged in Civil Disobedience, or 3. Under orders at the spinning wheel, or at some constructive work advancing Swaraj."

Preparation for action

(1) *Public opinion on swaraj*: Prior to the launching of this campaign, the sentiment for full independence was developed through discussion and the deliberations of the Congress Party. On 26 January the Congress, meeting in Lahore, had pledged its members to "carry out the Congress instructions issued from time to time for the purpose of establishing Purna Swaraj" (full independence).

(2) *Training courses*: Volunteers for satyagraha undertook courses of training for direct action, especially in methods of controlling large crowds. Satyagrahis drilled regularly, though they did so without arms.

(3) *Planning for civil disobedience*: The salt laws were selected for contravention. Gandhi planned to lead a march to the sea where satyagrahis would, in violation of the salt monopoly, prepare salt from sea water. Vallabhbhai Patel was chosen to prepare the way for the proposed march. He proceeded along the route to be taken, advising the people of the

objectives of the movement, and instructing them in the principles of satyagraha. They were urged to undertake constructive work, to abstain from intoxicants, and to overcome untouchability. (On 7 March Patel was arrested.)

(4) *The Satyagraha Pledge*: The All-India Congress Committee, meeting at Ahmedabad on 21 March 1930, drew up the following pledge to be taken by those volunteering for satyagraha:

1. I desire to join the civil resistance campaign for the Independence of India undertaken by the National Congress.

2. I accept the Creed of the National Congress, that is, the attainment of Purna Swaraj (complete independence) by the people of India by all peaceful and legitimate means.

3. I am ready and willing to go to jail and undergo all other sufferings and penalties that may be inflicted on me in this campaign.

4. In case I am sent to jail, I shall not seek any monetary help for my family from the Congress funds.

5. I shall implicitly obey the orders of those who are in charge of the campaign.

Preliminary action

(1) *Notice of civil disobedience*: Through the Congress independence resolution adopted at Lahore, subsequently advertised and discussed widely, the intention of the Congress Party to agitate for independence, if necessary through civil disobedience, was made known.

(2) *Gandhi's letter to Lord Irwin, the Viceroy*: On 2 March 1930, Gandhi apprised the Viceroy of the satyagraha plan and reviewed the grievances of the people. Non-violence, he wrote, could be "an in-

tensely active force." It was his purpose, he told the Viceroy, "to set in motion that force, as well against the organised violent force of the British rule as the unorganised violent force of the growing party of violence. . . . The non-violence will be expressed through Civil Disobedience, for the moment confined to the inmates of the Satyagraha Ashram, but ultimately designed to cover all those who choose to join the movement with its obvious limitations."

(3) *The ultimatum*: In his letter, Gandhi urged a negotiated settlement, barring which, he would lead a satyagraha movement. He further stated the exact day upon which he would proceed, with co-workers, to disregard the provisions of the Salt Acts. "It is, I know, open to you," he told the Viceroy, "to frustrate my design by arresting me. I hope that there will be tens of thousands ready, in a disciplined manner, to take up the work after me, and, in the act of disobeying the Salt Act, to lay themselves open to the penalties of a Law that should never have disfigured the Statute Book." He would, Gandhi said, welcome further discussion, and his letter was in no way a threat but a "simple and sacred duty peremptory on a civil resister." A young Englishman (Reginald Reynolds) who had joined the ashram was selected to deliver the letter.

Action

(1) *The march to the sea*: On 12 March, Gandhi and his co-satyagrahis left Ahmedabad for Dandi on the sea coast. He urged villagers along the way to pursue constructive work, to remain non-violent, and to participate in the civil disobedience following the initial breach of the law at Dandi. The march was considered a form of penance and discipline for the

93

beginning of civil disobedience. It also dramatized the issues and attracted nationwide attention.

(2) *The opening of civil disobedience*: The satyagrahis reached Dandi on 5 April. The following morning, after prayers, they proceeded to the beach where they prepared salt from sea water, thus technically breaking the salt laws.

(3) *Gandhi's statement to the press*: Upon breaking the law, Gandhi declared that it was then open to anyone who would take the risk of prosecution to manufacture salt wherever he wished. Villagers were to be instructed concerning the meaning of the salt tax and directed in methods of preparing salt.

(4) *Issuing of leaflets*: Instructions concerning the manufacture of salt were published in the various parts of the country.

(5) *Response from the people*: "It seemed as though a spring had been suddenly released," Nehru wrote. Everywhere people began to make salt. They collected "pots and pans and ultimately succeeded in producing some unwholesome stuff, which we waved about in triumph, and often auctioned for fancy prices." The main thing, Nehru continued, was to commit a breach of the "obnoxious Salt Law. . . . As we saw the abounding enthusiasm of the people and the way salt-making was spreading like a prairie fire, we felt a little abashed and ashamed for having questioned the efficacy of this method when it was first proposed by Gandhiji. And we marvelled at the amazing knack of the man to impress the multitude and make it act in an organised way."

(6) *Hartal*: Throughout the country shops closed in response to arrests of satyagraha leaders.

(7) *Resignation of offices*: Headmen in villages and subordinate officers resigned in large numbers in sympathy with satyagraha.

(8) *Symbolic acts*: In many parts of India dramatic demonstrations were conducted. In Bombay an "effigy" of the Salt Acts was thrown into the sea as a symbol that British law was dead in the land.

(9) *Succession in leadership*: Jawaharlal Nehru was arrested on 14 April and was succeeded by his father, Motilal Nehru. In other places, leaders of the satyagraha were replaced by appointment following the arrest of the initial leadership. Gandhi, arrested 5 May, was replaced by Abbas Tyabji.

(10) *Non-payment of taxes*: In some areas, as in Bardoli, a program of non-payment of taxes was undertaken.

(11) *Action to control rioting*: Leaders attempted to preserve the non-violent character of satyagraha. In response to the outbreak of riots in Karachi and Calcutta, Gandhi announced: "If non-violence has to fight the people's violence in addition to the violence of the Government it must still perform its arduous task at any cost." (17 April.) Gandhi later (26 April) announced that if satyagrahis who followed him did not fulfill the basic conditions, he himself would practice satyagraha against them.

(12) *Gandhi's second letter to Viceroy*: The Government, in a sort of non-cooperation of its own, refused to arrest Gandhi early in the campaign. The first week of May he explained in a second letter his next move—he would set out for Dharsana where the Government operated a large salt works. There he would demand possession of these works. It would be possible, he said, for the Viceroy to prevent this "raid" in one of the following three ways:

1. by removing the salt tax;
2. by arresting me and my party unless the country can, as I hope it will, replace every one taken away;

3. by sheer goondaism [hooliganism] unless every head broken is replaced as I hope it will be.

(13) *Raids on salt works*: Following Gandhi's arrest on 5 May (just after midnight), volunteers, led by Congress notables, marched to occupy the salt depots. Fresh volunteers stepped in as others were struck down by the police. Organized first-aid units worked to revive victims.

(14) *Non-violent persuasion of police*: Throughout the attack upon the satyagraha raiders, volunteers refrained from striking back or even from deflecting blows. They rushed onto the salt pans, wave upon wave. Where they could, they pleaded with the police to join them. Incidents were reported of policemen refusing to continue the assault. An American journalist, Negley Farson, recorded an incident in which a Sikh, blood-soaked from the assault of a police sergeant, fell under a heavy blow. Congress first-aid volunteers rushed up to rub his face with ice. ". . . he gave us a bloody grin and stood up to receive some more. . . ." The police sergeant was "so sweaty from his exertions that his Sam Browne had stained his white tunic. I watched him with my heart in my mouth. He drew back his arm for a final swing—and then he dropped his hands down by his side. 'It's no use,' he said, turning to me with half an apologetic grin, 'You can't hit a bugger when he stands up to you like that!' He gave the Sikh a mock salute and walked off."

(15) *Economic boycott*: When raids on salt works were halted upon the advent of the monsoon, civil disobedience took other forms including boycott of foreign-made products, especially cloth. Both cloth and liquor shops were persistently picketed.

(16) *Disobedience of ordinances*: As the campaign pro-

ceeded, special ordinances designed to suppress publicity and control assembly were promulgated by the Government. These were consistently disobeyed in a general movement to the jails.

(17) *Continuing activities*: The extensive campaign continued throughout the year and involved many manifestations of non-cooperation and civil disobedience.

(18) *Culmination of the movement*: A settlement was reached following talks between Gandhi and the Viceroy, and the Gandhi-Irwin Agreement was published on 5 March 1931.

Reaction of opponents

(1) *Arrests*: Initially, the Government avoided making mass arrests, partly in response to the "jail-courting" aspects of satyagraha. Finally, however, thousands of satyagrahis were arrested including hundreds of prominent Congress leaders.

(2) *Police action*: From the respective statements made on opposing sides of the movement, it is clear that the police reacted with determination and force. The official report does not acknowledge police excesses. Many non-Indian witnesses, however, testified to the contrary. The biographer of Lord Irwin notes that "the European Sergeants, provoked and overworked, did not always seem inclined to restrain their men." Gandhi, in his letter addressed to the Viceroy, asserted that "the rank and file has been often savagely and in some cases even indecently assaulted." An American journalist, Webb Miller, reported that after one raid on a salt depot he counted, in a hospital, 320 injured, "many still insensible with fractured skulls, others writhing in agony from kicks in the testicles and stomach . . ."

(3) *Determination of the Government*: The Viceroy, addressing both Houses of the legislature on 9 July

(1930), asserted that the mass action was "nothing but the application of force under another form, and, when it has as its avowed object the making of Government impossible, a Government is bound either to resist or abdicate." He concluded that the government must "fight it with all our strength."

(4) *Special ordinances*: In an attempt to control the situation, the Government issued numerous ordinances including those providing for press censorship and suppression of objectionable printed matter. In places a ban was placed upon wearing of the white Gandhi cap.

(5) *Viceroy announced Round Table Conference plans*: Lord Irwin announced (12 May) that steps were being taken to arrange a meeting in London of representatives to consider constitutional reforms for India.

(6) *Continuing repression of agitation*: Throughout the early months of 1931 civil disobedience was met by arrests, firings, *lathi* charges, and other police force.

(7) *Gandhi-Irwin Agreement*: Final settlement following talks between Viceroy and Gandhi.

(8) *Fulfillment of the Gandhi-Irwin Agreement*, including repeal of ordinances and release of satyagrahi prisoners.

Results

(1) *Modification of salt regulations*: The immediate objective of the salt satyagraha which opened the overall civil disobedience movement was, to a large extent, realized. The salt laws were not repealed, but a new official interpretation was effected in the settlement agreed to by Gandhi and Lord Irwin. That interpretation specified that "For the sake . . . of giving relief to certain of the poorer classes," the Government would "extend their administrative provisions, on lines already prevailing in certain places,

in order to permit local residents in villages, immediately adjoining areas where salt can be collected or made, to collect or make salt for domestic consumption or sale within such villages, but not for sale to, or trading with, individuals living outside them."

(2) *Other provisions of the Gandhi-Irwin Agreement*: According to the settlement arrived at in discussions between Gandhi and the Viceroy, the Government agreed to the following action:

(a) Amnesty to persons convicted of non-violent offenses in connection with civil disobedience.

(b) Withdrawal of the restraining ordinances.

(c) Restoration of confiscated, forfeited, or attached properties.

(d) Administrative concession to make salt in certain areas.

In return, civil disobedience was to be ended and, in particular, the following activities discontinued:

(a) Organized defiance of the provisions of any law.

(b) Movement for non-payment of land revenue and other legal dues.

(c) Publication of news-sheets in support of civil disobedience.

(d) Attempts to influence civil and military servants or village officials against government or to persuade them to resign their posts.

(3) *Constitutional reforms*: The settlement included a statement that in further discussions on constitutional reform, representatives of the Congress would be invited to participate, and that in the deliberations of the next Round Table Conference, such questions as federation, reservation of subjects (e.g. defense, external affairs), financial credit, and position of minorities would be included.

During 1930-31, satyagraha was employed throughout India to advance the cause of Indian independence. Thousands of localized campaigns in the over-all civil disobedience movement involved hundreds of thousands of persons, many of whom adopted satyagraha as a temporary expedient without fully understanding its basic philosophy. Nevertheless, the movement remained, for the most part, non-violent. The opening campaign led by Gandhi in the march to the sea provided a model of adherence to basic principles and brilliance of strategy. An outstanding characteristic of the other campaigns during these months was the assertion of strong and effective leadership by hundreds of provincial and local Congressmen.

As for the elements of true satyagraha, all are to be found in the salt satyagraha. The immediate objective was the removal of laws which worked a hardship upon the poor. The Salt Acts, establishing a government monopoly over a food necessity, symbolized the further injustice—the subjugation of India by a foreign power. It therefore became the duty of the satyagrahi to disobey the unjust salt laws and to cling to the truth understood to be the right of the Indian people to manufacture salt as they chose. The further truth implications were understood to lie in a people's right to self-government.

The volunteer satyagrahis who initiated the salt campaign rigorously abided by the principle of non-violence. During the later raids on the salt pans, some satyagrahis destroyed property by cutting wire and otherwise pulling down the fences surrounding the salt works. Gandhi himself did not lead the raids in which property was destroyed, and he might well have restrained property destruction or considered it a weakness in that phase of the campaign. Some satyagrahis justified the destruction of fences to gain access to the salt pans by arguing that the salt works were public property and should be made available to all citizens. There is no evidence, however, that any physical injury was inflicted by satyagrahis upon their opponents. Violence was, indeed, at work in the successive raids on the salt pans—but it was violence inflicted by police forces upon satyagrahis, many of whom sustained grave and agonizing injury. Wave upon wave of satyagrahis responded to the attack, their action remaining non-violent but nonetheless aggressive. They retaliated, not with violence, but with the several persuasive tactics at their command.

Self-reliance characterized the conduct of the satyagrahis. They signed a pledge to offer civil resistance without expectation of material help for themselves or their families. Again, organized propaganda was published and distributed in the form of bulletins and leaflets, and publicity was further supplied by the press throughout the country in detailed reporting of satyagraha activities. Suppression of satyagraha propaganda and censorship of the press served to extend the opportunities for contravention of the law.

Initiative was retained by the satyagrahis throughout this civil disobedience movement. That action which centered upon contravention of the Salt Acts, progressed from the initial march to the sea and the first production of contraband salt to the subsequent seizure of salt from government depots and the spread of salt-making. Action then extended into the realm of economic boycott accompanied by picketing of cloth and liquor shops. Direct action was not undertaken until every effort had been made for an honorable settlement through negotiation and appeal to the Viceroy. The demand of the satyagrahis that Indians should be free to manufacture salt at will, was at no time relaxed. However, Gandhi remained ever ready to negotiate with the government for a settlement.

This satyagraha proceeded through the early steps of attempted negotiation, of agitation and demonstration, and the issuing of an ultimatum. The opponent was kept informed of intention and procedure. When the settlement was finally effected, following discussions between Gandhi and the Viceroy, the immediate objective—redress of grievances arising from the Salt Acts—was to a substantial degree realized even though the Acts themselves were not abolished. The long-term objective of Swaraj (independence) was, of course, not at once achieved. However, the Gandhi-Irwin Agreement provided that the Congress should participate in the second Round Table Conference to consider constitutional questions involved in the advancement of India along the road towards full independence.

Concluding Note on the Five Campaigns

Satyagraha, as applied socio-political action, requires a comprehensive program of planning, preparation, and studied execution. To give active expression to the elements which inform the underlying philosophy of satyagraha, attention must be extended to a range of considerations from the choice of the objective through the selection of participants to the terms of final settlement.

Weaknesses in the campaigns examined appear especially where consideration of one or more of the stages of the campaign was slighted. The Vykom campaign showed signs of failure until participation in the satyagraha was narrowed to the religious community directly involved. The Ahmedabad labor satyagraha very nearly collapsed because participants had not been adequately prepared and a thorough-going constructive program had not been planned. The success of the Bardoli campaign was a result of careful attention to every stage of satyagraha. The Rowlatt campaign was discontinued because violence emerged due to inadequate preparation of satyagrahis, failure to delimit the extent of participation, and poor co-ordination of leadership. By 1930 the entire country had been exposed to something of the meaning of non-violent action. The country was more disciplined, as Nehru wrote, "and there was a clearer appreciation of the nature of the struggle." Not only was the technique better understood, Nehru continued, "but more important still from Gandhiji's point of view, it was fully realised by every one that he was terribly in earnest about non-violence. There could be no doubt about that now as there probably was in the minds of some people ten years before."[19] The initial action in the salt satyagraha was carefully organized with greater attention to preparation both of the participating satyagrahis and the villagers along the route of the march to the sea. The difficulties experienced later were, in large part, created by a participation more extensive than the leadership could at all times direct. The countrywide response resulted in elements joining the campaign which neither accepted nor fully understood the meaning of non-violent action. The civil disobedience movement extending beyond the initial phase of the salt satyagraha suffered, again, from the failure to develop sufficiently well-defined immediate objectives as intermediary steps to full independence.

The examination of the five campaigns has shown that individual participants in a satyagraha could include members of widely differing economic, social, and religious communities. We have noted participation in satyagraha by laborers, peasants, merchants; by women both from the peasantry and from highly educated and wealthy families; by untouchable Hindus, Brahmans, Muslims—indeed (as we shall see in Chapter IV) even by the redoubtable Pathan warriors of the Frontier. Leaders, as well as participants, included women and members of minority communities. Most of the participants in the campaigns reviewed were employing non-violence for the purpose of achieving specific objectives, and they adopted satyagraha because of its efficacy as a method. For most of those involved, non-violence was a policy, and not a creed. Gandhi's long-time secretary, Pyarelal, expressed this aspect of popular satyagraha movements in replying to a question I put to him with regard to the necessity of complete belief in non-violence: "It *is* possible to run a Satyagraha campaign with people who have no faith in non-violence as a creed provided they sincerely and implicitly follow the rules as a discipline and work under the leadership of unadulterated non-violence. . . ."[20]

The action undertaken in a satyagraha campaign varies distinctly from one circumstance to another. Tactics are evolved to meet the specific situation, both offensively and defensively. Strategy, however, remains broadly the same, based upon the considerations indicated above as steps or stages in a satyagraha campaign. We have noted that satyagraha has been successfully employed in opposition not only to the British Government in India, but against orthodox and entrenched Brahmans, against Indian mill-owners, and against local governments.

The techniques of non-violent action operating in situations of conflict employ force both defensively and offensively. In the case of Vykom the satyagraha was predominantly aggressive in character. In all cases the early emphasis was on persuasion. Non-violent coercion developed in the later phases of the campaigns, especially in the all-India satyagrahas. In the instance of the Ahmedabad satyagraha, Gandhi came to see that his fasting introduced an element of coercion which detracted from the true character of satyagraha. The adherence to persuasion as opposed to coercion was best exemplified in the Vykom satyagraha: after the State had withdrawn its support of the opposition and the roads had been legally opened to untouchables, the satyagrahis did not take advantage of this development to enter the roads against the persisting opposition of the Brahmans. They continued the satyagraha until they had persuaded their opponents that denial of passage to untouchables was morally indefensible.

In examining satyagraha in action, it becomes clear that satyagraha operates as a force to effect change. The effectiveness of its action is governed by criteria centering upon the degree of persuasion effected, the extensiveness of the constructive program, and the degree to which the non-violent character of the action has been preserved.

IV

HINDU TRADITION AND SATYAGRAHA: THE SIGNIFICANCE OF GANDHIAN INNOVATIONS

THE social and political developments of twentieth-century India are perhaps best characterized by the word "syncretic." The impact of the West upon the several traditions of India has elicited a response truly Indian; yet the result bears unmistakable traces of the thought and experience of modern Europe. The transplanting of social and political philosophies current in the West to the rich cultural soil of the Indian subcontinent has resulted in a growth both vigorous and productive. Perhaps nowhere has the syncretic product been more tellingly demonstrated than in the development of the Gandhian technique.

Reaction in the direction of the strictly traditional is certainly to be found in important corners of contemporary India. Efforts to revitalize Hindudom, to create a Hindu Raj, to recover the glories of an idealized Hindu past continue to be pressed by social and political groups: by the orthodox Hindu political parties and by Hindu cultural societies. However, Gandhi's experiments pursued an essentially different objective. The importance of differentiating the traditional on the one hand, and the Gandhian on the other, cannot be overemphasized. Gandhi used the traditional to promote the novel; he reinterpreted tradition in such a way that revolutionary ideas, clothed in familiar expression, were readily adopted and employed towards revolutionary ends. Gandhian developments are eminently syncretic. The traditional Indian and the modern Western both function within Gandhian philosophy. How the two streams of influence merge and how Gandhi's

creative leadership transformed elements from both to develop the satyagraha technique may better be understood by
exploring aspects of the Hindu tradition in Gandhi's background.

Commentaries on Gandhi agree that he had his roots deep
in traditional India. Gandhian concepts and slogans—*swaraj*
(self-rule), *Ramrajya* (godly rule), *aparigraha* (non-possession), *asteya* (non-stealing)—all are centrally familiar to Indian peasant and philosopher alike. *Satyagraha* alone in the
Gandhian nomenclature was coined for use in the early "experiments with truth," and its components are Sanskrit words
carrying ethical meanings from the body of Indian philosophy.
The influence of Western thinkers—of Tolstoy, Ruskin, Thoreau—has been repeatedly acknowledged by Gandhi himself. But in each case the influence was that of corroboration
of an already accepted ethical precept, a crystallization of
basic moral predisposition, or the formulation, for purposes
of specific application, of a nucleus principle.

Efforts have been made to claim extensive influence on
Gandhi for the Gospel teachings of the New Testament. And
Gandhi was aware that critics from among his more orthodox co-religionists regarded his interpretation of the Bhagavad
Gita as unduly influenced by the Sermon on the Mount.[1] But
repeatedly Gandhi asserted his essential attachment to Hinduism. In defining the concept *swadeshi*, Gandhi clarified his
position:

> After much thinking I have arrived at a definition of
> *Swadeshi* that, perhaps, best illustrates my meaning.
> *Swadeshi* is that spirit in us which restricts us to the use
> and service of our immediate surroundings to the exclu-
> sion of the more remote. Thus, as for religion, in order
> to satisfy the requirements of the definition, I must re-
> strict myself to my ancestral religion. This is the use of
> my immediate religious surrounding. If I find it defective,
> I should serve it by purging it of its defects. In the do-

main of politics I should make use of the indigenous institutions and serve them by curing them of their proved
defects. In that of economics I should use only things
that are produced by my immediate neighbours and serve
those industries by making them efficient and complete
where they might be found wanting . . . .[2]

An understanding of the success Gandhi achieved in mobilizing the Indian masses can be advanced by analyzing the
concepts basic to Hindu social and religious thought and their
exploitation in the Gandhian appeal. What were the elements
in the social milieu of all India which allowed for the impressive response of a people to an appeal to defy the Salt
Acts by reliance upon peaceful, persuasive tactics? Why did
the Bardoli peasants plead with Sardar Patel to lead their
struggle for revision of the tax assessments by methods of non-
violent resistance known as satyagraha? How could the unlet-
tered untouchable at Vykom persist in the challenge of Brah-
manical and political authority? Some of the answers to such
questions emerge in the course of examining the philosophical
concept of *satya*, the popular meaning of the Jain, Buddhist
and Hindu ideal of *ahimsa*, and the changing notion of *tapasya*
in the Indian ethos. The essential elements of satyagraha—
truth, non-violence, and self-suffering—had, for the Hindu,
roots in their corresponding traditional precepts. The assertion advanced by some that Gandhi was a Hindu revivalist
arises from a superficial understanding of the manner in which
he used these Hindu precepts. An exploration of Gandhi's
transformation or adaptation of Hindu tradition to develop a
social and political technique will make clear the inadequacy
of a characterization which would dismiss Gandhi as merely
a revivalist.

Jawaharlal Nehru reminds us that:

The business of philosophy in India was not confined to
a few philosophers or highbrows. Philosophy was an essential part of the religion of the masses; it percolated to

them in some attenuated form and created that philosophic outlook which became nearly as common in India as it is in China. That philosophy was for some a deep and intricate attempt to know the causes and laws of all phenomena, the search for the ultimate purpose of life, and the attempt to find an organic unity in life's many contradictions. But for the many it was a much simpler affair, which yet gave them some sense of purpose, and cause and effect, and endowed them with courage to face trial and misfortune and not lose their gaiety and composure.[3]

Gandhi went to the people of India with teachings phrased in terms reminiscent of the Vedas, with Upanishadic reminders, with quotations from the Gita and with exhortations familiar from the times of Manu. Indians responded to an appeal presented in the currency of Jain and Buddhist and Hindu ethics. *Satya, ahimsa,* and *tapasya* were common coin. But, into these traditional precepts Gandhi introduced considerations unfamiliar to Indian tradition and reminiscent of the rationalist, humanist tradition of the West.

Satya

Satyannasti paro dharmah: there is no religion or duty greater than truth. This is one of the essentials of Hinduism. The emphasis on truth is paramount in the writings of early Indian philosophers. In Manu's classification of duties, *Satya* held a prominent place. The vast body of philosophic commentary, the network of dialectic, the complex systems of logic and disputation which characterize Hindu philosophical and religious literature bear eloquent evidence to the lack of dogma and attest to a passion for truth arrived at through speculation.

In the philosophical systems of Hindu thought there are many treatments of the concept of truth. Most Indian writers tend to a position which has pragmatic bearing. Theoretical knowledge of the object is not enough. The Indian thinker goes beyond to see if the object so known is to be avoided or accepted: *heya* or *upadeya*.[4] We are concerned here not with the truth concept in Indian ontology or epistemology, but with the ethical system which bears upon the satyagraha notion and its acceptability to the Indian mind. In the Manu classification of duties, *satya* is listed among the *sadharana-dharmas* (duties of universal scope and validity) and is understood as *veracity*. In the Prasastapada classification of the duties, *satyavachana* or "speaking the truth" is one of the generic duties.[5]

The *satya* of satyagraha is understood in the ethical sense. As I have pointed out in Chapter II, the "Truth is God" concept resolved itself into a moral principle. The pursuit of Truth or God was, for Gandhi, as it was for the heart of Vedanta, the search for realizing the truth of human unity. With Gandhi, as we have seen, satyagraha was a means for achieving this realization. The realization itself—of God, or of Truth—was a consummation desired by the main body of Hindu thought.

Truth, moreover, figured widely in the traditional stories of India. The story of Prahlad, a young boy who suffered immeasurably the wrath of his father for the truth's sake, is one of the most famous in ancient Indian literature. It is known throughout the breadth of India, and Gandhi was fond of repeating the story to illustrate the meaning of satyagraha. His insistence upon "holding to the truth" was, then, broadly familiar, both to the Indian philosopher and to the simple villager.

Upon examining the Indian traditional approach, one finds the originality of Gandhi emerging in his formulation of satyagraha. The early *sadharanadharmas*, like the *samanya* duties, emphasize the attainment of the individual's own perfection.

There is practically no recognition of the social duties

proper, i.e. of the duties of social service in a positive sense as distinguished from negative toleration (Kshama) and non-appropriation (Chouryabhava). Even veracity does not necessarily imply positive social service and it may be practised purely as a dianoetic virtue of self-culture, i.e. as absolute self-dedication to Truth.[6]

Hindu ethics was aimed at self-sufficiency and freedom from external ties—at individual autonomy rather than the virtue of positive social service.

"Satyagraha" was, indeed, familiar to the ear of the Indian, but its meaning, in terms of truth-attainment, departed from the body of traditional Hindu notions of the function of the truth-ethic. Truth, *satya*, was the core of the Gandhian technique as of the over-all Gandhian philosophy. But satyagraha as a social instrument has projected the traditional ethical laws into the realm of social action.

> . . . religion that takes no count of practical affairs and does not help to solve them, is no religion.[7]

> The whole of the constructive programme—including handspinning and handweaving, Hindu Muslim unity, removal of untouchability, prohibition—is in pursuit of truth and non-violence.[8]

To realize the truth of human unity meant, for Gandhi, not only service to his fellow man, but the individual's effort to adjust his demands and his immediate position in the light of opposing demands which he took to be erroneous. Adherence to the truth meant adherence to the moral truth as originally understood by him who would assert it *until* persuaded by interaction with an opponent that he had erred. As we have seen in Chapter II, non-violent action was the means by which Gandhi advocated discovery of truth. "To me religion means truth and *Ahimsa* or rather truth alone, because truth includes *ahimsa, ahimsa* being the necessary and indispensable means for its discovery."[9]

Gandhi did not deny the orthodox Hindu philosophical position identifying truth with being or reality.* He claimed to demonstrate a way to discover truth by action in society. Gandhi was, indeed, a Karma-yogin—one who seeks God through action. The effect of the satyagraha formulation was to transform the absolute truth of the philosophical *Sat* to the relative truth of ethic principle capable of being tested by a means combining non-violent action with self-suffering.

Ahimsa

The term *ahimsa* appears in Hindu teachings as early as the Chandogya Upanishad, where it is listed as one of the five ethical virtues.† It is repeated throughout the Hindu scriptures. In the Prasastapada classification of the generic duties, *ahimsa* is noted as a duty "not simply in the negative sense of mere cessation from harm or injury (*himsabhaya*) but also in the positive sense of a definite *resolve* not to hurt a living being (*bhutanam anabhidrohasamkalpah*)."[10] Again, the Jain religion constitutes *ahimsa* the first vow. And it is a cardinal principle of Buddhism.

Together with the aphorism *satyannasti paro dharmah* (there is no religion greater than truth) the Mahabharata couples *ahimsa paramo dharmah* (ahimsa is the greatest religion or duty). This aphorism is known in every village in India, as are stories from Hindu, or Buddhist, or Jain classics illustrating the spirit and duty of non-violence. Gandhi himself was influenced by the teachings of the Jains whose adherence to non-violence towards living creatures reaches the furthest extremes. But, typical of his attitude towards religious authority, he wrote in 1916:

. . . though my views on Ahimsa are a result of my study

* The Sanskrit root *sat* means being or reality.
† The others are austerity, almsgiving, uprightness, and truthfulness (*Chandogya Upanisad*, III.18.4).

of most of the faiths of the world, they are now no longer dependent upon the authority of these works. They are a part of my life, and if I suddenly discovered that the religious books read by me bore a different interpretation from the one I had learnt to give them, I should still hold to the view of Ahimsa . . . .[11]

The especial contribution of Gandhi was to make the concept of *ahimsa* meaningful in the social and political spheres by moulding tools of non-violent action to use as a positive force in the search for social and political truths. While calling upon illustrations from Indian mythology, Gandhi transformed *ahimsa* into the active social technique which was to challenge both political authority and religious orthodoxy.

What is the meaning of Rama, a mere human being, with his host of monkeys, pitting himself against the insolent strength of ten-headed Ravan surrounded in supposed safety by the raging waters on all sides of Lanka? Does it not mean the conquest of physical might by spiritual strength? However, being a practical man, I do not wait till India recognises the practicability of the spiritual life in the political world. India considers herself to be powerless and paralysed before the machine-guns, the tanks and the aeroplanes of the English. And she takes up Non-cooperation out of her weakness.

. . . [But] I am not pleading for India to practise non-violence, because she is weak. I want her to practise non-violence being conscious of her strength and power. No training in arms is required for realisation of her strength. . . . My life is dedicated to service of India through the religion of non-violence which I believe to be the root of Hinduism.[12]

Nehru tells us that Gandhi based his firm belief in non-violence on the Bhagavad Gita.[13] Yet, that the Gita enjoins non-violence is not an orthodox interpretation. Gandhi insisted that *ahimsa* was even the religion of the *Kshatriya*.*

The discussion in Chapter II of non-violence as an element of satyagraha indicated the further meaning which *ahimsa* acquired in the Gandhian transformation. "I have been practising with scientific precision non-violence and its possibilities for an unbroken period of over fifty years," Gandhi wrote in 1940.

I have applied it in every walk of life, domestic, institutional, economic and political. I know of no single case in which it has failed. Where it has seemed sometimes to have failed, I have ascribed it to my imperfections. I claim no perfection for myself but I claim to be a passionate seeker after Truth, which is but another name for God. In the course of that search the discovery of non-violence came to me. Its spread is my life mission.[14]

The Indian cultural milieu was clearly infused with notions of the non-violence of *ahimsa*. We shall examine below the traditional ways in which *ahimsa* was exemplified and the specific uses of the non-violent methods which were forerunners of satyagraha tools.

Tapasya

A profound sense of asceticism permeates the Indian religious understanding. The classical Yogic law enjoins rigorous self-restraint. Whatever the path to realization of God—through adoration and faith (*bhakti*), through mystical intuition (*jnana*), or through deeds (*karma*) it is one of severe discipline. The concept of sacrifice evolved through the Vedic period from complex ritualism to self-imposed suffer-

* *Young India*, October 21, 1926. *Kshatriya* refers to the warrior caste, second in rank in the caste hierarchy. For an interesting commentary on the result of the restriction of the defense function to a small class within the society as rendering the Indian people averse to bearing arms, see Krishnalal Shridharani, *War without Violence* (New York: Harcourt, Brace [1939]), pp. 201-204.

ing. The many gods of Hinduism became important in enabling men to achieve the Absolute Godhead. "It was inevitable," Radhakrishnan tells us, "that sacrifice should come. For the depth of one's affection for God consists in the surrender of one's property and possessions to Him. We pray and offer."[15] *Tapas* in the Hindu scriptures refers variously to religious austerity, bodily mortification, and penance, and is closely identified with renunciation.*

> ... tapas only means the development of soul force, the freeing of the soul from slavery to body, severe thinking or energising of mind. ... A call to renunciation in the sense of killing out the sense of separateness and developing disinterested love is the essence of all true religion.[16]

Swaraj, which first acquired political meaning (of independence) through its use in that sense by the great Maharashtrian patriot, Tilak, is closely allied with the meaning of *tapas* as renunciation. *Swaraj* literally means "self-rule" and in its original connotation meant autonomy of the moral self (as in the Brihadaranyaka Upanishad) where strict control is exercised over the senses. As *swaraj* came to connote the political objective of Indian independence, so *tapas* came, in the Gandhian interpretation, to mean willingness to suffer in oneself to win the respect of an opponent. Gandhi extended suffering through sacrifice to the social and political sphere, where it became an essential element in the satyagraha technique. Once more we find Gandhi seizing upon a traditional religious notion and transforming it into a meaningful part of the technique which was to operate not for individual salvation alone, but within the sphere of social polity. Asceticism and sacrifice, which had characterized the efforts of the de-

---

* The original meaning of the word appears to have been warmth, or heat, and referred to the five fires to which a devotee exposed himself in the hot season: four fires lighted in the four quarters and the sun burning from above. (Monier Monier-Williams, *Sanskrit-English Dictionary, Etymologically and Philologically Arranged*, new ed. enl. and improved [Oxford: Clarendon Press, 1899], p. 437.)

votee withdrawn from social contact, were drawn back into the mundane arena and rendered means whereby common social ends might be attained.

The Concepts of Karma and Non-attachment

The law of *Karma* Radhakrishnan defines as "the counterpart in the moral world of the physical law of uniformity. It is the law of the conservation of moral energy."[17] The good action has a good reaction; evil results in evil. A man becomes good by good deeds, and bad by bad, as the Upanishads teach. This law of accumulated merit or demerit follows the individual from life to life and determines the fortune or misfortune which is his lot. But just as man cannot escape his individual responsibility for his actions, he can, by good deeds—by fulfilling the universal and especial duties which are assigned him—determine his future.

It is possible to interpret the law of *karma* in such a way that social service becomes irrelevant as a factor in man's salvation—for man may share none of the responsibility for another's burden. However, the Upanishads recommend service to others as the means by which freedom from *karma* may be attained. Unselfish performance of good deeds will lead him to his salvation. Gandhi attested his belief in such an interpretation.

> I firmly believe in the law of *Karma*, but I believe too in human endeavour. I regard as the *summum bonum* of life the attainment of salvation through *Karma* by annihilating its effects by detachment.[18]

Non-attachment to the fruits of action is the central theme of the great epic interlude in the Mahabharata, the Bhagavad Gita.

The technique of satyagraha admits of no determinist framework. Power in the hands of a satyagrahi to influence a situation is a paramount element. The holding of a moral truth, persisted in by non-violent action and supported by self-suffering, supplies a force which any individual can learn to wield against an opponent of any proportions with expectation of success in the struggle. *Karma* can be overcome by non-attached (selfless) action. The potential for such a force lies within the reach of every human individual. This, for Gandhi, was the message of the Gita.

Karma-marg, or the path of action, is explained as one of the ways through which self-realization or attainment of oneness with God may be achieved. *Anasaktiyoga*—or selfless action—is the character of that path. Gandhi's interpretation of the Gita is fully stated in Mahadev Desai's edited work *The Gospel of Selfless Action: The Gita According to Gandhi.*[19] Its bearing upon satyagraha is evidenced in the following passage:

> . . . I have felt that in trying to enforce in one's life the central teaching of the Gita, one is bound to follow truth and *ahimsa.* When there is no desire for fruit, there is no temptation for untruth or *himsa.* Take an instance of untruth or violence, and it will be found that at its back is the desire to attain the cherished end.[20]

Gandhi's translation and interpretation of the Gita is backed, as he tells us, by "the claim of an endeavor to enforce the meaning in my own conduct for an unbroken period of 40 years."[21] His interpretation breaks sharply with orthodox readings of the epic poem. He did not take the Mahabharata to be an historical work. The battle that was to take place on the field of Kurukshetra, where the Lord Shri Krishna unfolded the Gita truths to the despondent hero Arjuna, was not, according to Gandhi, an historical battle. Gandhi held the account to be purely allegorical and interpreted the war as a struggle between truth and untruth taking place in the heart of man.[22]

In the talks he had with Vincent Sheean shortly before his death, Gandhi repeated his belief that despite the millions of Hindus who take the whole of the Mahabharata to be historically and epistemologically correct, he viewed it as "fiction" leading on to the truth, containing significance but not historical fact. Sheean reports that he was "very shaken" by such "an extraordinary assertion."[23] In the light of Gandhi's frequent and persistent transformations of traditional precepts, together with his subordination of scriptural authority to his own experience, there is nothing startling about Gandhi's position with regard to the content of the Gita. Gandhi himself makes a noteworthy commentary on the progressive development and transformation of meanings to meet changing situations.

> Like man, the meaning of great writings suffers evolution. On examining the history of languages, we notice that the meaning of important words has changed or expanded. This is true of the Gita. The author has himself extended the meanings of some current words. We are able to discover this even on a superficial examination. It is possible that, in the age prior to that of the Gita, offering of animals in sacrifice was permissible. But there is not a trace of it in the sacrifice in the Gita sense. In the Gita continuous concentration on God is the king of sacrifices. The third chapter seems to show that sacrifice chiefly means body-labour for service. The third and fourth chapters read together will give us other meanings for sacrifice, but never animal-sacrifice. Similarly has the meaning of the word *sannyasa* undergone, in the Gita, a transformation. The *sannyasa* of the Gita is all work and yet no work. Thus the author of the Gita, by extending meanings of words, has taught us to imitate him. Let it be granted, that according to the letter of the Gita it is possible to say that warfare is consistent with renunciation of fruit. But after 40 years' unremitting endeavor fully to enforce the teaching of the Gita in my own life, I have, in all humility, felt that perfect renunciation is impossible without perfect observance of *ahimsa* in every shape and form.[24]

Into the great lesson of non-attachment offered in the Gita, Gandhi read the meanings of *ahimsa* and *satya*. Again he had found the elements of satyagraha in traditional scriptures.

The Traditional Methods of Hartal, Fast, Dharna

Turning now from the underlying philosophical attitudes in Indian culture, let us consider the traditional use of certain of the methods which later became the tools of satyagraha. Among the forms of resistance without overt violence known to ancient India are *dharna*, fasting, and *hartal*.

The word *dharna* comes from the Sanskrit root *dhri*, to hold, and means holding out. The method has been frequently used in India especially by creditors against debtors to bring pressure to bear upon the debtor to acknowledge the debt.* Sitting *dharna* describes the practice of sitting at the door of an opponent with the resolve to die unless the alleged wrong is redressed. It is significant to note that the method of sitting *dharna* is, basically, violent. For the attitude with which the method is employed is accompanied by the belief that should one die in employing the method, his spirit would remain to torment and afflict the unbending opponent. Basically the method is one of implicit revenge, whatever other intentions may accompany the act in terms of demonstrating sincerity or winning over the opponent through self-suffering.

What has been said of *dharna* may also be said of the ancient practice of fasting. We have noted Gandhi's caution in the use of the fast, for, as he never tired of insisting, the fast is a dangerous weapon which may be used to compel an opponent to capitulate against his will and without his having been persuaded of the moral superiority of the fasting opponent's position.

Hartal, a method which Gandhi employed in its traditional

* For a discussion of the uses of *dharna* to be found in classical Hindu literature, see Washburn Hopkins, "On the Hindu Custom of Dying to Redress a Grievance," *Journal of the American Oriental Society*, Vol. XXI, July-December, 1900, pp. 146-159.

form during satyagraha campaigns, resembles a strike, but has substantially different objectives. It is altogether a method of protest—a demonstration of extreme dissatisfaction. Its use in ancient India was against the Prince or King and was intended to draw attention to the unpopularity of an edict or other Government measure. The *hartal* is usually of short duration—a day or two. Shops close and work ceases. *Hartal* is also employed at times of national mourning.

Yet another method of peaceful demonstration against oppression is voluntary emigration—*hijrat* or *deshatyaga* (giving up the country). Where the people of an area were grievously oppressed and had no other recourse, they would all move from the place in a final effort of non-cooperation.

These techniques have the earmarks of what Gandhi would admit to be passive resistance. They do not, it is important to note, have certain of the necessary elements of satyagraha. The insistence upon non-violence in its positive meaning of considering the well-being of the opponent and not merely in the negative sense of refusing to do harm is not a necessary part of traditional tactics. Indeed, refusal to do harm to the opponent is clearly not an element of the traditional methods. In the several modes of *dharna* revenge is implicit. In the other forms of passive resistance—*hijrat,* or *deshatyaga,* as well as *hartal*—the emphasis is upon withholding cooperation and does not necessarily call for consideration of the opponent or insistence upon arriving at an adjustment mutually acceptable.

The very fact of Gandhi's use of traditional methods to effect the education of India in the ways of satyagraha may have functioned as a deterrent in transmitting the full implications of satyagraha to those who participated. Elements which were new in Gandhi's approach—the various emphases upon the well-being of the opponent and of mutual triumph—were oftentimes obscured by a ready understanding of the coercive character of traditional methods. Gandhi's refusal to take advantage of a misfortune or disability of the opponent was an element essential to satyagraha.* The constructive goodwill attitude so fundamental in the satyagraha approach was a novel introduction into social and political tactics, even to those which were characterized by passive resistance.

The Character of Gandhi's Appeal

An examination of the functioning of satyagraha in the Indian setting suggests questions concerning the conditions which allowed for the acceptance of the assumptions of satyagraha, the willingness to learn its technique, and the belief in its efficacy. The Indian ethos appears to have been eminently receptive to satyagraha notions. In his pertinent article,"Why India Follows Gandhi,"[25] H. N. Brailsford refers to the "ancient Hindu tactic" and the "mystical meaning of ahimsa" and reminds us that in India the saint who can control himself is considered capable of commanding the universe. Brailsford also notes the bearing of "economic nationalism" on those who followed Gandhi. Was, then, Gandhi's success as a leader determined by his ability to revive traditional ideals and to reaffirm inherent predispositions?

The authority supporting the explanation that Gandhi was a Hindu reformer, a revivalist who caught the imagination of the masses by incarnating the Hindu "ideal type," is preponderant and convincing. Jawaharlal Nehru writes in his autobiography,[26] "Gandhiji, indeed, was continually laying stress on the religious and spiritual side of the movement. His religion was not dogmatic, but it did mean a definitely religious outlook on life, and the whole movement was strongly influenced by this and took on a revivalist character so far as the masses were concerned." C. F. Andrews who knew Gandhi intimately writes:

* The writer has heard eyewitness accounts in India of proper satyagrahis refusing to take action in the midday sun because of the hardship this would work on European opponents who were less accustomed to extreme heat, and again, of satyagrahis postponing an action to spare the Englishman for his Easter Sunday services and celebration.

Thus Mahatma Gandhi remains rooted in the soil of India. He is not deraciné, like so many of those who have stayed for a long time away from India and have adopted wholesale Western customs. His mind stretches out in ever wider and wider circles . . . but the centre of his being ever remains fixed in Hinduism itself, which is his first and only love.[27]

Gandhi's Hindu fount remains unquestioned. But his continuing reaffirmation of traditional approaches must be placed over against the startling backdrop of the significant unorthodoxies which permeated Gandhian thinking.

We have already noted the fundamental transformations of traditional precepts and methods to forge the instruments of satyagraha. Gandhi repeatedly challenged scriptural authority. Yet another instance of Gandhi's choice of the criterion of reason as opposed to authority indicates his insistence upon making his own interpretations:

I do *not* believe in the exclusive divinity of the Vedas. I believe the Bible, the Quran, and the Zend Avesta to be as much divinely inspired as the Vedas. My belief in the Hindu Scriptures does not require me to accept every word and every verse as divinely inspired. Nor do I claim to have any first-hand knowledge of these wonderful books. But I do claim to know and feel the truths of the essential teaching of the Scriptures. I decline to be bound by any interpretation, however learned it may be, if it is repugnant to reason or moral sense.[28]

It is well to remark here that such an assertion is not altogether unusual in the annals of Hindu thought. Indeed, Hinduism is characterized, so-to-speak, by heretical commentaries. To a religion characterized by exclusiveness and limited by authority of original scriptures—as is Christianity—comments of the type above quoted would, indeed, be shaking. It is not so alien to a Hindu to hear at once the denial of scriptural authority and the assertion—such as Gandhi made at the time he wrote the above passage—that the speaker considers himself a *sanatani* (orthodox) Hindu. The force of Gandhi's insistence upon freedom from authority is tellingly illustrated by his position with regard to the injustice of untouchability. In his first important speech following a year of silence and withdrawal, Gandhi declared that ". . . even if all the Hindus of India were to be ranged against me in declaring that untouchability, as we know it today, has the sanction of the shastras or the Smritis, I will then declare that these shastras and these Smritis are false."[28a]

A religious reformer no doubt Gandhi was. But we may reasonably raise the question whether Gandhi's revivalist-reformer characteristics truly provide the solution to the question "why did India follow Gandhi?" Gandhi's identification of himself with the meanest peasant—his strict vegetarianism, his goat's milk, his spinning, his dress—indeed, his general asceticism and approximation to an Indian ideal-type comprise a leader-follower appeal most inviting to the Indian mind. But, on the other hand, there have been any number of personalities on the Indian scene who have presented a similar blend of characteristics, and who have been equally concerned with social service, yet who did not function with the degree of success which was Gandhi's. The key to Gandhi's leadership lay in his utilization of tradition, but utilization only to transform and to invite a mass following to partake of a philosophy and program of action.*

Gandhi's success in developing the use of satyagraha in India may have depended upon the happy circumstance that he was both a religious man and a politician. His appeal to the spiritual elements in the Indian make-up was combined with his apprehension of India's political and social prob-

---

* For an elaboration of this point, see my paper, "The Non-Conventional Political Leader in India," in Richard L. Park and Irene Tinker, eds., *Leadership and Political Institutions in India* (Princeton: Princeton University Press, 1959.)

lems. His immediate contact with the masses rendered him sensitive to their needs and desires, as well as to their capabilities. In an illuminating passage[29] Louis Renou explains Gandhi's "inner voice," upon which he claimed to rely for decisions and direction, as a feeling of what the masses expected of him. This analysis suggests the quality of *charisma*. There are indeed many ways in which Gandhi exemplifies the charismatic leader.

Max Weber, who introduced the term into sociological usage, applies charisma to "a certain quality of an individual personality by virtue of which he is set apart from ordinary men and treated as endowed with supernatural, superhuman, or at least specifically exceptional powers or qualities. These are such as are not accessible to the ordinary person, but are regarded as of divine origin or as exemplary, and on the basis of them the individual concerned is treated as a leader."[30] There is no doubt that the Indian villager looked upon Gandhi as just such an individual personality. They endowed him with the appellation "Mahatma"—literally, Great Soul. Instances have been recorded of Gandhi idols enshrined in village temples. Multitudes demanded his *darshan*, his blessing.

That Gandhi resisted attempts to deify or even to revere him does not detract from the persisting response of the Indian villager to the Mahatma. But Weber, in characterizing charismatic authority, seats its basis distinctly in the

> conception that it is the *duty* of those who have been called to a charismatic mission to recognize its quality and to act accordingly. . . . No prophet has ever regarded his quality as dependent on the attitude of the masses toward him. No elective king or military leader has ever treated those who have resisted him or tried to ignore him otherwise than as delinquent in duty. . . .[31]

On the part of Gandhi—in contradistinction to the position of many of those who followed him—there was repeated denial of charismatic qualification. In 1921, he wrote:

I have received a cutting, in which I am reported to be credited with being a messenger of God, and I am asked whether I claim to have any special revelation from God. As to this, the latest charge, I must disown it. I pray like every good Hindu. I believe that we can all become messengers of God, if we cease to fear man and seek only God's Truth. . . . I have no special revelation of God's will. . . .[32]

In 1924:

I lay claim to nothing exclusively divine in me. I do not claim prophetship. I am but a humble seeker after Truth and bent upon finding it. . . . The whole of my activity whether it may be called social, political, humanitarian or ethical is directed to that end. . . . I am no master. I am but a struggling, erring humble servant of India and therefore of humanity.

There is already enough superstition in our country. No effort should be spared to resist further addition in the shape of Gandhi worship. Personally I have a horror of adoration. I believe in adoring virtue apart from the wearer. . . .[33]

In 1927:

The Mahatma I must leave to his fate. Though a non-cooperator, I shall gladly subscribe to a bill to make it criminal for anybody to call me Mahatma and to touch my feet.[34]

In 1940:

Let no one say that he is a follower of Gandhi. It is enough that I should be my own follower.[35]

I am an erring mortal like you. I have never even in my dream thought that I was a Maha-atma (great soul) and that others were Alpa-atma (little souls). We are all equal before our Maker—Hindus, Musalmans, Parsis, Christians, worshippers of one God.[36]

It is not, of course, unlikely that a true charismatic leader would deny his charisma. But, again, Weber places charismatic authority

> . . . specifically outside the realm of everyday routine and the profane sphere. In this respect, it is sharply opposed both to rational, and particularly bureaucratic, authority, and to traditional authority, whether in its patriarchal, patrimonial, or any other form. Both rational and traditional authority are specifically forms of everyday routine control of action; while the charismatic type is the direct antithesis of this.[37]

In considering the character of Gandhi's influence, one should not lose sight of its organizational basis, the Indian National Congress. For there are aspects of this basic relationship which are antithetical to the charismatic type of leadership. The Congress was a democratically structured organization of long standing when Gandhi entered its ranks.[38] Gandhi did indeed transform it into a revolutionary organization which repudiated the existing Government of India: he was responsible for transforming the Congress into a popular movement.* During periods of all-out struggle, Gandhi was looked upon as the supreme commander, a status he held not through any control of the usual sanctions of force, but by virtue of his demonstrated ability and the effectiveness of his techniques. In more normal periods, the Congress functioned in the manner common to democratic political organizations. For all the attacks which Gandhi's opponents have levelled at his "dictatorial" control of the Congress, it is clear that

---

* See Sir Reginald Coupland, *The Indian Problem* (3 vols. in one; New York, London [etc.]: Oxford University, 1944), p. 92: "What gave the Congress its present strength was its conversion from a movement of the intelligentsia into a movement of the people; and that was Mr. Gandhi's doing, almost singlehanded."

he was greatly concerned that its democratic character be maintained:

> The Congress is no preserve of any single individual. It is a democratic body with, in my opinion, the widest intelligent franchise the world has ever seen.[39]

> No man, however great, be he even a *Mahatma*, is indispensable for a nation conscious of itself and bent upon freedom. Even as the whole is always greater than its parts, the Congress which claims to represent the nation is always greater than its greatest part. To be a living organisation it must survive its most distinguished members.[40]

Moreover, the satyagraha ideal concept of parallel government was basically of the rational-legal type defined by Weber, in contrast to the charismatic type of authority, as "resting on a belief in the 'legality' of patterns of normative rules and the right of those elevated in authority under such rules to issue commands (legal authority)."[41] The "Gandhian Constitution," as worked out by S. N. Agarwal and sanctioned by Gandhi, is distinctly rational-legal in character in that it adapts certain traditional Indian institutions (e.g., *panchayat*) to a democratic structuring.[42]

Whatever the degree of Gandhi's charisma, his leadership qualities cannot alone account for the magnitude of his achievements. Subhas Chandra Bose,[43] who broke with Gandhi over program and method, insisted that Gandhi's physical and mental conformity to the traditions and temperament of the Indian people was but one factor accounting for his success. The times were ripe, Bose held, for revolutionary tactics. The old methods had failed: constitutionalism proved sterile and violent resistance had been all-too-successfully suppressed. Satyagraha, with its armory of non-violent aggressive equipment, entered a fertile field.

Satyagraha did, indeed, offer a solution to the problems of the day. The economic boycott of British goods—the other side of the *swadeshi* coin—appeared to allow for a way out of economic depression. Indian mill-owners looked forward to a new indigenous market, while the Indian peasant through his patriotic spinning could approach a self-sufficiency in clothing. The early experiments with satyagraha in South Africa had already demonstrated the effectiveness of determined non-violent force against entrenched authority. And as Gandhi continued his experiments in India, the people became increasingly aware of satyagraha's effectiveness. By 1928 the people themselves clamored for leadership in non-violent action against government, as in the movement in Bardoli.[44]

Satyagraha had been recognized as an efficacious method. It will be recalled that the Bardoli peasants approached Sardar Patel to be their leader. This, no doubt, was so because Gandhi was not available. But the appeal in this case was largely an appeal for a method. Indian leaders accepted satyagraha even when they had little faith in the religious elements which appeared to infuse it. This was no doubt true, in the first instance, because Gandhi had done the thing which none of the intelligentsia had been able to do—he had awakened the masses. But as the method was applied, they began to have faith in satyagraha as a technique. We have noted the comments of Motilal Nehru at the time of the Rowlatt satyagraha.[45] Jawaharlal Nehru records in his autobiography[46] that in the beginning he had had keen misgivings about Gandhi's approach, but that he finally had come to embrace the method of satyagraha.

> What I admired was the moral and ethical side of our movement and of satyagraha. I did not give an absolute allegiance to the doctrine of non-violence or accept it for ever, but it attracted me more and more. . . . A worthy end should have worthy means leading up to it. That seemed not only a good ethical doctrine but sound, practical politics, for the means that are not good often de-

feat the end in view and raise new problems and difficulties.[47]

The undeniable spiritual well-springs of Gandhi's formulations and of his teachings to the people had their appeal. But those who adopted the method and, indeed, Gandhi himself, have not insisted upon any specific spiritual foundation. In an appeal for the absolute acceptance of "Gandhism," a proponent of satyagraha has written:

The only one exception that may be made to this general rule [of accepting Gandhism in all its aspects] is in the case of the spiritual aspect. The reason is that the spiritual aspect corresponds to one's personal spiritual life, and therefore, the acceptance of this aspect of Gandhism indicates the desire on the part of the individual for the development of the self along a different line—while all other aspects correspond to the social and political life of man in relation to his humanitarian activities and services to the country . . . in order to work for the amelioration of the conditions of the poor villagers of our country on the Gandhian principle one must [not necessarily] turn into a stern ascetic . . . [nor is] the essential precondition of the Gandhian way of service to the country . . . the practice of a severe austerity in personal life.[48]

Gandhi repeatedly assured non-believers that satyagraha did not require a man to declare a religious faith. As early as 1925 he replied as follows to an objection which had been raised to the wording of the satyagraha pledge, which began "with God as witness, I . . ."

So far as the conscientious objection [to the use of the "God as witness" declaration] is concerned the mention of God may be removed if required from the Congress pledge. . . . Had such an objection been raised at the time, I would have yielded at once.[49]

Gandhi, then, a religious man and a reformer of Hinduism, appealed to the religious mind and the secular alike. Although he claimed Hinduism as his religion, his teachings transcended sectarian bounds. From Islam, as well as from Buddhism and Christianity, Gandhi had drawn inspiration. His close friend, C. F. Andrews, has described Gandhi's sensitivity to the life and efforts of the Prophet Muhammad. Gandhi could appeal to the Indian Muslim through his respectful reminder of the self-denying manner in which the Prophet lived in the early days of Islam and of the heroic endurance of the early leaders of Islam. He held the deepest respect, Andrews has told us, for Muhammad's son-in-law, Ali and for Hasan and Husain.

> Furthermore, following the example set by the Prophet of Islam, Mahatma Gandhi has never for a moment separated the political from the spiritual, or failed to deal directly with the social evils which stood out before his eyes.[50]

Christ's Sermon on the Mount left its deep influence on Gandhi, as did the writings of Tolstoy following the Christian ethic. In an address to the Christian missionaries assembled in Calcutta at the YWCA on July 28, 1925,[51] Gandhi said:

> . . . I did not stop studying the Bible and the commentaries and other books on Christianity that my friends placed in my hands; but I said to myself that if I was to find my satisfaction through reasoning, I must study the scriptures of other religions also and make my choice. And I turned to the Quran. I tried to understand what I could of Judaism as distinguished from Christianity. I studied Zoroastrianism, and I came to the conclusion that all religions were right, and every one of them imperfect, because they were interpreted with our poor intellects, sometimes with our poor hearts, and more often misinterpreted. In all religions I found to my grief that there were various and even contradictory interpreta-

tions of some texts, and I said to myself, "Not these things for me. If I want the satisfaction of my soul I must feel my way. I must wait silently upon God and ask Him to guide me."

Gandhi's religious predilections did not obscure his reasonableness nor his willingness to accept the results of empirical tests. The element of appeal to reason is essential for the functioning of satyagraha. A well-considered eclecticism resulted in a denial of dogma. The technique of satyagraha, man-controlled and non-deterministic, operating to achieve a mutually satisfactory solution in a conflict situation, could appeal to a range of minds schooled in a variety of religio-philosophical systems.

Opposition to Gandhi's approach came from extremists in religion and in politics. The Hindu Mahasabha urged that Gandhi was a blight on the good name of Hinduism and that his "dictatorship" of the Congress had "weakened and humiliated Hindudom at every step."[52] "The world will not be saved by any utopian doctrine of non-violence that helps to emasculate a nation and deprive it of its will and power to resist evil."[53] "The Belief in Absolute Non-Violence condemning all armed resistance even to aggression evinces no Mahatmic saintliness but a monomaniacal senselessness!"[54] The characteristic slogan of the extreme Hindu groups is "Hinduise all politics and militarise Hindudom."[55] Such forces in extreme opposition ultimately effected the assassination of the Mahatma in January 1948.

The Hindu Sanghites and Gandhi alike utilized phrases and precepts to be found in Hindu scriptures, and with them Gandhi and Sanghites both made their respective appeals to the masses. It was the manner in which each used the traditional and familiar which set them at opposite poles. The innovations introduced through Gandhi's creative leadership resulted in the alienation of a substantial segment of the Hindu orthodox.

If Gandhi was rejected by Hindu extremists, he was also rejected by the leadership of the determined Muslim nationalists, who worked to establish a separate Islamic nation. Mohammad Ali Jinnah, the architect of Pakistan, asserted that Gandhi appealed with tremendous effect to Hindus, but only to Hindus. In a letter to Gandhi, Jinnah insisted:

It is quite clear that you represent nobody else but the Hindus . . .

As I have said before, you are a great man, and you exercise enormous influence over the Hindus, particularly the masses. . . .[56]

It was the persistent claim of Jinnah that only his Muslim League could truly represent India's Muslims. Nevertheless, that the Gandhian technique of satyagraha could appeal to a Muslim populace was demonstrated beyond question. For there emerged among the Muslims of the Indian northwest a remarkable movement infused with the principles and program of non-violent action. The development of satyagraha, and its acceptance as a social and political technique in India cannot be explained in terms of the Hindu roots alone, not even as these roots were fertilized by Western and Islamic notions. The soil which tolerated and then nourished the growth of the technique had universal elements. The further explanation of the function of satyagraha awaits exploration in the realm of the universal humus. But that satyagraha was adapted to the needs of a predominantly Muslim people to struggle against a political opponent on the Northwest Frontier of India (now Pakistan) is of enormous significance.

Satyagraha in an Islamic Setting

The development among the Frontier Pathans of a movement committed to the use of satyagraha as the means for promoting social and political objectives, demonstrates the potential appeal of the technique among a people unfamiliar with a tradition or philosophy enjoining non-violence. Indeed, the Pathans of the Frontier have long had the reputation of being masters in the art and science of violence. "The true Pathan is perhaps the most barbaric of all the races with which we are brought into contact," wrote William Crooke.

> ... he is cruel, bloodthirsty and vindictive in the highest degree. ... He leads a wild, free, active life in the rugged fastnesses of his mountains; and there is an air of masculine independence about him ...[57]

War had been traditionally the "normal business of the land"[58] among this proud people which had "no hesitation to kill when the provocation causes sufficient wrath."[59]

Within this Pathan society—within a reasonably well-defined area characterized by a relatively homogeneous Islamic culture—the son of a respected chieftain organized the Khudai Khidmatgar, or Servants of God.* This leader—Khan Abdul Ghaffar Khan—has been contrasted with Gandhi:

> As Gandhi was of the soil and sand of India, Ghaffar Khan is of its rocks and crags and raging torrents. The hot blood of sharpshooting, trigger-happy mountaineers courses in his veins but he has adopted the philosophy of complete non-violence and so have the thousands of brother Pathans whom he organized as the Khudai Khidmatgar or Servants of God.[60]

Ghaffar Khan, a man of great physical and moral stature, first undertook work among his people as a social reformer. As his efforts in education and social reform progressed, he determined that a new approach must be introduced and that such an approach must be political. In 1926 he laid the foundation for a political party and in 1929 organized the Khudai Khidmatgar as its direct action branch. The purpose of this organization was to effect the political, social, and economic reforms which had become paramount to the people of the Frontier.

---

* *Khidmatgaran* is the correct plural form of Khidmatgar. The organization is usually referred to as Khudai Khidmatgar.

The three conditions of membership in the Khudai Khidmatgar were: signing of the Khudai Khidmatgar pledge, ability to speak Pushtu, and freedom from membership in any other organization.[61] The membership pledge read:[62]

1. I put forth my name in honesty and truthfulness to become a true Khudai Khidmatgar.
2. I will sacrifice my wealth, life, and comfort for the liberty of my nation and people.
3. I will never be a party to factions, hatred, or jealousies with my people; and will side with the oppressed against the oppressor.
4. I will not become a member of any other rival organization, nor will I stand in an army.*
5. I will faithfully obey all legitimate orders of all my officers all the time.
6. I will live in accordance with the principles of non-violence.‡
7. I will serve all God's creatures alike; and my object shall be the attainment of the freedom of my country and my religion.¶
8. I will always see to it that I do what is right and good.†
9. I will never desire any reward whatever for my service.

* Another translation reads "shall not furnish security or tender apology in the non-violent fight." This translation is given both by R. R. Diwakar, *Satyagraha: Its Technique and History* (Bombay: Hind Kitabs [1946]), p. 194, and Pyarelal, *A Pilgrimage of Peace: Gandhi and Frontier Gandhi among N. W. F. Pathans* (Ahmedabad: Navajivan [1950]), p. 50.

‡ The translation given in Diwakar, *op. cit.*, and Pyarelal, *op. cit.*, reads: "I shall always live up to the principle of non-violence."

¶ The translation given in Diwakar, and Pyarelal reads: "I shall serve all humanity equally. The chief objects of my life shall be attainment of complete independence and religious freedom."

† The translation given in Diwakar, and Pyarelal reads: "I shall always observe truth and purity in all my actions."

10. All my efforts shall be to please God, and not for
     any show or gain.

This pledge reveals major characteristics of the organization. It had, first of all, a religious basis. It took as its objective
both local socio-economic reform and political independence.
At the height of the movement in the 1930's political independence came to mean freedom for the whole of India from
British rule. Its adoption of non-violence was more thorough
than that of the Indian National Congress inasmuch as the
Khudai Khidmatgar pledged themselves to non-violence not
only as a policy, but as a creed, a way of life.* And, finally,
the Khudai Khidmatgar required of its members complete
devotion.

> The ideal of the Khudai Khidmatgar as their name im-
> plies, was to become true servants of God—in other
> words, to serve God through service of humanity. They
> were regularly drilled and taught to take long marches
> in military fashion. But they bore no arms, carried no
> weapons, not even a *lathi* or a stick.[63]

The membership of the Khudai Khidmatgar in the early
1930's is reported to have been but 500. By 1938 the numbers
had risen to well over 100,000.[64] The Khudai Khidmatgar was
organized in Peshawar district, but its influence spread first
throughout the rural sub-districts of Peshawar and then into
the other districts of the Province. British sources[65] indicate
that it was influential in Malakand Agency and penetrated
into Swat and Mohmand tribal territory. The movement's
strength was greatest in the villages. Women participated as
active members.

---

* Attention may also be called to the fact that the Khudai Khidmatgar
had a frankly religious basis in contradistinction to the Indian National
Congress which was strictly secular in its creed. The Congress adopted
non-violence as a method for conducting the independence fight during
certain periods in the struggle: at no time did the Congress declare
non-violence to be a permanent creed.

The Khudai Khidmatgar resembled the military in organization. Its hierarchy of command was established by appointment from above and discipline was strict. It is worth noting, however, that the fifth point in the pledge bound the member to obey *legitimate* orders. The ultimate allegiance of the Khudai Khidmatgar was not to the organization but to God and to service of fellow man.* The discipline was self-imposed. Smith comments: ". . . the movement, sounding somewhat romantic, is in practice strict."[66]

The training program of the Khudai Khidmatgar included instruction in the religion of unity and of brotherhood. Forgiveness was one of the virtues which was to distinguish the "Servant of God." "He who forgives and is reconciled, his reward is with God."[67] Such quotations as this from the Quran were invoked by leaders of the movement and instances of toleration and forgiveness in Islamic history were woven into the training.

The Islamic character of the Khudai Khidmatgar is highlighted by the attitude of the few Hindu members in its ranks. The percentage of non-Muslim Pathans was almost negligible. The Hindu members complained that the movement was too Islamic. In response, Khudai Khidmatgar leaders replied that, inasmuch as the overwhelming majority were Muslim, the appeal had to be made through Islam.[68] Although the character of the movement was intensely Islamic, it was also consistently non-communal and one of the objectives of the organization was the promotion of Hindu-Muslim unity.

The action on the Frontier during the 1930's followed a pattern similar to that in the rest of India. In the towns there

* In this connection it is instructive to note the following comment by the Turkish scholar, Halidé Edib, *Inside India* (London: Allen and Unwin [1937]), p. 333: "The name of the Society once more brings us to the psychology of the Muslem. The first allegiance must be to the supreme 'Idea,' not to any symbol of it. All the rest is secondary. And that is what makes Abdul Ghaffar Khan what he is. That is what made the simple Muslems of Benares stand out as more uncompromising and distinct than the older and better organized Hindu workers."

was liquor-shop picketing, processions, *hartal*, jail-courting, singing of national songs, and general non-violent resistance to the efforts of the authorities to interfere with demonstrations. "If any member broke the rules of non-violence," Halidé Edib, the Turkish observer, reported, "he was dismissed at once."[69]

Pathan women participating in non-violent action campaigns would frequently take their stand facing the police or would lie down in orderly lines holding copies of the Quran. The flag which commonly appeared in demonstrations on the Frontier, was similar to the Indian National Congress flag used in satyagraha demonstrations excepting that the *charkha* (spinning wheel), central in the flag pattern, was replaced by the crescent of Islam. Slogans used in the Frontier campaign frequently included the Islamic cry: Allah Ho Akbar! (God is most great!)[70]

The period from March to December 1931 marked the climax of activities for the Khudai Khidmatgar in the Civil Disobedience movement. The official Government report notes that "probably at no time since British influence was first extended to the Frontier have conditions given cause for such acute anxiety as during [this period]."[71] In the words of the Government account:

> ... acts of lawlessness and defiance of authority increased with extraordinary speed, and organizations affiliated to the Congress gained greatly in prestige and popularity. The volunteers known as the *Khudai khidmatgaran*—or "Red Shirts," owing to their distinctive uniform—were enrolled in unexpectedly large numbers, particularly in the Charsadda and Mardan subdivisions of the Peshawar District, and figured prominently in the innumerable anti-Government demonstrations which took place. Abdul Ghaffar Khan, it may be mentioned, after having held a series of mass meetings in and around Charsadda during the third week of April, had been arrested there, with

several of his supporters, on the same day as that on which the Peshawar riots occurred.[72]

The action was highly developed in the city of Peshawar. Despite the determined resistance of British troops patrolling the city, and repeated firings, picketing persisted with fresh volunteers replacing those who had fallen. The action resulted in the complete seizure of the city by the Khudai Khidmatgar. From an unsympathetic British report of the events in Peshawar we have this description:

> On April 23rd last riots broke out in Peshawar city after the arrest of certain orators and office bearers of the Provincial Congress Committee. There were troops in the city, but some thirty hours later these were withdrawn—two of the platoons of the Garhwal regiment had refused to support the police. The Congress Committee thereupon assumed the virtual control of the city; volunteers were posted in the main streets to direct traffic; patrols policed the streets at night and bulletins from the Congress office were placarded every day in the principal square purporting to announce events of interest. This state of things went on for nine days. . . .[73]

Another British report describes the extensive activities of the Khudai Khidmatgar in other areas where Ghaffar Khan's followers "held large camps" at which "manoeuvers in military formation were carried out. The campaign for the non-payment of revenue and water-rates and for the refusal to take government canal water was steadily pursued." This report describes the success of Khudai Khidmatgar officers in establishing revenue offices and collecting revenue from landholders.[74]

Such reports indicate that the Khudai Khidmatgar were able to carry through a satyagraha program to the extent of establishing parallel government for a short period in the city of Peshawar. It should be noted that the soldiers of a Garhwal regiment refused to fire upon the satyagrahis.[75] The details of that refusal have especial bearing upon the functioning of satyagraha in general. A British Civil Servant, describing the behavior of the Garhwal soldiers as "refusal . . . to do their duty in face of the mob," continues with this tribute to the men involved:

> Hardly any regiment of the Indian Army won greater glory in the Great War than the Garhwal Rifles, and the defection of part of the regiment sent a shock through India, of apprehension to some, of exultation to others.[76]

It was an experienced soldiery which refused to fire upon a crowd which had demonstrated itself unwilling to retaliate with violent means, and which was led by disciplined satyagrahis.[77] What British observers chose to call a "mob" subsequently organized the administration of Peshawar to the extent of setting up a parallel government. This was in the face of civil police and frontier constabulary reinforced by an entire division of troops and a detachment of the Air Force at Risalpur.[78]

The Khudai Khidmatgar had, in fact, suffered the most severe of all repressions in the Indian independence movement. "Some of the stories of the wholesale shootings and hangings last year," reported one British journalist following his tour of the Frontier, "made me—rapidly becoming a hard-boiled and cynical journalist—hang my head in shame."[79] There were repeated instances of police firing, with figures for casualties high, even according to the official record.[80] But despite an ordinance outlawing the Khudai Khidmatgar, the movement increased in popularity and in numbers.[81]

Gandhi himself did not go to the Frontier until 1938. When he did, he found there an organization already tried in the techniques of satyagraha. Abdul Ghaffar Khan's belief in non-violent action had been developed over a number of years of experience and experiment. He wrote in *Young India*:

My non-violence has become almost a matter of faith with me. I believed in Mahatma Gandhi's *ahimsa* before. But the unparalleled success of the experiment in my province has made me a confirmed champion of non-violence.[82]

Both Gandhi and Abdul Ghaffar Khan commented upon the novelty of non-violence to the Pathan temperament. Gandhi was concerned that satyagraha should be fully understood and that the Pathan should be made fully aware that passivity played no part in the satyagraha technique.

"At every meeting I repeated the warning that unless they felt that in non-violence they had come into possession of a force infinitely superior to the one they had and in the use of which they were adept, they should have nothing to do with non-violence and resume the arms they possessed before. It must never be said of the Khudai Khidmatgars that once so brave, they had become or been made cowards under Badshah Khan's influence. Their bravery consisted not in being good marksmen but in defying death and being ever ready to bare their breasts to the bullets."[83]

Ghaffar Khan recounted to Gandhi an experience he had had in discussing his movement with a Punjabi Muslim:

"He was full of denunciation of me saying that I had undermined the spirit of Islam by preaching non-violence to the Pathans. I told him that he knew not what he was saying and that he would never have talked like that if he had seen with his own eyes the wonderful transformation that the message of non-violence has worked in the midst of the Pathans, to whom it has given a new vision of national solidarity. I cited chapter and verse from the Quran to show the great emphasis that Islam had laid on Peace, which is its coping stone. I also showed to him how the greatest figures in Islamic history were known more for their forbearance and self-restraint than for their fierceness. The reply rendered him speechless."[84]

Analyzing the curious and stimulating development of the Khudai Khidmatgar and their use of satyagraha in an environment in which such techniques appeared strange indeed, Halidé Edib found that the "psychological aspect of the movement was more interesting than its political significance."[85] She came away from the Frontier convinced that the movement indicated the existence among the indomitable Pathans of "a new interpretation of force, which is very unexpected."

> Non-violence is the only form of force which can have a lasting effect on the life of society and man. And this, coming from strong and fearless men, is worthy of study.[86]

The point of greatest significance for a study in the philosophy of action is that satyagraha could be, and was, adopted by a people to whom the concepts of *ahimsa, tapasya,* and *satya* were unfamiliar. If satyagraha could be supported by Islamic scripture, it required a complete reinterpretation of the familiar teachings, and an abrupt reorientation in things religious as well as social and cultural. That this was achieved is a matter of primary interest for those who are concerned with the conditions under which the technique may be employed and by whom it may be adopted.

The Pathans of the Frontier were traditionally trained in the use of weapons and they had easy access to arms. In contrast to the Indian of the plains, who had virtually no training or background in the use of violent weapons, the Pathan had grown up in the tradition of tribal organization which was part of what may be called a military confederacy.

The Hindu notion of *karma,* which attaches responsibility to the individual for his actions and attributes to a universal law the assignment of reward and punishment, is replaced in the Pathan philosophy with the rule of "an eye for an eye." The Muslim Pathan did not, moreover, have either the concept of *ahimsa* or the tradition of *tapasya* or self-suffering. Finally, the Islamic faith does not imbue the Pathan with any notion akin to the divinity of man which would give him faith in the ultimate goodness of human nature. The Pathan is trained to defend himself and to establish his position in his society through skillful and ruthless use of violence. The British claimed never to have been able to pacify the Frontier peoples and made their violent character and contentiousness the reason for continuing military rule.

Further differences between Hinduism and Islam are manifold: the metaphysical speculations of Hinduism as contrasted with the straightforward notions of unity, transcendence, and omnipotence of God in Islam; the elaborate appeal of Hinduism to the masses through music, ritual, and idolatry as contrasted with Islam's stern austerity, puritanism of unaccompanied prayer, and an absolute rejection of idolatry; the freedom of Islam from racial and caste distinctions; and finally the proselytizing zeal of Islam, with its insistence upon a vigorous, and even ruthless, extension of a victorious creed as contrasted to the inherent tolerance and inclusive character of Hinduism. There could scarcely be two more different religious backgrounds than the Islam which lies behind the Frontier Pathan and the Hinduism which infuses the culture of the Indian Hindu.

> The gulf, indeed, between Mr. Gandhi's philosophy and the outlook of the average Pathan could scarcely be wider. The principle of "non-violence" is almost unintelligible on the Frontier where most men carry firearms and the maintenance of the blood-feud is still regarded as a sacred duty.[87]

This observation by the well-known British constitutional historian of India, Sir Reginald Coupland, is typical of the British incredulity that a society so infused with respect for violence could be to any degree receptive to non-violence.

Pyarelal, who accompanied Gandhi on his tour of the

Frontier, records this remark by a high official from Southern India:

"As I move from the south northwards, I seem to confront a different humanity altogether. There seems to be no meeting-ground between the type here and that found in the south. Will the twain ever meet?

Gandhi is reported to have replied:

. . . whilst apparent difference was there, non-violence was the golden bridge that united the ferocious and war-like Pathan and the mild and intellectual South Indian. The Khudai Khidmatgars who had accepted non-violence as their creed ceased to be different, except in the degree of their non-violent valour, from people in other parts of India."[88]

If the Indian satyagraha was based upon *ahimsa, satya,* and *tapasya,* the technique as it operated on the Frontier was supported by Islam—"peace"*—and was backed by Ghaffar Khan's appeal to Islamic sanctions. The hardy Pathans were convinced by their stalwart Pathan leader that it was more courageous to die than to kill. The Pathan warrior was persuaded to substitute for the certainty which he found in the rifle and dagger, a faith in the power of a moral force. This he was ready to accept because he trusted a leader who knew of its efficacy and taught its divine sanction.

* The interpretation of Islam by the leaders of the Khudai Khidmatgar was, in some respects, close to that of the eminent Indian Muslim, Syed Ameer Ali, who wrote in his famous work *The Spirit of Islam*: "In order to form a just appreciation of the religion of Mohammed it is necessary to understand aright the true significance of the word Islam. *Salam* (salama), in its primary sense, means, to be tranquil, at rest, to have done one's duty, to have paid up, *to be at perfect peace*; in its secondary sense, to surrender oneself to Him with whom peace is made. The noun derived from it means peace, greeting, safety, salvation. The word does not imply, as is commonly supposed, absolute submission to God's will, but means, on the contrary, striving after *righteousness.*" (Syed Ameer Ali, *The Spirit of Islam*, Calcutta: S. K. Lahiri, 1902, pp. 117-118.)

The role of Khan Abdul Ghaffer Khan on the Frontier is significant for a study of leadership. The work of Ghaffar Khan was characterized by tolerance and catholicity. His was a straightforward, unequivocal position of freedom from bondage, service to all humanity, and reconciliation of varying creeds and races. His appeal to Pathans was that of the religious, national leader mixed with the rational appeal which a new method offered for achieving popular goals. Halidé Edib summed up his achievements:

> Although he based his simple ideology on religion, his interpretation of it was so universal, that instead of separating the Muslims from the rest of the world, he tried to make them so that they could cooperate with their fellow-men for the good of all. For the writer, his supreme importance lies in his having brought the simplest and truest conception of Islam into the lives of a most elemental people . . .[89]

As we have seen with Gandhi, the leadership of Ghaffar Khan was, above all, creative. He used Islamic precepts to communicate to his people the need for changes in the traditional. The effect which the Khudai Khidmatgar had on Frontier society is incalculable. The movement not only introduced women into political action—a far cry from the seclusion of purdah—but it posed a challenge to other social and economic institutions. The movement took the form of occasional revolutionary action of peasant against landlord. Wherever the Khudai Khidmatgar believed there to be injustice, action by satyagraha was initiated. Satyagraha for the Khudai Khidmatgar was at all times a method, not an objective, a means and not an end. The objectives of the organization were both social and political. That the adoption of satyagraha transformed those objectives could well have been expected as a natural consequence of the use of satyagraha. Advancement towards the originally-held ends of social uplift became, for Abdul Ghaffar Khan, adjudged in terms of moral progress. Moral progress came to mean the effective utilization of satyagraha in its total form including substantial efforts in the constructive program.

The achievement of the Khudai Khidmatgar was nothing less than the reversal in attitude and habit of a people steeped in the tradition of factious violence. For competition in force, they substituted cooperation in constructive action. The Khudai Khidmatgar achieved a discipline for hot-tempered discontents and directed it into channels which proved effective not only in social organization but in political action. The instrument for this achievement was a Pathan version of satyagraha.

Conclusion

The complex Indian ethos has lent itself to several appeals. The claim which Gandhian satyagraha can make is that, of all the efforts to forge instruments of change, satyagraha has gained the greatest response and has achieved the most far-reaching successes on the several levels of social and political action in India. The emergence of satyagraha cannot be explained in terms of the Indian traditional ideal alone. Western objectives—social equality, economic prosperity, basic popular social action—played their role. Yet, the Vykom satyagraha for removal of Harijan disabilities, the satyagraha for a fair living allowance for the Ahmedabad textile workers, the political campaigns of mass non-cooperation, the over-all program of constructive work—these efforts were not predominantly Western in influence nor did they issue from Hindu revivalism or religious reform. All of those elements were, indeed, strands in the complex fabric of the Gandhian movement. But the essence of the Gandhian *karma-yoga*—the way of the deed—is a technique of action the key to which is a synthesizing approach which attacks all problems of social conflict with the active dialectic of non-material suasion. Its elements are truth, non-violence, and self-suffering. These could, indeed, be found in the Indian ethos, as could the circumstances which supplied conflict and cried for its resolution. Gandhi responded with a constructive technique and used elements familiar to his ethos punctuated by influences from other cultures. But the method of satyagraha which evolved in the early decades of twentieth-century India was adopted by people of a very different background: it was used with equal success and with greater consistency by the Khudai Khidmatgar. Thereby is illustrated the further significance of satyagraha.

V

CONSERVATIVE OR ANARCHIST?
A NOTE ON GANDHI
AND POLITICAL PHILOSOPHY

In the realm of political thought it is substantially easier to say what Gandhi was than what he was not. He was in one sense a conservative, in another a philosophical anarchist; he was on the one hand a socialist, and on the other, a capitalist; and yet again he was a primitive communist. For each of these assertions some evidence can be culled from his writings and speeches. He belongs at once to all these camps and to none of them. For whatever else may be said of him, Gandhi was not a political theorist. He entered the practical realm suggested by one political creed only to make his own constructions and move into the next. It is as inaccurate as it is insufficient to infer that he wished only the idealization of a system. He had no time and but little patience with theoretical formulations. That he had scant interest in academic analyses was borne home to me in 1946 at the outset of my exploration—and academic analysis—of satyagraha. For when I explained my purpose, during a brief talk with Gandhi at Sodepur ashram,[1] he directly responded: "but satyagraha is not a subject for research—you must experience it, use it, live by it."

Gandhi saw at every hand the inequities and imperfections of political and social organization. He raised, then, questions of *how* but only occasionally those of *what*. "How can we transform the system?" superseded "What is the form of an ideal organization?" Gandhi was, in the judgment of the man best qualified to assess his impact upon the Indian scene, "the greatest revolutionary" India has yet produced. He not only "shook" India, Jawaharlal Nehru has said, "he brought about great changes," and "this is revolution."[2] Gandhi set out to transform the social and political system in which he found himself. An abiding awareness of social and political disabilities had first been forced upon him in South Africa. As he forged the tools with which he could fight such disabilities, he did not concern himself with questions of ideal social and political organization. It is possible that more than one "ideal" system could be formulated to meet Gandhi's requirements. But essential to such a system would be a non-violent sociopolitical technique of action in the hands of the members of that society. Gandhi himself had "purposely refrained from dealing with the nature of Government in a society based on non-violence," he wrote in 1939.

> When society is deliberately constructed in accordance with the law of non-violence, its structure will be different in material particulars from what it is today. But I cannot say in advance what the Government based wholly on non-violence will be like.[3]

Gandhi's political philosophy is, indeed, elusive. To the scholar who seeks internally consistent, systematized bodies of thought, the study of Gandhi is unrewarding. As I shall try to show, the most serious efforts to classify Gandhi in terms of exclusive schools of political theory have failed. Nevertheless, I suggest, once more, that in the Gandhian development lies a contribution of great significance for political philosophy. The contribution centers upon the role which satyagraha as a technique of action, together with the philosophy of conflict which lies behind it, may play in a social and political system based upon them.

If one is to understand the significance of Gandhi's "experiments" for political thought, he must focus upon the potential of a dynamic end-creating method. To think of Gandhi and communism, or of Gandhi as a conservative, or of anarchist elements in Gandhian thought—to think in this manner of Gandhi will bear little fruit. One must frame the questions in terms of conservatism or communism or anarchism or capitalism or any other "ism" *plus* satyagraha—to discover the potential of the Gandhian approach. For the introduction of satyagraha into any system would necessarily effect modifications of that system. It could alter the customary exercise of power and bring about a redistribution and a resettling of authority. Satyagraha would guarantee the adaptation of the system to citizen demands and would serve as an instrument of social change. The implications of the role which satyagraha might play within a system of political thought will be suggested in the course of analyzing two of the most common classifications of the thought of Gandhi. It has frequently been said that Gandhi was a conservative. On the other hand, there are those who place him within some school of philosophical anarchism. As we examine these assertions, light may also be shed upon certain weaknesses inherent in the recognized schools of conservatism and anarchism.

Gandhi and Conservatism

There were several aspects of conservatism at work among the influences which shaped Gandhi's development. The Vaishnavite, Jain society in which young Gandhi grew up is one of the most conservative in the whole of the Indian subcontinent. The social milieu into which Gandhi was born may be characterized as religiously orthodox and politically reactionary. However, there were other elements which conditioned Gandhi and among them was the impact of the writings of three Westerners whom Gandhi recognized as having substantially influenced his thought: Tolstoy, the Christian Anarchist, Thoreau, whose experiments with civil disobedience attracted Gandhi, and John Ruskin, the only systematic political theorist of the three.

In investigating the extent to which Gandhian thought is conservative, a further question is suggested: what, if any, modifications would be required of conservative principles for them to be properly characterized as Gandhian?

The problem of definition is delicate. In the following examination of conservative elements in Gandhian political thought, I am aware of the limitations of an approach which takes the sum of several characteristics to represent the whole of a political philosophy. But it is necessary to adopt some criteria by which to judge the degree to which the Gandhian political approach agrees with what is generally considered to be conservatism.

Conservatism, then, let us take to be an attitude toward political institutions and a philosophy of social relationships which include (1) a respect for the wisdom of established institutions, especially those concerned with religion and property, (2) a strong sense of continuity in the historical changes of the social system, (3) belief in the relative impotence of individual will and reason to deflect societal change from its course, and (4) a keen moral satisfaction in the loyalty that attaches the members of a society to their stations in its various ranks.[4]

RESPECT FOR THE WISDOM OF ESTABLISHED INSTITUTIONS

The revolutionary character of the Gandhian movement in India does not in itself determine the political genre of Gandhi or Gandhism. For when out of power, conservatives tend to become revolutionaries[5] in an attempt to re-establish a *status quo ante*. From a quick reading of some of Gandhi's writings, one might conclude that such references as those to "Panchayat Raj" and "Rama Raj" suggest political reaction. His nostalgic recollections of India's past, coupled with his comments urging the rejection of aspects of modern technology, have led some observers to label Gandhi a traditionalist and a reactionary. But let us examine Gandhi's position more closely.

Panchayat Raj is ordinarily taken to mean a political structure, probably a federation, which has at its base the village panchayat, that is, the village council.[6] Traditionally the panchayat consisted of five elder statesmen of the community, who functioned in the triple capacity of legislature, executive, and judiciary. The number varied from place to place and from time to time as, indeed, did the manner of the panchayat's constitution and function. Now it is doubtful that Gandhi had any systematic notion of the political and sociological implications of the traditional village panchayat.[7] The historical record, incomplete though it is, shows a range of variations in the manner of selection and operation of this institution. However, a few predominant elements stand out as characteristic of the ancient panchayat system. The village panchayat was traditionally organized with the group and not the individual as the unit. It was, in many respects, an extension of the Indian family system, and was strictly patriarchal in character.[8]

Now Gandhi's concern, as we shall see, was consistently for the individual. By freedom he meant to no inconsiderable extent individualism. How, then, could he reconcile this position with that of the revival of the ancient panchayat? The answer is, that he did not. For the panchayat of his conception was very different from that typical of the ancient system. Gandhi drew upon his experience with and knowledge of the institutions of his own society for terms to express the concepts and objectives which emerged from his own "experiments with truth." He seized upon Panchayat Raj to indicate a type of political organization of his own conception. The panchayat Gandhi envisaged was to be annually elected by all the adult villagers—"male and female alike." "This village democracy," he wrote,[9] "will be based on individual freedom and will be able to defy the might of a world because both the individual and the village will be ruled by the law of nonviolence." The contrast between the panchayat of Gandhi's conception and the patriarchal "assemblage of co-proprietors" of the traditional system[10] is to be found at the very heart of the institution.[11]

In like manner, Gandhi used the term Rama Raj to communicate with a largely illiterate populace steeped in India's epic lore. The term Rama Raj derives from the Ramayana's classic depiction of the victory of Rama, symbolizing the forces of good, over Ravana, symbolizing the forces of evil, and the consequent establishment of a reign of goodness and justice in the land. To orthodox Muslims, Gandhi's reference to Rama Raj, deriving as it did from Hindu scripture, aroused the fear that Gandhi intended a Hindu-dominated state with Hindu leadership. Gandhi found it necessary explicitly to state that by Rama Raj he did not mean Hindu Raj; he meant merely "the Kingdom of God," Rama and Rahim [one of the Muslim names of God] were the same, he said, and he acknowledged "no other God but the one God of truth and righteousness."[12] The ideal which Gandhi referred to as the kingdom of heaven on earth was defined, not in the traditional Hindu manner, but in his own way on the basis of social and political desiderata.

We find again and again Gandhi's use of the traditional to communicate new ideas, his use of phrases emerging out of established ways and familiar institutions to transmit newly created values. The question of Gandhi's conservative character may be further pursued through an examination of his position with regard to the institutions of religion and property.

Religious institutions. Gandhi insisted that there was, for him, no politics without religion and that he had entered politics because he was a religious man.[13] Certainly he had the conservative's respect for religion as an essential element of society.* Yet, when we enquire further into Gandhi's attitude towards religion and its institutions in the Indian setting, we discover less the conservative approach than that of the liberal, less the reformer than the revolutionary. Gandhi de-

---

* In this connection it is pertinent to recall what U. N. Ghoshal has called "the pronounced disinclination of the Hindu mind to conceive the secular life as the antithesis of the religious." *A History of Hindu Political Theories: From the Earliest Times to the End of the Seventeenth Century A.D.* (London, New York [etc.]: Humphrey Milford; Oxford University Press, 1927), p. xi.

fended "the irreligious brother"[14] and, in defining God, he wrote:

> To me God is Truth and Love; God is ethics and moral-
> ity; God is fearlessness. God is the source of Light and
> Life and yet He is above and beyond all these. God is
> conscience. He is even the atheism of the atheist.[15]

Repeatedly Gandhi expressed his belief in the "fundamental truth of all great religions of the world,"[16] and urged his fol- lowers to "remember that his own religion is the truest to every man even if it stands low in the scales of philosophical comparison."[17]

Allied with this belief in the fundamental value of all reli- gions was Gandhi's insistence upon equality among the vari- ous religious and racial communities of India. His was a constant struggle against the divisiveness of communalism. "In the Congress," he wrote, "we must cease to be exclusive Hindus or Musalmans or Sikhs, Parsis, Christians, Jews." And, he added, "while we may staunchly adhere to our respective faiths, we must be in the Congress Indians first and Indians last."[18]

Gandhi did not hesitate to attack orthodox positions, and as we shall see later, his position on such religiously sanctioned social institutions as caste gave serious alarm to orthodox Hindu elements—an alarm which, fed from several sources of Gandhian activity, grew to such proportions that it ulti- mately effected Gandhi's assassination. Again and again Gandhi indicated that for him an ethic-principle superseded tradition. "Let us not deceive ourselves into the belief that everything that is written in Sanskrit and printed in Shastra has any binding effect upon us," he wrote. "That which is opposed to the fundamental maxims of morality, that which is opposed to trained reason, cannot be claimed no matter how ancient it may be."[19] We have seen, in analyzing the Gandhian non-violent technique, how the inner dynamics of satyagraha may lead to the setting aside of customary practice or the precipitating of resistance to legal rules. The Gandhian philosophy of conflict renders impossible a rigid, unquestioning adherence to traditional institutions. It is bound to weaken, if not transform, this aspect of conservatism.

Property. Gandhi's economic doctrines have received some of the most serious of the attacks made by his critics. The Gandhian doctrine of "trusteeship" has overtones of a conservative position with respect to property. By virtue of this doctrine zamindars (landholders) had found in Gandhi at once a protector and a reformer. Zamindars, Gandhi said,

> should give their tenants fixity of tenure, take a lively interest in their welfare, provide well managed schools for their children, night school for adults, hospitals and dispensaries for the sick, look after the sanitation of villages and in a variety of ways make them feel that they the Zamindars are their true friends taking only a fixed commission for their manifold services.[20]

They should, in short, act as trustees. What, then, if the zamindar should fail to perform his duties as a trustee? The zamindari system, Gandhi said, "should be mended, not ended."[21] The answer to the further question, to what extent should the zamindari be mended, is suggested by Gandhi's position on economic equality.

Economic equality was one of the objectives outlined in Gandhi's practical constructive program.[22] But, he wrote, "economic equality must never be supposed to mean possession of an equal amount of worldly goods by everyone."

> It does mean, however, that everyone will have a proper house to live in, sufficient and balanced food to eat and sufficient Khadi with which to cover himself. It also means that the cruel inequality that obtains today will be removed by purely non-violent means.[23]

Gandhi would regulate the zamindar by non-violent tactics. He would tolerate landholders if they became trustees; they could be persuaded to become trustees through non-violence. But should they refuse to serve their tenants properly the tenants could, through non-violent techniques, justifiably end the zamindari. Gandhi even suggested that a non-violent state might find it necessary to equalize land distribution if both tenants and zamindars were to fail in their efforts.[24] Though he resisted any abrupt expropriation, Gandhi favored sweeping land reform. With non-violent techniques in the hands of the peasants, the zamindar would, indeed, be mended or ended.

Further evidence relating to Gandhi's position with regard to property is found in his doctrine *aparigraha* (non-possession), "bread-labor," and equitable distribution. Gandhi certainly did not consider property a good in itself. On the contrary, he taught, and in his own life very nearly achieved, the ideal of *aparigraha*: non-possession or voluntary poverty. This is consistent with his effort to achieve freedom from attachment to material things. It is the very negation of the institution of property. Recognizing that absolute non-possession is an abstraction and unattainable, Gandhi suggested that "if we strive for [non-possession], we shall be able to go further in realizing a scale of equality on earth than by any other method."[25] Gandhi held as an ideal, he tells us, equal distribution. But he recognized that "it is not to be realized." And so, he worked for "equitable distribution."[26] His objective was that "everybody should be able to get sufficient work to enable him to make two ends meet." He reasoned that

this ideal can be universally realized only if the means of production of elementary necessaries of life remain in the control of the masses. These should be freely available to all as God's air and water are or ought to be; they should not be made a vehicle of traffic for the exploitation of others. Their monopolization by any country, nation or group of persons would be unjust. . . .[27]

In examining Gandhi's views on industrialization one is at

once reminded of John Ruskin. Gandhi could embrace without qualification Ruskin's functional view of property. Tools in the hands of those who can use them and wealth restricted within fixed limits are principles which Ruskin and Gandhi held in common. Ruskin's attack on the assumptions of political economy and the industrial system are systematically set forth in his *Unto This Last*. It was this work which found its way into Gandhi's hands in South Africa, and which he credits with having inspired him to establish the community of Phoenix in Natal on principles of bread-labor and the responsibility of the community organization to provide for the physical welfare of the worker who is its member. Gandhi's response to Ruskin is a striking example of the realism and vitality which characterized Gandhi's leadership. He tells us in his autobiography that he discovered some of his deepest convictions reflected in *Unto This Last* and that the book "captured" him. He understood the message of Ruskin's work to be

1. That the good of the individual is contained in the good of all.
2. That a lawyer's work has the same value as the barber's, inasmuch as all have the same right of earning their livelihood from their work.
3. That a life of labour, i.e., the life of the tiller of the soil and the handicraftsman, is the life worth living.[28]

The first of these, he explains, he knew; the second he had "dimly realized"; but the third had never occurred to him. *Unto This Last* made it "as clear as daylight . . . that the second and third were contained in the first." And then Gandhi concludes this chapter on "The Magic Spell of a Book" by recalling this action so typical of him: "I arose with the dawn, ready to reduce these principles to practice."

It has been suggested by scholars who have written on the Victorian era that Ruskin's *Unto This Last* influenced the Labour members of Parliament of 1906 more than any other book and foreshadowed the Socialist movement.[29] Ruskin's influence may be seen to have extended even further into the socialist realm if one traces the extraordinary effect which Gandhi has had upon the Praja Socialist leadership in India, and if one explores the recent developments in "Gandhian socialism" as manifest in the sarvodaya movement.[*]

It is important to note here that it was Ruskin's ideas on political economy, and not his authoritarianism, which Gandhi assimilated into his own thinking. Ruskin provided Gandhi with ideas which were to reinforce the economic principles of ashram organization throughout the Gandhian development. As we shall see, Gandhi did not share the more conservative views of Ruskin which held the common man inferior, erected an aristocratic hierarchy, and denied the masses any political control on grounds of incompetence.

The duty of physical labor, a precept Gandhi adopted from Ruskin, was also an essential principle for Tolstoy who used the term "bread-labor" to describe it.[30] Gandhi understood bread-labor to mean "that everyone is expected to perform sufficient body-labor" to entitle him to his daily bread. It is not necessary to earn one's living in this manner, but "everyone must perform some useful body-labor."[31] This principle entered into the development of "khaddar" (handspun) economics with its tool and symbol the charka (spinning wheel). With Gandhi and Ruskin alike, bread-labor fitted into the trusteeship approach. "If all worked for their bread," suggested Gandhi, "distributions of rank would be obliterated; the rich would still be there, but they would deem themselves only trustees of their property, and would use it mainly in the public interest."[32]

In his application of the bread-labor principle, Gandhi

[*] Sarvodaya is the word which Gandhi used for the title of his translation into Gujarati of Ruskin's *Unto This Last*. For an analysis of "Gandhian socialism" and the influence of Gandhian principles upon Praja Socialists, see Margaret W. Fisher and Joan V. Bondurant, *Indian Approaches to a Socialist Society* (Berkeley: Indian Press Digests, 1956).

went so far as to suggest it as a qualification for the franchise, a qualification which he urged, "should be neither property nor position but manual work . . ." In this way "all who wish to take part in the Government and the well-being of the State," could prove themselves, and the labor-test would be far superior to that either of literacy or property.[33] Gandhi held that the voters, by becoming self-reliant through this principle, could not become pawns in the hands of politicians. He argued that the people would thereby have the capacity to resist misuse of authority and prevent the division of the state into a small class of exploiting rulers and a large class of exploited subjects.[34] There is perhaps no more telling an illustration of the inaccuracy of reading strict conservatism into Gandhi's approach than this suggestion about the use of manual labor. For beyond the explicit statement, there lay implicit in Gandhi's suggestion a potential anything but conservative—the undermining of caste itself.

With all Gandhi's respect for the dignity of labor and for the need for men to partake of physical labor, he had an essentially utilitarian attitude towards machinery. Gandhi could have no consideration, he tells us, for machinery "which is meant either to enrich the few at the expense of the many, or without cause to displace the useful labor of many." However, he explained further, "the heavy machinery for work of public utility which cannot be undertaken by human labour has its inevitable place, but all that would be owned by the State and used entirely for the benefit of the people."[35]

Gandhi's attitude towards capital and labor was consistent with his views on the zamindari and the trusteeship ideal. He held that capital "should be labour's servant, not its master," both labor and capital should act as mutual trustees and should work in the interests also of consumers. The worker, however, need not wait for the gradual conversion of management.

If capital is power, so is work. Either power can be used

destructively or creatively. Either is dependent on the other. Immediately the worker realizes his strength, he is in a position to become a co-sharer with the capitalist instead of remaining his slave.[36]

Both Ruskin and Gandhi sought the "conversion" of the upper class. Ruskin appealed for a change of heart and a transformation through which justice, rather than profit would be paramount.[37] But Ruskin could not consider the masses of men as ends in themselves; rather, did he treat them as means to the ends of others.[38] Gandhi conceded the possible result that voluntary transformation might fail. He recognized the power of the common man and placed before him the means whereby he could assure himself the "justice" about which Ruskin could only speculate. Gandhi believed in the worth of the individual man and considered his welfare the ultimate social goal. The element which distinguished the Gandhian approach is, again, the provision of a means to achieve that end—a technique of direct social action.

Gandhi extended the conservative position that every right carries with it a corresponding duty to include the further "corresponding remedy for resisting any attack" upon the right. Different situations and relationships produced different correlative rights, duties, and remedies. Applied to the realm of industrial relations, this approach led Gandhi to reason that, were he a laborer, "the corresponding duty is to labour with my limbs and the corresponding remedy is to non-cooperate with him who deprives me of the fruit of my labour."[39] The non-violent strike was a tool available to the satyagrahi. The Ahmedabad textile workers strike outlined in Chapter III was an instance of a Gandhi-led satyagraha movement in industrial conflict. Gandhi held that there was "fundamental equality" between the capitalist and the laborer and, recognizing this, the laborer must strive for the "conversion" of the capitalist. Moreover, Gandhi said, "destruction of the capitalist must mean destruction in the end of the worker."[40] He urged that labor should have a right to share in the administration and control of industry, as well as a right to leisure, wholesome living conditions, a living wage, and the other benefits for which the Ahmedabad Textile Union under his leadership began to seek.

In this brief examination of Gandhi's approach to established institutions and traditional approaches, especially with reference to religion and property, unorthodoxy has emerged as the predominant characteristic. Gandhi's action, through the series of satyagraha movements he led or inspired, effected revolutionary changes. The satyagraha of the Champaran peasants against an established system in the indigo fields of Bihar effected a revision of revolutionary proportions. The applied Gandhism of non-violent strikes of labor upset the traditional pattern which assured a submissive labor force. The satyagraha of Vykom for the right of untouchables to use a temple road undermined the entrenched Brahmanic authority. Where satyagraha is applied to a system a change unpredictable in specific content may result. When Gandhi set out to reform, or as some might say, to "react," he did it with methods which he well recognized might lead to basic changes. He would "mend, not end" the zamindari; but if reform failed to mend the system, Gandhi was prepared to bring about its end. Willingness to admit flexibility of ends is essential for those who believe that means are ends in the making.

CONTINUITY IN THE HISTORICAL CHANGES OF THE SOCIAL SYSTEM

The mainstream of conservative thought has been concerned centrally with the social organism. Edmund Burke treats society as such an organism governed by laws of growth beyond the competence of the individual will to alter.[41] Law is typically the essence of social continuity and to break the law constitutes a breach of the overriding moral law. For Burke the study of the history of each people is essential for an understanding of its politics,[42] and progress necessarily proceeds from long-established foundations and is determined by gradual trends within the historical depths of a nation.

We have seen how Gandhi used traditional precepts yet sought to change established institutions to make them subservient to the needs of the members of society—to the common good defined in terms of individual welfare. He insisted that he was not a worshipper of all that goes under the name of ancient,[43] though he made reference to ancient Indian institutions and appealed to his countrymen to reject vain imitations of Western patterns. He urged the abandoning of custom when it proved detrimental to the social welfare. "We must gladly give up custom that is against reason, justice, and religion of the heart," he said. And he urged Indians "not ignorantly to cling to bad custom" but to part with it "when we must, like a miser parting with his ill-gotten hoard out of pressure and expedience."[44]

The treatment of society as an organism, a treatment common to many schools of conservatism, is also familiar in traditional Indian thought. A general, if rudimentary, organismic theory of the state and society is to be found throughout the history of Hindu political theory. The *varna* (caste) scheme of social organization lends itself to an organismic interpretation, for society is conceived as a unit consisting of differentiated classes, each functioning in its specific sphere for the good of the entire society.* Gandhi occasionally used familiar organismic analogies when he considered the role of the individual in his society. "True social economics," he said, "will teach us that the working man, the clerk and the employer are parts of the same indivisible organism," where "none is smaller or greater than the other." Their interests, he

---

* The Rig-Veda (X, Purusha Sukta) describes the creation of the four varnas in terms of an organism: the Brahman as the mouth, the Kshatriya (Rajanya) the arms, the Vaisya the thighs, and the Sudra the feet.

For further comment on the notions of the integration and differentiation of the elements in the Manusamhita and the rudimentary biological analogy in the late Sukraniti, see Ghoshal, *op.cit.*, pp. 234-235.

added, "should not be conflicting but identical and interdependent."[45]

Yet, Gandhi did not conceive of an organismic growth of society in the usual conservative manner with irreversible laws governing that growth. His emphasis was consistently on the equality of the members. Nor did he understand equality in terms of a *suum cuique* (to each his own) formulation or of determined "place" in the social structure. Where he does make use of the biological analogy he takes care to explain that he decries "distorted notions of superiority and inferiority."*

For those who find in the organismic theory a doctrine repugnant to individual liberty, the greatest danger lies in the concept of the state as a natural organism, and the imputing to the state a supra-life—an hypostatization which lends itself, as in Hegel, to the transformation of the "is" into the "ought." However, Gandhi made the essential distinction between state and society, a distinction implicit in his doctrine of disobedience. When Gandhi writes, as he did in 1939, "I value individual freedom but you must not forget that man is essentially a social being," he sets himself in agreement with the "new" liberalism of T. H. Green rather than with the metaphysical theory of Hegel. Man has "risen to the present status by learning to adjust his individualism to the requirements of social progress," continued Gandhi.

Unrestricted individualism is the law of the beast of the jungle. We have learnt to strike the mean between individual freedom and social restraint. Willing submission to social restraint for the sake of the well-being of the whole society, enriches both the individual and the society of which one is a member.[46]

* See, for example, *Young India*, May 3, 1928, a passage in which Gandhi describes man as "a wonderful organization" and compares social and political organizations to the human body. "An organization which has no directing mind and which has no members cooperating with the mind, suffers from paralysis and is in a dying condition."

For Gandhi, society must provide opportunities for the maximum growth of the individual, and the final decision as to what constitutes that growth lies with the individual. "If the individual ceases to count," Gandhi asked, "what is left of society?" It is by virtue of individual freedom alone that an individual will be prepared to "voluntarily surrender himself completely to the service of society." And if that freedom is "wrested" from him, he becomes merely an "automaton" to the ruin of society.

> No society can possibly be built on a denial of individual freedom. It is contrary to the very nature of man. Just as a man will not grow horns or a tail, so he will not exist as man if he has no mind of his own. In reality even those who do not believe in the liberty of the individual believe in their own.[47]

T. H. Green's concepts of positive freedom, and the realization of the individual's fullest potential as possible only within the social structure, are very close to those of Gandhi. The idea of collective well-being or the common good as underlying any claim to private right is again congenial. Like Green, Gandhi would have no part in glorifying the State. The community ought simply to secure the conditions for the realization of an individual's best potential. For both, the aim was to make life morally meaningful for all people, and both viewed the community as held together not by compulsion but by the sense of a common interest or good.[48]

Although Green may be ranked on the side of liberalism, certain aspects of his thesis have conservative connotations. There is the danger inherent in identifying political and moral obligation and linking this to the concept of collective well-being. But, for Gandhi, such difficulties were neatly averted, first by avoiding the confusion between society and state, and finally by the introduction of the technique of satyagraha based upon a philosophy of relative truths. A Gandhian tradition of civil disobedience secures the precedent for distinguishing moral from political obligation, and in this too, Gandhian thought deviates from characteristic conservatism.

For Burke, law is the essence of continuity and to break the positive law involves a breach of the moral law. The social and political circumstances in which Gandhi developed his ideas and his techniques precluded any possibility of retaining this conservative characteristic. Resistance to the British regime was the central effort. Civil disobedience became one of the primary tools by which that resistance was manifested. But there are, as well, other elements in the Gandhian philosophy which call for a rejection of any especial reverence for law. Gandhi was of the opinion that progress was impossible without the right to err, and an essential of political organization was "freedom to err and the duty of correcting errors."[49] This concept follows from the Gandhian philosophy of conflict where "truth" is relative and satyagraha serves as a technique for discovering truth in a given conflict situation.

Gandhian thought is not in any real sense conservative by this second criterion. Throughout occasional references to the social structure as organism, the emphasis is upon elements which are characteristic of the "new" liberalism common to T. H. Green, and to a further extent, to that other British liberal thinker, L. T. Hobhouse. Virtue was for Gandhi, as it was for Hobhouse and for Green, essentially social. But the concept of a collective well-being, as in Green, or the state as the guarantor of the rights of its members, as with Hobhouse—neither of these concepts requires a trust in "the inherent logic of social growth"* or other Hegelian conclusions necessitating obedience to destiny or respect of the law as sacred. Similarly, the Gandhian insistence upon selfless service to society, upon duty to the community as the more important correlative of right, and the final concept of a social well-being—these moral incentives provided by Gandhi, as by Green, could lead to a nationalization of industries, social-

---

* Such a position was basic, for example, to the political thought of Bernard Bosanquet.

ization of health and education, and, in general, a form of Liberal Socialism.[50] The philosophy underlying the method of satyagraha once more sets the Gandhian approach out of the mainstream of conservatism. For, whatever the significance of history, whatever respect for laws, and whatever the organismic nature of society, the individual may assert his freedom to test, to challenge, to disobey, and this is not only his prerogative, but his foremost duty. "It is not that I harbor disloyalty towards anything whatsoever," Gandhi asserted, "but I do so against all untruth, all that is unjust, all that is evil." He wanted to make clear that he remained loyal to an institution "so long as that institution conduces to my growth, and the growth of the nation." Immediately upon finding that the institution "instead of conducing to its growth impedes it," he considered it his "bounden duty to be disloyal to it."[51]

Truth, with Gandhi, is the one persisting goal. But conservatives are often seekers for peace rather than truth. This was so for Plato and it tended to be so for Burke. That "truth" was, for Gandhi, relative truth is of striking significance. For absolutes are more congenial to the conservative mind. The development of a technique for discovering relative truths, and for resolving conflicts among them, is Gandhi's especial contribution.

IMPOTENCE OF INDIVIDUAL WILL AND REASON

Gandhi is surely not conservative by this further criterion of belief in the impotence of individual will and reason to deflect historical changes in the social system. We have already touched upon Gandhi's reliance upon reason and his belief in the capacity of the individual to bring about fundamental change. The evidence is extensive and compelling.

Conservative thought assigns to man a very limited role. The locus of rationality for the conservative lies outside of man—in the social process, in history, in the reified state. For Gandhi, however, man is the measure and, as he tellingly demonstrated, the individual is capable of and, under some circumstances, responsible for pitting himself against the state.

There is a strain in Hindu political thought which is idealist in form and conservative in effect. The concept of *dharma* which lies at the heart of ancient Hindu polity is reminiscent of aspects of the Hegelian metaphysical theory which L. T. Hobhouse has summed up in this manner: The individual attains his true self and freedom in conformity to his real will. This real will is the general will and the general will is embodied in the state.[52] The eminent Indian historian of philosophy Sarvepalli Radhakrishnan has defined *dharma* as the complex of influences which shape the moral feeling and the character of the people and serve as a code of conduct, supported by the general conscience of the people. It is not a fixed code of mechanical rules, but a living spirit which grows and moves in response to the development of society.[53]

The Hegelian metaphysical theory endeavors to exhibit the state as the embodiment of greatness and glory and an expression of the Spirit or the Absolute. The Hindu metaphysical concept of *dharma* could lend itself to a similar development. But the Gandhian approach could scarcely be reconciled with such an interpretation. As Hobhouse shows in his critique of the metaphysical theory of the state, there is no distinction between the real will and the actual. The will of the individual is not identical with the general will, and the rational order is not confined to the state organization. The Gandhian position is basically in agreement with critics of the metaphysical theory. Gandhi held that "submission to the state law is the price a citizen pays for his personal liberty." Therefore, he argued, submission "to a state wholly or largely unjust is an immoral barter for liberty."

A citizen who thus realizes the evil nature of a state is not satisfied to live on its sufferance, and therefore appears to the others who do not share his beliefs to be a nuisance to a society whilst he is endeavoring to compel the state, without committing a moral breach, to arrest him. Thus considered, civil resistance is a more powerful expression of a soul's anguish and an eloquent protest against the continuance of an evil state.[54]

The technique of satyagraha presupposes the will of the individual as apart from that of the general will, and predicates a rational order not confined to state organization. Reason is the very basis of the satyagraha method, and reason is defined, not in terms of history or hypostatized organizations, but in terms of the individual himself.

In the Gandhian view, the purpose of the state is to establish conditions under which man may realize to the fullest his potential, and the state should secure obedience from its members in return. When the state fails in achieving this objective, the individual must challenge its authority. It is for him to determine when disobedience is in order, and this he is increasingly better able to do as he gains experience with satyagraha.

I have found that it is our first duty to render voluntary obedience to law, but whilst doing that duty I have also seen that when law fosters untruth it becomes a duty to disobey it. How may this be done? We can do so by never swerving from truth and suffering the consequences of our disobedience. This is Civil Disobedience. No rules can tell us how this disobedience may be done and by whom, when and where, nor can they tell us which laws foster untruth. It is only experience that can guide us, and it requires time and knowledge of facts.[55]

Gandhi had no sympathy for the conservative principle that man is impotent to influence the course of change in society. For Gandhi, satyagraha, a technique which may be wielded by an individual, precludes historicism, a metaphysical explanatory principle. Satyagraha may become an instrument of social change, and through it untruth can be deflected. Untruth is determined by the extent to which the needs of society's members are left unfulfilled. Oppression ceases, Gandhi taught his followers, "when people cease to fear the bayonet."[56] Satyagraha, which disciplines the emotional response, is built upon reason—the reason of the individual operating in any given social milieu.

ATTACHMENT OF MEMBERS OF A SOCIETY TO THEIR STATIONS

The fourth characteristic of conservatism is a keen moral satisfaction in the loyalty that attaches members of a society to their stations in its various ranks. It is this characteristic which is most clearly evinced in Plato's well-structured class society. The Platonic concept of justice in the state is built upon the establishment and maintenance of the class-structure. When each class in the city-state attends to its own business, including the money-earning class as well as the auxiliaries and the guardians, then justice is realized.[57] Edmund Burke later argued that the perpetuation of society itself was largely dependent upon an hereditary landed aristocracy, whose duty and function it was to transmit social virtue. It was upon such a principle, he tells us, that the English House of Lords was based.[58] The conservative view holds that duty is of greater importance and priority than right. The citizen finds his duties as a member of a given section of society. It is his moral obligation to fulfill these duties.*

In traditional Hindu polity, emphasis upon duty is extended to the King. The King, above all others, is obliged to fulfill his kingly duties towards his people, and proper fulfillment of such duties is the sole justification for expecting his subjects to obey him. Gandhi, who would make every man a king, consistently emphasized duties as prior to rights. But the effect of his reasoning was not precisely conservative in nature. "Rights accrue automatically to him who duly performs his

---

* Hobhouse has pointed to the fallacy of identifying moral and political obligation, in his argument against the metaphysical theory.

duties," he wrote.[59] These rights were not to be rigidly confined to rank and order, as we shall see in examining Gandhi's position on that conservative structuring of society arising out of caste.

Varna was the ancient social organization of the Hindus based upon the four class divisions. The institution degenerated into a rigid but fragmented caste structure which resulted in serious social disabilities for those of lower or of no caste. When Gandhi wrote of varna, he tended to defend the ideal system of functional division into the prototypes, Brahman, Kshatriya, Vaisya, and Shudra. In an article in *Young India* Gandhi expressed his belief in varna which, he explained, "marks four universal occupations—imparting knowledge, defending the defenceless, carrying on agriculture and commerce, and performing service through physical labour." These occupations, he said, are common to all mankind and Hinduism had recognized them in the form of "the law of our being" and had further used this law to regulate social relations and conduct. But Gandhi did not stop here in his commentary—nor should the reader who wishes to understand the manner in which Gandhi seized upon the traditional only to transform it. At the same time that Gandhi found value in an ideal, he looked about him to assess the real situation. His assessment with regard to the institution of caste led him to conclude (in the same article on varna), that he did not believe in caste "in the modern sense." "It is an excrescence and a handicap on progress," he explained, and summed up his position with yet another assertion of the principle of equality:

Nor, do I believe in inequalities between human beings. We are all absolutely equal. But equality is of souls and not bodies. Hence, it is a mental state. We need to think of, and to assert, equality because we see great inequalities in the physical world. We have to realize equality in the midst of this apparent external inequality. Assumption of superiority by any person over any other is a sin against God and man. Thus caste, in so far as it connotes distinctions in status, is an evil.[60]

The revolutionary character of the Gandhian approach may be seen once more in his opinion on the orthodox rules governing inter-dining. Such rules were, he held, hygienic in origin. "Given a proper confirmation with the rules of cleanliness there should be no scruple about dining with anybody."[61] Even restriction upon intercaste marriage Gandhi held to be "no part of Hindu religion." The restrictions "crept into Hinduism when perhaps it was in its decline" and were weakening Hindu society.[62] Gandhi himself promoted many marriages across caste lines and his ashram society was organized entirely without caste distinction. The continuing campaign Gandhi conducted against untouchability is, again, telling evidence of his abiding concern for the reconstruction of the institutions and approaches of his own society. He himself had suffered the bitter humiliation of discrimination. As he forged the tools with which the struggle could be pressed against social injustice, there emerged a philosophy of conflict which was further to influence the development of his thought. The experience of social disability and the idea of structured class positions offended Gandhi's reason. He held the Harijan (untouchable) as capable of exercising responsible functions as the Brahman. He knew no argument, he tells us, in favor of the retention of untouchability and he had "no hesitation" in "rejecting scriptural authority of a doubtful character" if it supported a "sinful institution." Here once more we find him asserting his rejection of all authority "if it is in conflict with sober reason or the dictates of the heart," and adding that "authority sustains and ennobles the weak" only when it is the "hand-work of reason," for when it supplants reason, it serves only to degrade.[63]

The law of varna Gandhi believed to establish "certain spheres of action for certain people with certain tendencies," which had the effect of avoiding "all unworthy competition."[64] But in insisting upon flexibility in refusing to countenance any deferential privilege for a member of one group as opposed to a member of another, and by rejecting birth as the determining factor, he completely upset the traditional approach:

> One born of Brahman parents will be called a Brahman, but if his life fails to reveal the attributes of a Brahman when he comes of age he cannot be called a Brahman. . . . On the other hand, one who is born not a Brahman but reveals in his conduct the attributes of a Brahman will be regarded as a Brahman, though he will himself disclaim the label.[65]

When Gandhi was challenged by those truly conservative elements among the Hindu orthodox, he urged upon them constructions and interpretations which they were unprepared to accept. "What is this Varnashrama?" Gandhi wrote in reply to one orthodox Hindu. "It is not a system of watertight compartments," and, he explained:

> A Brahman is not only a teacher. He is only predominantly that. But a Brahman who refused to labour will be voted down as an idiot. . . . Nor have I the least hesitation in recommending handweaving as a bread winning occupation to all who are in need of an honest occupation.[66]

And so Gandhi pressed his campaign to overcome discrimination and the fear and weaknesses which arise from it. In so doing he undermined some of the most sacred institutions of his society.

One further aspect of the criterion of conservatism we are here examining is a confirmed attitude towards the selective nature of leadership. To some extent Gandhi could agree with Ruskin and Carlyle that a rule of the wisest is the best rule. But, for Gandhi, wisdom did not necessarily inhere in those of superior birth. Nor did it bear any necessary relationship to the level of formal education. Criteria for leaders lay less in birth or station than in personal qualities. "Courage, endurance, fearlessness and above all self-sacrifice are the qualities required of our leaders," Gandhi wrote. "A person belonging to the suppressed classes exhibiting these qualities in their fulness would certainly be able to lead the nation; whereas the most finished orator, if he has not these qualities, must fail."[67] Nor did Gandhi share the conservative's distrust of the masses. Gandhi's faith in the people was, as he said, "boundless." "Let not the leaders distrust them," he urged, for "theirs is an amazingly responsive nature."[68] Gandhi believed that the people often know what they want, but "do not know how to express their wants, and less often how to get what they want." Herein, he argued, lay the need for and the purpose of leadership. "The masses are by no means so foolish, or unintelligent as we sometimes imagine," and, Gandhi added, "disastrous results can easily follow a bad, hasty, or what is worse, selfish lead."[69] He further believed that leadership comes only through service, and for himself he places service at the forefront of all his efforts, claiming leadership to be a less important by-product. Finally, his attitude towards the common man and towards leadership is reflected in the role assigned to public opinion. For Gandhi, "every ruler is alien that defies" public opinion, for a government is dependent upon it.[70]

In summary, Gandhi insisted that the individual look first to duty and not concern himself with rights. Nevertheless, it is clear that Gandhi believed the individual to have many claims upon the state in terms of rights. As we have seen, he believed that the state should exist to fulfill the needs of its members, that "the supreme consideration is man,"[71] and that when the state ceases to perform services for its members which will fulfill their needs, then the individual has the duty to disobey and to resist. This duty has the force of prerogative. The Gandhian philosophy of conflict makes duty imperative, but the technique of satyagraha assures the acquisition of right. The Gandhian conservatism—if, indeed, the description can be used at all—would lead directly out of and beyond the conservative effect into the newer liberalism, the results of which might look very much like the welfare state.

We are now somewhat closer to the answer to our question, was Gandhi a conservative? Had he not undertaken his "experiments with truth" the answer might have been "yes." Early in his life Gandhi discarded the belief in the relative impotence of individual will and reason to deflect the course of historical change. Once he had abandoned this criterion of conservatism, his experiments began. From those experiments emerged a philosophy and a technique which were to transform the conservative and to fashion a radical in the truest sense of striking at the root.

Anarchist Elements in Gandhian Thought

In one of the few analytical works on Gandhian political thought,[72] G. N. Dhawan asserts that Gandhi was a philosophical anarchist. He reminds us that Gandhi strove for "the greatest good of all" and held that this end could be realized "only in the classless and Stateless democracy of autonomous village communities based on non-violence instead of coercion, on service instead of exploitation, on renunciation instead of acquisitiveness and on the largest measure of local and individual initiative instead of centralization."[73] Dhawan suggests further that where Gandhi did condone a degree of state organization he did so because he believed that an anarchical society was ideal but unattainable. He therefore sought to mitigate the oppressive nature of the state organization and to reduce government to the barest minimum. Dhawan shows the anarchist trend in Gandhi's position, but he overlooks the key to "Gandhian anarchism" and fails to formulate the significance of the Gandhian modifications at work upon a familiar political approach. I shall try to show that the Gandhian approach points the way towards reconciling political organization with the ideals of anarchism. The maximum cooperation of individuals operating through an organization based not upon the violent force of the state, but upon a non-violent sanction supplied by satyagraha, allows for the realization of the fundamental objectives of anarchism. Dhawan errs first in not recognizing the relative unimportance of end-structure in the Gandhian approach to the state, and again when he suggests that Gandhi's democracy would be ". . . based on non-violence instead of coercion . . ." For in the Gandhian ideal an element of coercion is, in fact, retained. The distinguishing character of that coercion is its non-violence.*

In Western political thought there have been some seven distinct schools of anarchism, ranging from the irrational, intuitionist egoism of Max Stirner to the empirical, rational, evolutionary communism of Pietr Kropotkin. I shall try here only to suggest the elements essential to all these schools, and to cite comparisons and contrasts between Gandhi and certain Western anarchist theorists where that may serve to place or elucidate the Gandhian position.

Anarchists firmly hold the undesirability of a state organization. They urge the necessary superiority of voluntary association or mutualist agreement. They differ from those political philosophers who hope that freedom will be won *after* the establishment of certain economic principles or programs, by insisting that freedom is a fundamental condition upon which all else must follow. They urge freedom from politics, rather than political freedom. Beyond these essential characteristics there is considerable variation among the several anarchist schools of thought. We shall see how Gandhian thought stands in opposition to that of Bakunin, who considered direct violent action necessary to abolish the state. We shall note the extent of agreement with the Christian anarchists as exemplified by Tolstoy, and the dissimilarity between Gandhian associationist thought and the Proudhonian theory of "mutualité."

---

* For a discussion of physical and psychological violence and the element of coercion in satyagraha, see above, Chapter I, pp. 9-11.

Finally, we shall discover the essential contribution which Gandhi has made, how it solves the anarchist dilemma and points to success where anarchist programs have failed.

In a conversation reported by Mahadev Desai,[74] Gandhi asserted that "a society organized and run on the basis of complete non-violence would be the purest anarchy." When asked if he considered this a realizable ideal, he replied:

> "Yes. It is realisable to the extent non-violence is realisable. That State is perfect and non-violent where the people are governed the least. The nearest approach to purest anarchy would be a democracy based on non-violence. The European democracies are to my mind a negation of democracy."

Now it is clear that by a "democracy based on non-violence" Gandhi referred to a social and political structure developed through voluntary association. "Society based on non-violence," he said, "can only consist of groups settled in villages in which voluntary cooperation is the condition of dignified and peaceful existence."[75] We shall see later, in a discussion of decentralization, some of the characteristics of a federation based upon Gandhian principles.

Gandhi agreed with the anarchist emphasis upon the individual. As we have already seen, Gandhi held that "no society can possibly be built on a denial of individual freedom."[76] In an interview with N. K. Bose, he made explicit his fear of the state and the danger to the individual of an increase in state power:

> Q. Then, Sir, shall we take it that the fundamental difference between you and the socialists is that you believe that men live more by self-direction or will than by habit, and they believe that men live more by habit than by will, that being the reason why you strive for self-correction, while they try to build up a system under which men will find it impossible to exercise their desire of exploiting others?

A. While admitting that man actually lives by habit, I hold it is better for him to live by exercise of the will. I also believe that men are capable of developing their will to an extent that will reduce exploitation to a minimum. I look upon an increase in the power of the State with the greatest fear, because, although while apparently doing good by minimizing exploitation, it does the greatest harm to mankind by destroying individuality, which lies at the root of all progress.[77]

It is in Gandhi's approach to the individual vis-à-vis society and his especial interpretation of individualism that we find a distinct difference between Gandhi and that school of anarchism which follows Proudhon in his concept of "mutualité." For Gandhi, individuality is necessarily accompanied in any non-violent organization by service to the group. We recall Gandhi's assertion, "I value individual freedom, but you must not forget that man is essentially a social being," and his reminder that man "has risen to the present status by learning to adjust his individualism to the requirements of social progress."[78]

Service to the group without demand for return, without suggestion of a necessary reciprocity, is central in the Gandhian approach. It is a position directly opposed to Proudhon's doctrine of mutualité. Proudhon defined his concept of mutuality "rather in an exchange of good services and products than in a grouping together of forces and in a community of labours."[79] The concept is further described as a "reciprocity of services," based upon a "reciprocity of respect" which "carries into the real order of economics the principle governing personal relations among individuals themselves . . ." Mutuality, then, is a different thing from association, and it is clearly different from Gandhi's conception of a society organized on the basis of a functioning non-violent sanction. Instead of transforming the social order into a community, Proudhon would have society become a "vast network of organized exchanges."[80]

> ... service for service, produce for produce, loan for loan, assurance for assurance, credit for credit, security for security, guarantee for guarantee, etc. It is the ancient talion, an *eye for an eye, a tooth for a tooth, a life for a life*, in a way reversed, transferred from the criminal law and the atrocious practices of the *vendetta* to the economic law, to the works of labour and the good offices of the fraternity.[81]

For Proudhon, individual rights were everything. The one norm which Proudhon set above all else and, indeed, the only norm he recognized, was *pacta sunt servanda*—agreements are binding. In a societal network of individual agreements Proudhon found the solution to the problem of unity. Everywhere else he saw only "the materialism of the group, the hypocrisy of association, the weighted fetters of the State." It was only through his pattern of individual agreements that Proudhon could hope to find "the real brotherhood."[82]

Proudhon recognized, as did Gandhi, the "social bond" as the underlying principle of the "political" order. But Proudhon's emphasis on the "social bond" as uniting "reasonable and free creatures" held the ideal to be that of freedom from all constraint. This suggests that Proudhon might have disagreed with Gandhi's principle of satyagraha. For in satyagraha there is a force capable of operating to effect constraint. It is at just this point that Gandhian thought is most fundamentally non-anarchist. (This is not to say that it is anti-anarchist.) And it is in the coercive possibilities of the technique of satyagraha that Gandhian doctrine stands where anarchism falls under the attack of those critics who demand assurance that anarchism is not simply an idealization of chaos. For the "no authority" concept which is central to the theory of anarchism issues ideally in complete freedom of individual action against which there is to be no restraining force.

The anarchist usually professes an abiding faith in the essential goodness or reasonableness of man in supporting his belief that societal life can proceed without external sanction. For Kropotkin, the element which assured order resulting from freedom was a sense of reasonable "social solidarity"—a formulation of the basic nature of man through which the principle of mutual aid necessarily operated. And for Proudhon, "freedom was the mother, not the daughter of order." Once more, we find that Gandhi could agree with this essential of anarchism *if* we add to it the technique of satyagraha to utilize man's good and reasonable nature.

Now if anarchists oppose constraint because constraint by necessity implies violence, then we may suggest that they could, without contradiction, accept the Gandhian introduction of a coercion characterized by non-violence. (There is no evidence that they have, hitherto, considered constraint to be possible without violence.) It is significant that one of the most serious failings of anarchists lies in their repeated resort to violence in attempting the annihilation of the system which they hold to be the root of societal evil. Their argument against authority usually centers upon and always entails opposition to violence itself and the resulting destructiveness, for the individual, of the state and of government based upon violence. But anarchists have no positive alternative. It was a weakness perceived by two outstanding anarchists in America, Emma Goldman and Alexander Berkman, who, after persistent efforts to propagate the abolition of government through violence, recognized that the method had failed. Even those anarchists who opposed violence as a method had only a negative solution of withdrawal from the existing state organization, and their efforts to establish anarchist communities suffered from the failure to develop a method of active resistance. Anarchists may claim a positive philosophy, but they, like other political theorists, have rarely sought a positive *technique* whereby a system could be realized.

We have to go back to William Godwin, whose work *An Enquiry Concerning Political Justice* is considered the first systematic exposition of anarchism, to find a suggestion which appears familiar to the Gandhian approach of non-violent action. Godwin's insistence upon the priority of individual "private judgment" and his reliance upon reason as the dynamic operating force in society is remarkably Gandhian. We have seen the significant place reason holds in Gandhian thought. With the anarchism of Godwin we again find this emphasis. It is suggested in Godwin's formulation of "private judgment"; it is again suggested in his insistence upon the propagation of truth through discussion. "The only substantial method for the propagation of truth," he reasoned, "is discussion, so that the errors of one man may be detected by the acuteness and severe disquisition of his neighbours."[83] Having rejected force as "scarcely under any circumstances to be employed," he went on to ask "of what nature is that resistance which ought constantly to be given to every instance of injustice?" Godwin's answer followed: "The resistance I am bound to employ is that of uttering the truth, of censuring in the most explicit manner every proceeding that I perceive to be adverse to the true interests of mankind."[84]

In his *Political Justice*, Godwin emphasizes the necessity for gradual and non-violent elimination of political institutions. That the process should be gradual and non-violent is an aspect of Godwin usually neglected in commentaries on his political thought.[85] Indeed, non-violent and gradual procedure is popularly considered to be antithetical to anarchist doctrine. This follows from the tendency to regard Bakunin and the anarchist development subsequent to the split in the Second International as representative of essential anarchism. However, there are other branches of anarchist thought, for anarchism is a philosophy which has in many ages and in many places attracted philosophers of politics.

Among the Christian anarchists, Tolstoy is perhaps the most notable. In addition to his emphasis upon non-violent, non-resistant efforts to negate the state, Tolstoy assigned to reason a primary role. Man cannot deny reason by the use of reason, Tolstoy held, for reason which "illuminates our life and impels us to modify our actions, is not an illusion, and its authority can never be denied." Tolstoy took as "the substance of the teachings of all the masters of humanity" the injunction "to obey reason in the pursuit of good."[86]

In Gandhian thought, as in all anarchist thought, there is an effort to dispense with government. For Godwin, as for Tolstoy, as for Gandhi, the problem became one of how and to what extent government can be eliminated. We have seen how each put forward reason as a determining element in societal organization. Gandhi could agree wholeheartedly with Godwin's assertions regarding political authority: that all men have the faculty of reason, that no man is to preside over the rest, that government is for the security of individuals, so that each man should have a share in providing for his own security, and that exercise of private judgment and public deliberation are essential.[87] He would also agree that "Private judgment and public deliberation are not themselves the standard of moral right and wrong; they are only the means of discovering right and wrong. . . ."[88] The contribution of Gandhi lies in his transformation of just such principles as these into the dynamic technique of action, satyagraha.

There are many other points of similarity between Gandhian thought and Godwin's *Political Justice*. Priestley's statement that "Godwin's economic thought, like his politics, is a branch of moral philosophy," and, further, that "he is not concerned with economic problems as such, but with the correlated problems of morals and politics,"[89] applies equally well to Gandhi. It may, of course, be added that Gandhi was much more directly concerned with the practical aspects of the economic well-being of his fellow-man than was Godwin. There are many further points of similarity between Gandhian thought and Godwin's *Political Justice*. I have been concerned here only with those elements which are germane to anarchism.

Gandhi's emphasis was consistently upon individual effort, local reform, and village-centered activity. He worked towards a societal organization based upon decentralized village industries and self-sufficient rural communities. Swaraj (self-rule) implied something beyond independence for India—it carried the meaning of an all-embracing self-sufficiency down to the village level. Self-sufficiency translated into a concrete program of action in the Indian circumstance led to the swadeshi (home production) movement, and the central effort during the years of the nationalist struggle for swaraj lay in the propagation of khadi (hand-spun cloth). Swadeshi not only served an economic function in the actual supply of cloth, it also carried significant ideological implications.

Where orthodox anarchists most seriously failed—in supplying a positive alternative program of social organization—Gandhi again met with a measure of success. The constructive program was an essential component of the Gandhian revolutionary struggle for Indian independence. It was the constructive program which gave content to the satyagraha framework and applied Gandhian principles to the Indian circumstance. This program, designed for conditions peculiar to the time and place, was subject to revision and adapted to changing conditions. In general, the program included the following points:[90]

1. Communal unity
2. Removal of untouchability
3. Prohibition
4. Khadi
5. Other village industries
6. Village sanitation
7. New or basic education
8. Adult education

9. Uplift of women
10. Education in health and hygiene
11. Propagation of Rastra Bhasha (national language)
12. Promotion of economic equality

Among these items, the production of khadi—the over-all khaddar program of hand-spinning and hand-weaving—was central. If Proudhon's exchange bank would, in theory, "absorb" the state, dissolving the government in the economic organism,[91] khadi and the voluntary organization which grew up around it was used by Gandhi for much the same purpose. The khaddar program pointed the solution to the Indian social and political problem. In hand-spinning Gandhi saw at once not only the economic salvation of India, but also an answer to the psychological and political problems of the nationalist movement. The Khadi Bhandar organizations which flourished in India were reminiscent of Proudhon's Exchange Bank. To these Khadi centers anyone could take thread spun by hand and directly exchange it for woven saris or dhotis or piece goods which, in turn, had been produced by hand-weavers from the hand-spun yarn so collected. In an illuminating exchange of letters between Gandhi and S. Saklatvala,* Gandhi replied to a Communist criticism of his khaddar program by emphasizing its capacity to organize the country.

Khaddar has the greatest organising power in it because it has itself to be organised and because it affects all India. If khaddar rained from heaven it would be a calamity. But as it can only be manufactured by the willing co-operation of starving millions and thousands of middle class men and women, its success means the best organisation conceivable along peaceful lines. If cooking had to be revived and required the same organisation, I should claim for it the same merit that I claim for Khaddar.[92]

* Shapurji Dorabji Saklatvala, a Parsi from Bombay, was a Communist member of Parliament elected from a London constituency.

For Gandhi, non-violence and centralized industry were incompatible. Mass production degrades the worker, he argued, and results in an implicitly violent power-construct. Small-scale village industry, on the other hand, allows little opportunity for fraud and speculation.[93] In the national khaddar program, he explained, ". . . millions of people can take their share in this work and progress can be arithmetically measured."[94] Gandhi also insisted that decentralization of industry "preserves the purity and compactness of domestic life, artistry and creative talent as well as the people's sense of freedom, ownership and dignity."[95] Such points as these favoring decentralization are clearly in agreement with anarchist doctrine.

S. N. Agarwal, whose *Gandhian Plan for Economic Development of India* may be taken as the orthodox Gandhian position, likens the Gandhian plan's stress upon small local units to that of Syndicalism, Guild Socialism, and Anarchism.[96] As has often been observed, the followers of Proudhon and Kropotkin were attracted by that type of small community organization represented in the old Russian mir. The Indian village with a functioning panchayat is similar to the early Russian system. The system designed by Agarwal took the panchayat as its basic unit and altered this traditional institution in the Gandhian manner which has already briefly been noted in the discussion of conservative approaches. The suggested organizational structure clearly indicates wherein the Gandhian plan differs from true anarchism. In many respects, it more nearly approximates the Guild Socialist program, though we do not find in the Gandhian plan the essential principle of functional representation. The panchayat of the Gandhian system was viewed as representing a self-sufficient village community—self-sufficient at least in the basic necessities of life. Economic reconstruction would be "from the bottom upwards" and the village unit would constitute the "foundation of our Planning."[97] The panchayat would be autonomous in internal village administration. The departure from the anarchist tradition is marked in the hierarchical pattern to be established through linking the village panchayat with the taluka, district, division, province, and nation "for purposes of common policy and interests" and by a system of indirect elections except at the village level. The necessity for government—and for an administrative hierarchy, albeit characterized by evolutionary rather than devolutionary power channels—is recognized in this Gandhian approach.

As do anarchists, Gandhi opposed the absolute sovereignty of the state. However, he could not accept the over-all philosophical anarchist position. Dhawan, in his frequent assertions that Gandhi was a philosophical anarchist, finally concludes that he would "decide every case on its own merits," and, despite his distrust of the state, would "welcome" state action where it is "likely to advance the welfare of the people."[98] It is indeed clear that Gandhi held essential ideals in common with anarchists but that he was willing, as they are not, to accept a degree of state organization and control. He believed that government to be best which governs least, and yet he held that "there are certain things which cannot be done without political power," even though there are "numerous other things which do not at all depend upon political power." A nation is truly democratic, he said, when it "runs its affairs smoothly and effectively without much State interference."[99]

Dhawan suggests that Gandhi has retained the state as a second best society, a middle way. It would, of course, be incorrect to suppose that Gandhi thought of retaining the state as some intermediate step in a determined progress towards anarchical society, in the manner of Marxist thought. Satyagraha eliminates the ultimate danger which the anarchist fears from the state. The satyagrahi need not wait until the state is abolished before he acts upon his principles of voluntary association and opposition to authority. A given political system may immediately be attacked by non-violent direct action. Moreover, such action is not merely in the nature of attack. For at the same time that resistance against the state is launched, satyagrahis may undertake to establish a parallel system based upon the principles of non-violence. There is never the need for the satyagrahi to wait until all opposition has been liquidated. He proceeds by methods of direct resistance to that portion of state authority which he holds to be unjust. The constructive work not only accompanies and follows direct action to eliminate state authority, but it precedes it as well. Gandhi described this process as "one of automatic adjustment." "If the Government schools are emptied," he said, "I would certainly expect national schools to come into being. If the lawyers as a whole suspended practice, they would devise arbitration courts and the nation will have expeditious and cheaper methods of settling private disputes. . . ."[100] In the course of satyagraha during the Indian independence struggle, parallel public service organizations were actually set up in districts where non-cooperation had paralyzed the government. This was one of the most vital functions of Congress organizations entrusted with the various aspects of the constructive program.

The anarchist fear of political means was minimized for Gandhi who evolved the technique of satyagraha whereby control could be exercised and constructive results assured. Anarchist criticism of Gandhi still centers upon his use of political means. Undoubtedly Gandhi did, explicitly and intentionally, use such means. "To me political power is not an end," he said, "but one of the means of enabling people to better their condition in every department of life."[101] And one of the steps in a satyagraha movement which dealt with grievances against an established government included attempts at political negotiation. It was only when such negotiation entirely failed that Gandhi found it necessary to reject constitutional political means and to depend solely upon the direct action of civil disobedience and other satyagraha direct action methods.

Recent anarchist criticism of Gandhi's political methods reflects a disappointment that he "retained faith in the State as an instrument of justice." It is the political element, argued Robert Ludlow, writing in *The Catholic Worker*, that "will destroy Gandhi's teachings in India," for "he did not realize that Satyagraha must be united with an anti-State philosophy . . ." Ludlow continued with an identification of political methods with violent methods:

> . . . political methods are bound to fail because they carry with them the elements of himsa (hate) and that in personal action alone and action by the people themselves will society be transformed. He understood well these things—it is only that he did not realize that political and personalist action must inevitably clash.[102]

Contemporary critics appear almost unwilling to understand the implications of the Gandhian method. In anarchist criticism, of which the above is one of the more sympathetic, there is an honest failure to recognize the potential of satyagraha. Political methods, as we find them conventionally practised, are, indeed, based upon *himsa* (which means more precisely injury or violence, and includes hate). It is just in this understanding that satyagraha makes its unique contribution. For politics *based on* satyagraha does *not* carry with it elements of *himsa*, but of *ahimsa*. It still remains politics and may involve a government, state structure. Instead of violent sanctions, non-violent sanctions operate. Such a system is immensely difficult of conception for those of us who are steeped in the processes of modern politics and who understand law as a violently coercive order. But it is just this which anarchists should be brought to understand—for it is the solution to the problem of method which anarchism has consistently failed to solve.

Occasionally anarchist thinkers have attempted to formulate a technique of resistance other than the destructive methods made popular by terrorist tactics. Benjamin Tucker in America recommended, as did Thoreau, a passive resistance to modern governments. He, and, of course, Tolstoy and other Christian Anarchists, enjoined refusal to pay taxes and the withholding of all other cooperation with governmental functions. With Tolstoy non-violence meant a quite different thing from Gandhian satyagraha. It meant avoidance of all force in any form. It was in no case a technique for mass positive constructive action. Godwin, as we have seen, held that discussion must be employed to arrive at truths, but Godwin was structuring ideal processes and had no intention of developing a method of direct action.

The anarchists following Bakunin were well aware of the force inherent in any non-cooperation of labor. Syndicalists operated with the objective (real or ideal) of the general strike. Even Max Stirner, whose extreme individualist anarchism allowed him little concern for social techniques, held that "the laborers have the most enormous power in their hands, and, if they once became thoroughly conscious of it and used it, nothing would withstand them."[103] And Godwin had stated a basic element of civil disobedience when he reasoned that "if government be founded in the consent of the people, it can have no power over any individual by whom that consent is refused."[104]

Anarchists were, then, essentially aware of the strength of a people, or a section of a people (notably labor), to resist government authority. But even in those cases where anarchists attempted something more than a negative resistance policy (as they did in anarchist settlements, especially those founded in Canada and the United States), the weakness of the effort lay in the failure to develop a technique of resistance or to delineate a method. Gandhian satyagraha meets this problem, and the non-cooperation of satyagraha has the necessary concomitant of cooperation among the resisters themselves. Cooperation functions not only in organizing the resisters for establishing a parallel social structure, but also in the program of persuasion and conversion of the system against which the group is resisting.

The Christian Anarchist Ludlow[105] tells us that if we were to subtract the socialist elements from Gandhi's thought we would have left "an ideology and plan of action that would be truly anarchist and would thus reject the State as a form of government." It is true, as we have seen, that there are essential socialist elements in Gandhian thought, and that Gandhi was not prepared to abandon political means or the state as an organizing factor. Nevertheless, with satyagraha as the functioning socio-political technique of action, anarchism could conceivably result. We may also challenge the anarchist to show us how he intends to realize anarchy: what, indeed, is the "plan of action" of anarchists?

Among the weaknesses of anarchist thought has been the persisting inability to show how the present state could be eliminated without violence. Anarchists have not denied that violence tends to militate against the very possibility of annihilating the present authority without substituting another authority equally objectionable. They, further, have not faced the problem of tactics—even violent tactics—insofar as they appear to expect a revolution to succeed without discipline and authority. It was such a faith which most notably marked the failure of Bakunin's practical efforts. There is no assurance that at the critical moment each individual will come forward to fulfill his function spontaneously and without disciplined direction. Yet, to be consistently anarchist means to refuse a coercive organization implied in disciplined effort.

Whenever we find attempts at application of anarchist theory we find that the failure has been one of method. Conflict, for the anarchist, was not only apparent but was essential. The anarchist has no constructive technique whereby he can struggle towards anarchist goals. Destruction is not enough, for the use of violence would necessarily subvert anarchist ends. In contrast to the Gandhian approach, the anarchist has not recognized the necessity for centering his prior consideration upon the development of constructive techniques.

Conclusion

Gandhi's "experiments with truth" led him to sample many political approaches. We have examined Gandhian political thought by measuring it against two trends in Western political theory—conservatism and anarchism. Was Gandhi, then, either the conservative or the anarchist that he has been labelled? We have seen that at the heart of his "experiments" lay an insistence that individual will and reason can effect social and political change. The touchstone which resolves what otherwise might seem to be basically contradictory positions is the technique of non-violent action. The political label did not matter—Gandhi accepted them all and insisted only that those who wished him to lead them into conflict should accept his weapons. Once satyagraha is introduced into a system by satyagrahis who maintain their self-imposed and exacting requirements, the system becomes metamorphosed.

Gandhi would have had no patience with attempts to classify him as conservative, liberal, socialist or anarchist. He was all these and none of them for he never lost his profoundly revolutionary character. If the technique of satyagraha is resolutely pitted against injustice, then conservatism, liberalism, socialism, or anarchism might serve as matrix from which human indignation, guided by reason, might carve out an ever-approaching nearness to the ideal.

VI

THE GANDHIAN DIALECTIC
AND POLITICAL THEORY

GANDHI did not proceed from any specific political ideology, and yet the significance, for political theory, of his action on the practical field of politics, is inestimable. The contribution has been not alone to the development of a social and political method. It extends further into the realm of political thought and challenges the substantial presuppositions of the mainstream of political theory.

Political thought has heretofore made requisite these two irreducible essentials: reflection upon the ends of political action, and the means of achieving them. It is to this basic dichotomy that the ultimate failure of historical schools of political theory may well be traced. Traditional political thought, assuming a separation of ends and means, has proceeded to eclipse means consideration by emphasizing concern for ends. Where political theory has evidenced an awareness of the unity of ends and means, the problem has tended to be stated in terms of machinery or of form and device. The challenge of Gandhian satyagraha centers upon the necessity of reconciling ends and means through a philosophy of action.

The foregoing chapters have analyzed precepts basic to the Gandhian technique and have dealt with historical instances of satyagraha in action. It is suggested that the success of the technique depends to no inconsiderable extent upon the manner in which the essential elements are applied and manipulated during the course of a given satyagraha action. An integral part of Gandhian satyagraha is necessarily a philosophy of conflict. There have been few efforts to systematize that philosophy, though it lies implicit in Gandhi's experiments. The formulation which follows is an attempt to introduce a theoretical framework which serves further as a point of departure for the concluding critical comments on the failure of traditional political theory.

A Theoretical Statement of Satyagraha

Satyagraha refers, not to an end-product, but to a means for achieving agreement. It is dynamic, not static. It allows for the fullest realization that means are ends-in-the-making, or ends in process.[1] Analysis of satyagraha suggests that its essence may be cogently described in terms of dialectic.

What I shall now call Gandhian dialectic does not refer to any phenomenal or noumenal system; it does not describe a metaphysical order. The Gandhian dialectic, which lies at the heart of satyagraha, is a process to be made explicit by human action, not to be found as implicit either in the nature of things or the progress of time. It partakes of prescription, rather than description. These distinctions are essential if one is to understand "dialectic" as applied to the action technique of Gandhi. The contrast between the Gandhian dialectic and that of Marx or his forerunner, Hegel, is striking. Each deals with a different level of abstraction and by comparing them the dynamic quality of satyagraha may be illuminated.

Sidney Hook, in discussing criteria of dialectical thinking, remarks:

> Only when that whole or unit or continuity which has been destroyed by the presence of conflicting factors has been restored or re-established in another whole . . . can we claim validity for our procedure.[2]

And he proceeds to define the heart of the Marxian dialectic thus:

> For Marx any material which is the subject of man's activity generates its own normative ideals in relation to the way it succeeds in fulfilling human needs. From the

reciprocal influence and interaction between the ideal and the actual a new subject matter is produced out of which in turn are born the means by which it will be changed.[3]

Marx was critical of the Hegelian dialectical method because it did not allow for empirical approach. He believed that he had resolved the problem by interpreting the dialectic in such a way as to allow the dialectical process to control both the thought and the action. Marx retains the dialectic as a system of logic and applies it to human activity solely as an interpretation. The interaction is expressed in terms of social environment on the one hand, and human needs on the other. For Marx, the class struggle results.

Whether or not Gandhi would have accepted the Hegelian dialectic or the Marxist critical adoption and interpretation of the dialectic, is not our present concern. There is much in Hegelian dialectical idealism which Gandhi might well have accepted, had he been given to formulations and interpretations of systematized philosophy. He could, no doubt, have accepted the criterion for a dialectical approach as stated above, recognizing its applicability to his method of satyagraha. He could also have accepted the Marxian assertion of dialectic as a social relation. But Gandhi could not have travelled far with either Hegel or Marx.

Gandhi could agree with Marx that the dialectical concept must have a social orientation, must relate to human action. He could accept the convenient structure of thesis and antithesis as expressing elements in the continuing process of growth through conflict and, again, the idea of synthesis as the welcomed result. But, inherent in the Gandhian approach, is a rejection of the Marxian (as well as the Hegelian) development of dialectic in the direction of predetermining the content of both thesis and antithesis—a development which, in Marx, defines class struggle and anticipates a synthesis in the realization of a classless society where, of course, the dialectical process must, for Marx, end.

The dialectical materialism of Marx bends the dialectic in a direction which, at first glance, might appear to gratify the Gandhite. The dialectic is projected beyond the realm of logic into the field of social and political action. The Marxist dialectic as a process involving social action is relieved of the Hegelian philosophical system which obscured it as a method. But, again, with Marx the dynamic quality of the dialectic is only partially retained, for the content of the process is supplied through the dogma of the class struggle. It is here—at the point where Marx introduced content—that Gandhian satyagraha strikingly departs. The method loses its true dynamic, creative quality when it becomes entangled with historicism.[4] The dialectic as a method relating directly to conflict is shorn of its dynamic character when the substance of conflict is specified. With Marx conflict is inevitably *class* conflict, and the direction in which such conflict can move is irrevocably determined.

We may say, then, that Hegelian dialectic is a system of logic describing inherent, natural processes; Marxian dialectic is a method embracing not only man's original nature, but his class relationships, an historical method by which both the direction and the structure of conflict are predetermined. Gandhian dialectic, as distinct from Hegelian logic on the one hand and the Marxist adaptation on the other, describes a process resulting from the application of a technique of action to any situation of human conflict—a process essentially creative and inherently constructive.

HOW THE GANDHIAN DIALECTIC OPERATES

The dialectic implicit in the Gandhian method of satyagraha is not dependent upon Gandhi's metaphysical assumptions, nor upon his Hindu-based theology. It could operate in non-Hindu societies, as it did among the Muslim Pathans of the Northwest Frontier Province. Despite the tremendous faith Gandhi had in divine power, the technique of satyagraha is based upon the admission of relative truths and the rejection of absolutes which are not knowable for mortal man. God was, in Gandhi's definition, even the atheism of the atheist. There was no insistence upon an objective absolute. Absolute truth cannot be known absolutely to mortal man. Yet, satyagraha means clinging to the truth. The problem was practical, for Gandhi—as it was for Marx. For both, criteria of truth lay in the meeting of human needs. But whereas Marx accepted a philosophy of history which defined the content of those needs and indicated their satisfaction, Gandhi perceived the necessity for developing an approach, a tool, a form whereby the content (substantial human needs) could be met and the truth (relative truth in terms of substantial human needs) of any situation could emerge. Gandhi could reject the Hegelian concept of reality and reason to agree with Feuerbach that "man is the measure of reason." For, despite the ever-present overtones of religion in Gandhian thought, concern for human needs lies at the core of Gandhian teaching.

Perhaps the most persistent element in Gandhi is the recurring theme that non-violence is truth-creating. Here again, we find an expression not of absolutes and substance, but of relatives and process. By non-violence Gandhi means, as we have seen, the technique of conducting social relations characterized by constructive, peaceful attitudes, and infused with the determination to enlarge areas of agreement and to achieve resolution of conflict by persuasion.

Means and ends in Gandhian satyagraha are distinguishable only temporally. Both means and ends partake of a continuous process. The means precede the end in time, but there can be no question of moral priority. Truth is inseparable from non-violence, and the method of achieving and clinging to the truth is non-violence. Non-violence becomes both the means and the end, and the terms become convertible. Non-violence is the heart of a technique. The Gandhian philosophy of conflict accepts the Hegelian position that "every relation may be viewed from two opposite aspects, i.e. from the point of view of the two terms it relates. Each term regards the relation as internal to itself and the other term as external to itself. An antinomy results which can be solved only by reinterpreting the situation and by looking at both terms and their relation from the point of view of a wider relation . . . But one antinomy is solved in order to make way for another. Opposition breaks out between the terms on a higher level."[5] Hegel, however, made his interpretation and left the rest to the inexorable march of history and, in the last analysis, to formulation by historicists. The Gandhian philosophy, accepting the dynamics of the dialectical situation, and taking man as the measure of reason, centers upon a technique whereby one or both sides in a conflict can resolve the antinomy into a reinterpretation (which, in turn, gives rise to another antinomy). The technique, for Gandhi, necessarily involved an active exercise of non-violence.

Again, Gandhi could agree with Marx that through action alone can beliefs be tested. Gandhi went further to supply the empirical control which Marx sacrificed to historicism. Where Marx introduced subject and content, where he predetermined the structure and direction of conflict, the Gandhian philosophy insists that the process and technique must suffice. A technique such as satyagraha could only lead to solutions yet unknown.

The inference in all that has been said above is that Gandhian satyagraha assumes the rationality of man. This is not to say that satyagraha denies large areas of non-rationality in human motivation and behavior. It requires simply the assumption that man is endowed with reason, that man can utilize reason to direct his actions, and that a technique for conducting conflict can appeal to the rational in man.

The first step for any satyagrahi is an analysis and a reflection upon the character of the total conflict circumstance. He must clarify his understanding of his own position and his own immediate objective and consider these carefully in the light of the total situation.[6] Whatever the subject of a specific conflict, understanding of the nature of conflict in general and of the objective to be attained in the given conflict situation is prerequisite. The force within any dialectical situation is derived from the clash of opposing elements within that situation. In every case of satyagraha the conflict is to be understood in dialectical terms. The immediate objective is a restructuring of the opposing elements to achieve a situation which is satisfactory to both the original opposing antagonists but in such a way as to present an entirely new total circumstance. This is, in Hegelian terms, an aiming at synthesis out of the conflict of thesis and antithesis. The claim for satyagraha is that through the operation of non-violent action the truth as judged by the fulfillment of human needs will emerge in the form of a mutually satisfactory and agreed-upon solution.*

* Samuel Beer, in his provocative work, *The City of Reason* (Cambridge: Harvard University Press, 1949), has developed "the philosophical ideas which support the theory of a free society." These ideas, based upon A. N. Whitehead's metaphysics of creative advance, suggest the direction in which an extensive philosophy embodying the Gandhian dialectic might well be developed. Beer's thesis is that "man is inwardly free and, therefore, ought to be free outwardly. Man is inwardly free by virtue of his reason. Hence, the liberal ideal is a society which protects and promotes the exercise of that capacity: The City of Reason." [p. vii]. Beer draws upon Dewey's analysis of purposive action to state the technics of problem-solving and to suggest a process which is truly "stability in change." Compare the Gandhian dialectic on the field of action with the following treatment Beer makes of the process of inquiry and solution of problems: "An enquiring mind comes to a problem with certain purposes, but in its contact with fact those purposes are modified and enriched. New traits in a situation may be perceived and that perception will modify the purposes which were brought to the situation. Thus creative solutions arise. In the continuum of inquiry, the inquirer's perspective is continually developed. The purposes and interests which he brings to inquiry guide him in his contacts with the facts. But what he learns about the facts in turn guides the development of his interests and purposes. If he is to learn, he must start from what he already knows. In that sense his approach to the facts is limited and biased and he is 'blind' to many aspects of the facts. But we must not forget that he can learn and that in the course of learning his initial purposes may be greatly enlarged and deepened." [p. 42].

The political theory which Beer derives from Whitehead's meta-

The satyagrahi must recognize that elementary to his technique is the first step of a full realization that his immediate goal is not the triumph of his substantial side in the struggle—but, rather, the synthesis of the two opposing claims. He does, then, all he can to persuade the opponent of the correctness of his own position, but, while he carries on his own persuasive activity, he allows the opponent every opportunity and, indeed, invites him to demonstrate the correctness of his (the opponent's) position and to dissuade him of his own position. He is at all times prepared to depart from his own position and to embrace the opponent's position should he be persuaded, by the opponent, of his error. This may, of course, be achieved totally or partially; the satyagrahi may be persuaded to abandon certain parts of his original position. He recognizes, and attempts to demonstrate to his opponent that he recognizes, the desirability of a resulting synthesis, and that he is not seeking a one-sided triumph. His effort is to allow for the emergence of the best restructuring of the situation. He seeks a victory, not over the opponent, but over the situation in the best (in the sense of the total human needs of the situation) synthesis possible. As I shall show below, this differs acutely from the notion of compromise.

SATYAGRAHA VERSUS COMPROMISE

It was Feuerbach's view[7] that "That is true in which another agrees with me—agreement is the first criterion of truth; but only because the species is the ultimate measure of truth."

---

physics is "based on reason and directed toward liberty." The ethics of politics outlined for his City of Reason, though it has content and meaning, yet "is not committed to the legal structure or economic system or customs of any particular age. The philosophy on which this ethics is based emphasizes the relativity of all institutions. . . . The gulf between the ideal and the actual is never bridged, although the duty of man is continually to try to bridge it." [p. 213]. That central area of Gandhian thought which I have called the Gandhian philosophy of conflict could be supported and informed by a "philosophy of liberalism" such as that presented by Beer in *The City of Reason.*

Agreement is an essential element in the objective of Gandhian satyagraha. In a conflict situation agreement is achieved through non-violent persuasive action, possibly involving aggressive non-violence. Agreement, in the Gandhian philosophy, is in the nature of adjustment and is of a quite different character from compromise in the usual sense of that word. Gandhian philosophy does not exclude compromise as a device for the accommodation of differing positions at a point where conflict has not become explicit and basic principles have not been challenged. But once conflict materializes the Gandhian technique proceeds in a manner qualitatively different from compromise. What results from the dialectical process of conflict of opposite positions as acted upon by satyagraha, is a synthesis, not a compromise. The satyagrahi is never prepared to yield any position which he holds to be the truth. He is, however, prepared—and this is essential—to be persuaded by his opponent that the opponent's position is the true, or the more nearly true, position. In the working out of the Gandhian dialectical approach, each side may, of course, yield through dissuasion any part of its position. But this is not compromise. When persuasion has been effected, what was once the opponent's position is now the position of both antagonist and protagonist. There is no sacrificing of position, no concession to the opponent with the idea of buying him over. Non-violent resistance must continue until persuasion has carried the conflict into mutually agreeable adjustment. Such adjustment will be a synthesis of the two positions and will be an adjustment satisfactory to both parties in the conflict. There is no victory in the sense of triumph of one side over the other. Yet, there is no compromise, in the sense in which each side would concede parts of its previous position solely to effect a settlement. There is no "lowering" of demands, but an aiming at a "higher" level of adjustment which creates a new, mutually satisfactory, resolution. (Compromise will be treated in more detail below, in the discussion of Liberal Democratic Theory.)

THE ELEMENT OF SACRIFICE

It may be pertinent here to comment again upon the element of sacrifice in Gandhian thought.* The non-violent technique requires the same preparation as does violent conflict for offering the highest sacrifice—life itself—as a possible outcome of using the technique. The satyagrahi will cling to his own position so long as he holds it to be true. He must not offer violence in opposition to his adversary. This may require endurance even to death. Marx, for one, bitterly opposed sacrifice in, we suppose, just this sense. Yet Marx clearly calls for sacrifice in circumstances of class struggle— a sacrifice of the individual life to the irrevocable march of history toward predetermined goals. Sacrifice enters as an element of both approaches.

HEGELIAN, MARXIAN, AND GANDHIAN DIALECTIC

Conflict ensues when customs and institutions due to one circumstance or another frustrate rather than fulfill basic impulses or desires. Such conflicts result in violence when no effective means exist for their peaceful (nonviolent) resolution. The development of such means needs not be left to the blind operation of impulsive forces. Reason, the logical testing of reality may play an important role in their discovery.[8]

It is by just such criteria that the Gandhian dialectic seeks to weigh, to judge, and to establish the framework for action. The *method* is that of testing reality; the *technique* of non-violent persuasion is that of holding to the "truth," yielding only when full conviction is carried by the opponent.

The historicism of both Hegel and Marx denied access to the heart of the problem of social and political conflict. Hegel discovered reason in things themselves, equated real with rational, and understood the progress of history in terms of

* See above, Chapter II.

the dialectic as a method of logic. Marx sought for an empirical approach. Yet, he allowed the dogma of the class struggle and the absolutism of his philosophy of history to strangle the development of the dialectic on the level where it could enter into a technique of action. In contrast, the dialectical approach which is central to the Gandhian philosophy provides dynamic control on the field of action through the fashioning of techniques for the creative resolution of conflict.

The Failure of Traditional Political Theory

In Chapter V, I argued the poverty of Anarchist philosophy in the realm of means consideration, and suggested the distinctive superiority of the Gandhian approach. In the paragraphs above I have, on the other hand, treated the same problem in Marxist thought—a political philosophy which does concern itself with the problem of means, but which obscures an adequate solution by centering upon a dialectic dependent upon a determinist philosophy of history. To further elucidate my proposition that political theory has failed to deal adequately with the question of means, I shall examine three other examples of Western political thought to ascertain how each proposes to achieve the political goals which it takes as desirable, and what each has to say about the ends-means relationship: Conservatism, Authoritarian Idealism, Liberal Democratic Theory.

A word may be said here by way of recognizing the limitations of this brief analysis. I attempt only to offer illustrative material and to point the direction in which the Gandhian development of satyagraha has posed its most serious challenge. I have, in the selection of these illustrations, attempted to include those theories which have most seriously contested for consideration in the area of the means-ends relationship: Anarchism (discussed in Chapter V) for its vehement denials, Marxism as the most vigorously prosecuted political philosophy in the current world ideological struggle, Conservatism for its genuine sensitivity to change and its concern for effecting peace through stability, Authoritarian Idealism for its extreme emphasis on ends, and finally Liberal Democracy for its valiant efforts to solve the ends-means problem through political engineering. I repeat that these analyses are intended to be no more than illustrative.

The selection has had to be further limited to specific theories within the broader schools of political thought. In this further selection, I have tried, in general, to settle upon those theories which fall within the mainstream of their respective schools. Where there is an occasional introduction of extreme theoretical statement, the purpose has been to illustrate the result of a prosecuted emphasis within a school. Such, for example, is the purpose of including a consideration of de Maistre's absolutist thought under Conservatism. It has also been necessary to introduce certain formal breakdowns in order to discuss with some degree of precision the objectives of given theories. In the analysis of Conservatism the imposition of a basic structure, such as was used in Chapter V for the analysis of Gandhian conservative elements, has seemed desirable. It is recognized that the subtleties and often the dynamics of political thought elude such a bald treatment. The most that an analysis of this type can hope to do is to bring into focus the more obvious characteristics of the theory under examination and to describe them with reference to the problem at hand. Here that problem concerns the treatment each theory affords the ends-means relationship.

CONSERVATISM AND THE PROBLEM OF MEANS

The edifice of Conservative theory is grounded solidly on a belief in the wisdom of historical experience and inherent social processes. It emphasizes respect for established institutions, especially religion and property, and takes as an essential virtue of the political relationship a loyalty that attaches a society's members to their especial stations in the life of that society. Conservatism holds that individual will and reason are relatively impotent to deflect society from its appointed course.[9] Order and stability are its highest values. Tradition and the power of custom are the elements which secure these values.

As in the political theory of Edmund Burke, an area of civil liberty may be recognized by the Conservative approach. Such liberty, however, is limited, and, ultimately, it is to be understood in terms of the proper ordering of society. The doctrines of Conservatism do "suppose indeed a certain portion of liberty to be essential to all good government; but they infer that this liberty is to be blended into the government; to harmonize with its forms and its rules; and to be made subordinate to its end."[10]

> . . . the liberty, the *only* liberty I mean, is a liberty connected with *order*, and that not only exists *with* order and virtue, but cannot exist at all *without* them.[11]

Conservative freedom is a passive value. It is the freedom of the member of society within the limits of the realm to which his station in life has assigned him. The end of civil society is "the establishment of liberty for the realization of moral duties."[12] "To be attached to the subdivision, to love the little platoon we belong to in society, is the first principle (the germ as it were) of publick affections."[13] Duties, moreover, are not voluntary, but assigned to each member of society by a Supreme Ruler. "The place of every man determines his duty."[14]

The tendentious effect of the Conservative position is to make the community, or society—and not the individual—the ultimate consideration. Above all, the culture of a nation must be preserved—conserved—and the meaning of continuity in the social process is in these terms. The locus of rationality is to be found, not in man himself, but in the course of history and the social process. De Maistre—that French Restoration philosopher whose absolutistic theory represents the last defense of classical Conservatism—lashes the Jacobin "gratuitous" conception of democracy—as though liberty were to be gained by a sudden, mortal effort, challenging the centuries of tradition. Burke's respect for the laws is typical of the attitude which poses what Godwin called "that most palpable of all impostures—collective wisdom."[15] And de Maistre defends the "bad" parts of any constitution for, if they are parts of a people's constitution they must necessarily be a reflection of that people's traditionally accumulated wisdom.

If, then, the ends which Conservative theory takes to be desirable are the stability of society secured by perpetuating traditional order as manifested in its historically-developed institutions, and if this is understood to result in a political structure which finds every member of the society realizing himself and his freedom within the limits of his assigned sphere, what are the means which Conservative theory envisages to achieve these ends?

Ruled out by one of the inherent characteristics of Conservatism as a means for realizing desired ends, is the exercise of man's own reason or will to control or direct the course of political development. Constitutionalism, as much as revolution, are condemned by Conservative theory as means for achieving their social and political objectives. With only the variant of degree, both de Maistre and Burke (as well as contemporary Conservatives typified by T. S. Eliot) explicitly attack constitutional *a priorism*. A constitution cannot be "made." It "grows" out of the national spirit and is identical with its development, identical with the immanent spirit and with history. Into constitutional theory Conservative thought breathed the spirit of a force moving over and above the will of the people. For the obscurantist theory of a Maistre, that spirit was a divine mystery of indivisible sovereignty, unpenetrable by man's reason. The roots of political constitutions exist prior to all written law, de Maistre wrote. A constitutional law is and can be only the development or sanction of a pre-existing and unwritten right, and the weakness and frailty of a constitution are in exact proportion to the number of constitutional provisions that are written.[16]

For Burke, too, there is a mystical strain. In the development of the constitution of England the social and political forces have operated with a natural regularity.

> By a constitutional policy, working after the pattern of nature, we receive, we hold, we transmit our government and our privileges, in the same manner in which we enjoy and transmit our property and our lives. Our political system is placed in a just correspondence and symmetry with the order of the world, and with the mode of existence decreed to a permanent body composed of transitory parts. . . . Thus, by preserving the method of nature in the conduct of the state, in what we improve we are never wholly new; in what we retain, we are never wholly obsolete.[17]
>
> Each contract of each particular state is but a clause in the great primeval contract of eternal society, linking the lower with the higher natures, connecting the visible and invisible world, according to a fixed compact sanctioned by the inviolable oath which holds all physical and all moral natures, each in their appointed place.[18]

If, then, man must not interfere with this process of a natural ordering, there can scarcely arise the question of man's assuring stability by his own devices. The preservation of the political order is a natural functioning of a society's ancient institutions. For the reactionary absolutism of a Maistre or a Bonald, these institutions are rooted exclusively in the religion of each culture. De Maistre points to the constituent and infallible power of the Pope and the Church as the agent through which order is ultimately established and preserved. Hand-in-hand with faith in the temporal representatives of God goes an exaltation of political faith and a mysticization of patriotism.

For Burke, the procedure is less dogmatic. Change is explicitly allowed for[19] and though Burke held a rigorous contempt for theories of popular sovereignty, his was a broader conception of the constituent power—a power vested not in an individual, but in a class: the "natural" aristocracy with the "noblesse qui oblige." He held that ". . . the people of England well know, that the idea of inheritance furnishes a sure principle of conservation, and a sure principle of transmission. . . ."[20] The agents to secure the preservation of liberties belong, necessarily, for Burke, to the propertied aristocracy.

> The power of perpetuating our property in our families is one of the most valuable and interesting circumstances belonging to it, and that which tends the most to the perpetuation of society itself. It makes our weakness subservient to our virtue; it grafts benevolence even upon avarice. The possessors of family wealth, and of the distinction which attends hereditary possession . . . are the natural securities for this transmission. With us, the house of peers is formed upon this principle.[21]

In a similar way, the contemporary Conservative thinker, T. S. Eliot, seeks to preserve the social and political order and to conserve that which will lend itself to stability by establishing a rigid class distinction wherein the culture of one class is perpetuated by that class, and where no perversions such as occur in Western "popular" culture may arise. He seeks an interrelated class structure, each class coming into contact with the other but each knowing and keeping its place, and each propagating itself within its class. In this way the transmission of the culture is handed on from generation to generation.[22]

Such, then, are the Conservative suggestions as to how the objectives of stability and order are to be achieved. Thus far we find little more than a faith in established institutions on the one hand, and on the other a belief in a growing organic structure of societal relationships following upon an understanding of the "natural," divinely sanctioned order and process of traditional developments. What, then, does this mean in terms of political action or of specific power techniques?

With de Maistre, the application of "spontaneous" rather than "rational reason" and the mystical apprehension of a nation-spirit issues in frank nationalism or, more precisely, supra-nationalism. The nation lives through "rational reason." The view of patriotism in de Maistre approaches that of Nietzsche. Individual will and reason are reduced to subjects for contempt. The meaning of de Maistre's political philosophy in terms of action technique is not far to seek. For the key figure in de Maistre's ideal society becomes the hangman.[23] It is the hangman who instills the State's members with proper respect for their stations in life and their respective duties. The exercise of individual will and reason is not only degraded but actively suppressed. The means for de Maistre are clearly those of autocratic violence.

Continental classical Conservative thought had been presaged by the embodiment of the reactionary ideal in the Holy Alliance created by the treaty of September 1815. That convention declared the intention

> to take as their sole guide in both internal and external relations of their governments, the precepts of justice, Christian charity and peace; to treat one another as brothers, and to act toward their respective subjects as fathers of families; to regard themselves as delegated by Providence to govern three branches of one family, whose sole sovereign should thus confessedly be God.[24]

The will was understood to be that of the king acting with the absolute power, however benevolent, of a father over his child; it was not the will of the people or the nation. Nor was the authority ultimately derived from the people but through direct delegation from God.

The technique which, for Restoration Philosophers, was to assure the functioning of the State along the lines determined by history, tradition, or extra-human spirit was that of violence applied by an all-powerful State force controlled by the chosen few. The techniques of modern Fascism are reminiscent of this aspect of earlier absolutist thought. In flouting the individual will of members in society, absolutist theory brought upon itself the full force of man-directed counterviolence, both from within and from without. The ideal of order and security in the end dissolved in a realized chaos and destruction.

What, then, of English Conservative theory which denied absolutism and irrationalist elements ultimately defended by a Maistrian hangman? Burke set the standard of the statesman in "a disposition to preserve, and an ability to improve . . ."[25] Where de Maistre would suppress, Burke would reform. English Conservatism conceived of eliminating revolution through evolution. Parliamentary reform, then, could become part of the Conservative program. Indeed, Burke was less occupied with abstract ends than he was with the practical arts of government; he was concerned with results which could be obtained through the cautious development of the devices through which a people are governed. But improvement should be undertaken only where necessity and utility indicate that change is desirable. It must be done through a careful understanding of the past and concern for the future.

Let us improve it [the constitution] with zeal, but with fear. Let us follow our ancestors . . . who, by respecting the reason of others, who by looking backward as well as forward, by the modesty as well as by the energy of their minds, went on, insensibly drawing this constitution nearer and nearer to its perfection by never departing from its fundamental principles, not introducing any amendment which had not a subsisting root in the laws, constitution, and usages of the kingdom. Let those who have the trust of political or of natural authority ever keep watch against the desperate enterprises of innovation: Let even their benevolence be fortified and armed.[26]

If, then, stability is to be achieved and improvement carried out through reform determined by aristocratic "responsible" rule, is there anything further said about the principle of means which may assure the evolutionary process? However much Conservative thought may be concerned with device— and result—Conservatism does not, as we have seen, consider techniques of social action. The social process is controlled by inherent principles and not by deliberate contrivances of man. Basic to the treatment of means in Conservative theory is the doctrine of obedience — no resistance to established law and consent to traditional rule. It is obedience which secures the stability of the State. "'Resistance is nowhere enacted to be legal'," Burke quotes Walpole at the trial of Dr. Sacheverel, "'but subject, by all the laws now in being, to the greatest penalties. It is what is not, cannot, nor ought ever to be described, or affirmed, in any positive law, to be excusable. . . .'" And then, Walpole is quoted as adding,

". . . when, and upon what *never-to-be-expected* occasions, it may *be exercised, no man can foresee; and it ought never to be thought of, but when an utter subversion of the laws of the realm threatens the whole frame of our constitution, and no redress can otherwise be hoped for*."[27]

This admission of an exception characterizes the English Conservative position: no resistance until some overwhelming necessity presents itself. Burke's cleverly contrived defense of the revolution of 1688 is, despite his protestations, the admission of the necessity for revolutionary action. Burke's argument that the action of 1688 was anti-revolutionary in its effect, that it did not "dissolve the whole fabrick" but "regenerated the deficient part of the old constitution"[28] is a statement about the necessity for placing in the hands of the "natural rulers" a means for securing the end of conserving the "true constitution."

Summing up his position on the revolution of 1688, Burke wrote:

That the fundamental subversion of this antient constitution, by one of its parts, having been attempted, and in effect accomplished, justified the revolution. That it was justified *only* upon the *necessity* of the case; as the *only* means left for the recovery of that *antient* constitution, formed by the *original contract* of the British state; as well as for the future preservation of the *same* government.[29]

The English Conservative position as typified by Burke, may, then, be summarized. The political ends to be secured are stability and a natural hierarchical order. The means for achieving these ends are, for the most part, not the concern of man, for historical movement and the social process, if not tampered with, will assure good government and the realization of the individual's good within his appointed sphere. Obedience is the citizen's clear duty. But if a "never-to-be-expected" circumstance should arise wherein the "natural" order of things is being subverted, then those in positions of responsibility—those endowed with *noblesse qui oblige*—necessarily take the lead in setting things right. When such a circumstance does arise, the technique is, perforce, that of violence.

The ceremony of cashiering kings . . . can rarely, if ever, be performed without force. It then becomes a case of war, and not of constitution. Laws are commanded to hold their tongues amongst arms; and tribunals fall to the ground with the peace they are no longer able to uphold. . . . The question of dethroning, or, if these gentlemen like the phrase better, "cashiering kings," will always be, as it has always been, an extraordinary question of state, and wholly out of the law; a question (like all other questions of state) of dispositions, and of means, and of probable consequences, rather than of positive rights. As it was not made for common abuses, so it is not to be agitated by common minds. The speculative line of demarcation, where obedience ought to end, and resistance must begin, is faint, obscure, and not easily definable. It is not a single act, or a single event, which determines it. Governments must be abused and deranged indeed, before it can be thought of; and the prospect of the future must be as bad as the experience of the past . . . a revolution will be the very last resource of the thinking and the good.[30]

Can the full force of Burke's revulsion for the French Revolution be explained by reference to the Conservative position of tradition-sanctioned institutions? Can the horror with which Burke viewed the effects of the Revolution be understood in terms of Conservative ends alone? In many areas Burke is hailed as a champion of Liberal thought and a defender of civil rights. Can we, then, discover the substantial element in Burke's reaction to the means principle operating to effect revolution? It was the realization of human savagery with which revolution tore down the traditional structure, the continuing effects of spreading violence, the transformation of stated objectives by the methods which were used to achieve them, the chaos and bloodshed of a social fabric rent on every side without compensating construction that aroused Burke's righteous wrath and threw him headlong into the eloquent fulminations of his *Reflections*. Again, the caution with which he reluctantly admits extreme necessity for revolution, reveals a fear of destructive means as much as it does a reverence for established ends. If "constitution" is to be revered, respected, and defended it is as much because its antithesis is war as it is that established law is in the natural order of things.

Burke was forced to a position of preferring peace to freedom. And yet, he could not abandon himself to the absolutism which characterized the Continental reactionary Conservatives. Burke did not embrace a principle of infallibility. And so, for Burke, stability based upon unswerving obedience was not quite enough. His real dilemma arose after he attempted to place the decision for resistance. He could restrict resistance to its barest "never-to-be-expected" circumstance, he could turn to the nobility to take up the responsibility for the ultimate decision. But beyond this Burke could not go. For the effect of violence, as Burke all too clearly saw, was chaos. That violence had been reduced to a minimum in the revolution of 1688, and that the result had been controlled, was so gratifying to Burke that he was seized by the belief that it was a revolution to end all revolution. Nevertheless, an inference of fallibility underlies Burke's admission of revolution even as a last resource.

There is only an implied answer to the question "what if the nobility subvert the constitution?" A popular revolution could never be tolerated. Indeed, the question of means in the sense of social action had gone a-begging. In the realm of techniques of action, whether in the hands of the few or the many, Conservative theory presents us with an eloquent void.

The poverty of Conservative theory is most evident and most serious in its failure to approach a philosophy of action. In the extreme Conservatism of the Continental reactionaries non-resistance on the one hand, and autocratic violence on the other, represent the means for securing the desired political ends. But in the mainstream of English Conservative thought, one cannot find a definitive statement regarding this aspect of the means principle. The residual feeling in the English Conservative appears to be one of hatred of violence, but agreement to its use as a last resort. This is more clearly expressed when the use of violence is in defense of established institutions. There is nothing more than an implied, uneasy agreement to use violence in order to "correct" subversions of those institutions.

Not only is the weakness of English Conservatism reflected in its failure to formulate a policy of political action, but there is every suggestion that such failure further influences the priority structure of desired ends. Can we believe, for instance, that Burke truly preferred peace to freedom? There is the suspicion that he felt only that there was no alternative to peace but chaos. The suggestion that a rigorous consideration of a technique of action might present him with the possibility of both peace and freedom appears not to have occurred to him.

Conservative theory is, then, taken up with a consideration of ends and of institutional devices. Its difficulties in allowing for change—and change is accepted as desirable by most Conservatives—its fear of extended freedoms, its failure to meet or to deny the growing insistence of the developing social forces demanding participation—these are all failures traced to an insensibility, an inability or an unwillingness to face the question of "how" to tackle the problem of means in the aspect of social action and to consider the relationship of such means to Conservative ends.

AUTHORITARIAN IDEALISM AND THE PROBLEM OF MEANS

That branch of Idealist thought which issues in authoritarianism reaches its apogee in the writings of Georg Wilhelm Friedrich Hegel. Hegelian political philosophy goes beyond the idealism of Kant and of Fichte to embody an historical, evolutionary doctrine which transforms the will into an aspect of pure abstract intelligence.[31] The State is the embodiment of this will "having its reality in the particular self-consciousness raised to the place of the universal."[32] The State is "absolutely rational" and is "substantive will" realizing itself through history and is therefore eternal. "This substantive unity is its own motive and absolute end. In this end freedom attains its highest right. This end has the highest right over the individual, whose highest duty in turn is to be a member of the state."[33]

Hegelian metaphysical theory has been even less concerned than has Conservatism with the problems of positive means for man's achieving political ends. For the State is an end in itself; it is Mind realizing itself through history. The locus of rationality lies, as it does to a less well-defined extent in Conservatism, elsewhere than with man. For Hegel, history is the regulative factor. That which is realized—the real—is the rational, and the most that individual reason can do is to understand the course and the meaning of that realization. In such an effort and only in such an effort can man achieve freedom. For freedom is service to the State. Political ends are not to be contrived by man; they are to be apprehended by a process which is inseparable from the system of which the process is a part. The Hegelian dialectic is the logical apparatus according to which the laws of history move.

The Idealist conception of the State is, moreover, organismic. Not only is the State an end in itself, but the organic form in which it is conceived necessarily provides that its members be distributed according to functionally differentiated parts. This means, of course, that an individual within a State is performing his proper, necessary function through service to the State within his own proper sphere of endeavor. The State has "the highest right over the individual, whose highest duty in turn is to be a member of the State."[34]

The constitution of a State is, then, determined by its own nature and by its own rationality. The divisions of legislative, executive, and princely power combine to form a unity and work together according to the particular nature of the organism. That Hegel imposes a hierarchy and places the princely power at the top[35] is merely indicative of his motivation in glorifying the Prussian State of his day. But it is to be noted that his approach was one of discovering the true nature of the State, not of inventing techniques by which desired political ends might be achieved.

The lack of concern for means characterizes Hegelian Idealism. Hegel's insistence upon the distinction between the State and civil society is yet another case in point. The State, as Sabine describes Hegel's approach, "was no utilitarian institution, engaged in the commonplace business of providing public services, administering the law, performing police duties, and adjusting industrial and economic interests. All these functions belong to civil society."[36] They must, however, be adjusted to the needs of the State which regulates and supervises them but does not perform them. Indeed, the individual citizen and the civil servant each has an important duty to perform in these functions of civil society. But this is so because they are the agencies upon which the State depends. And service to the State is the citizen's realization of freedom.

Throughout the Hegelian argument the question of individual judgment is treated with righteous scorn. Individual choice is nothing more than caprice. The next step can only be the recommendation of simple obedience.*

What, then, does this theory have to say about ends and means? The question of means is, for the Hegelian Idealist, impertinent and sentimental. The only means which Hegel recognizes is, on the one hand, a method of explaining the movement of History—the dialectic—and, on the other, a structuring of society in the political hierarchy of a Constitutional Monarchy where the constitution is not determined by the citizens of the society it regulates but by the natural progression of the Spirit of that society.[37] In no case does Hegel concern himself with a technique of action whereby specific ends could be achieved.

* Sabine suggests (A History of Political Theory, New York, Henry Holt, 1947, p. 640) that Hegel failed to make clear a belief that the modern State does protect the right of choice. The effect of Hegelian theory emerging in authoritarian systems has been to reaffirm the expressed belief that individual choice is caprice and sentimentality.

The effect of the Hegelian metaphysical system on later strands of political theory is painfully recalled. The "real is rational" had its corollary of "might makes right." Authoritarian theories invoked the Hegelian glorification of the nation as an end in itself. The metaphysical explanation of the State as realization of abstract will, and of service to the State as the realization of the freedom of the individual, resulted, on the one hand, in an appeal to obedience and non-resistance, to blind adoration of the State and its leaders. On the other hand, the Hegelian metaphysic, when "set right side up" by Marx, lent itself to an activism directed towards intervention at the psycho-historically ripe moment wherein the masses were to function as the midwives of History to deliver the dialectical child onto a further stage in the progress of Society towards a preconceived socio-political end.

Authoritarian Idealism, then, resolves the question of "how" by adopting a determinist philosophy. The manifold exceptions to the patterns which Hegel found in history have suggested the failure of his system. More than this, man's search for freedom continues despite the metaphysical solution that it cannot realize itself save in the pattern of determined State evolvement. The practical experiment with glorified nation-states supplying all needs, including man's urge for liberty, have destroyed States and members alike.

The refusal to deal with man-determined ends, together with the failure to understand the function and importance of a man-controlled technique for achieving ends understood in terms of man's needs, have signalled the terrible defeat of an impressive political philosophy.

LIBERAL DEMOCRATIC THEORY

With the theoretical formulations of Conservatism and of Authoritarian Idealism, it has not been difficult to point to eminent failure to deal adequately with the problem of means. But what of Liberal Democratic theory? Here, if anywhere in the course of Western political thought, it is argued, is a theory which is distinguished by its efforts to establish techniques for accommodating change, to develop means for achieving desired ends. With Liberal Democratic theory we are brought to the heart of Western theory's efforts to answer the ends-means question. It is, then, in a comparative analysis of Liberal Democratic method and Gandhian satyagraha that the significance of the Indian development for Western political thought is most pointed.

Simply stated, the principles which infuse Liberal Democratic theory are those of equality on the one hand and of liberty on the other. Its operative ideals, as A. D. Lindsay calls them,[38] follow a pattern of belief in free associations, in the instrumental and secondary function of the State, in the superiority of the voluntary principle over force, in tolerance, and in diversity. As Liberal philosophy moved from the negative position it took in the earlier days of its historical development when it sought freedom of contract, right of non-interference, and when it carried on the struggle against oppressive government, through the modifications effected in its theory by J. S. Mill, and finally to its reorganization beginning with T. H. Green and the introduction of the positive welfare concept, its attitudes were reflected in a changing notion of the Liberal Democratic State. Different concepts of government were fashioned accordingly, as the theory emphasized the libertarian or the egalitarian aspects of its basic philosophy. But, throughout, Liberal Democracy has meant political freedom, equality before the law, freedom of assembly, and free elections. These are basic tenets in a philosophy aimed at the elaboration of instruments which are intended to assure both liberty and equality. Those instruments are familiar to us in various forms of representative government including such devices as delegacy, recall, referendum.

Above all, Liberal Democracy is characterized by its recognition of change: the substantial body of Liberal Democratic theory centers upon the development of political machinery, the arrangement of social interrelationships, the invention of adequate devices to assure the optimum articulation of the liberty-equality nexus in a changing environment.

It is the purpose of a vast body of polemical literature—and not my purpose here—to debate the relative merits of specific contesting democratic devices. From the earliest days of Liberal Democratic thought, controversy over methodology has played an eminent part in the structuring of its theory. The psychological method which infused Locke's theory of politics was replaced for the Utilitarians by a method borrowed from physics leading to an insistence upon scientific administration as assuring the Benthamite "greatest good of the greatest number" principle. J. S. Mill's subsequent modifications of Utilitarianism were propelled by a methodology which derived much from history. Mill recognized that society must be considered in terms of an historical interaction between men and institutions. With the advent of T. H. Green, Liberal Theory acquired an organic view which, in L. T. Hobhouse, proceeded upon a methodology borrowed largely from biology. With each change in method came a shift of emphasis in the regulation of social interrelationships, and with each change in method came, too, new suggestions for constructing instruments through which the objectives of Liberal Democracy could be realized. And each method attempted to make possible the most effective expression of the will of the people —for consent is a necessary fundamental of democracy.

What, then, is the degree of adequacy Liberal Democratic theory has attained in satisfying the ends-means question? Is this theory free from the weaknesses which characterize Anarchism, Conservatism, Authoritarian Idealism, and Marxism in the safeguarding of ends which they take to be desirable by a means compatible with those ends?

Inasmuch as I am treating here of theory, it is not pertinent to dwell at length upon the current threats to Liberal Democratic institutions. And yet, it is my suggestion that these institutions and what is, in the cliché, called the "democratic way of life," are so seriously threatened in the current clime because Liberal Democratic theory has, indeed, failed to deal adequately with the question of ends-means relationship. It has, I submit, failed in the area where it might well have been expected to achieve its greatest triumph: in the development of means whereby desirable ends of Liberal Democracy may be secured. Methodological development on the one hand, and structuring of social and political machinery on the other, have by-passed the most fundamental of all facets in the means-ends problem. For Liberal Democratic theory has failed to develop an adequate technique of action as distinct from the structure of political machinery.

Liberal Democratic theory has been concerned with mechanism, not with action, with form rather than performance, with instrument more than with technique. It has raised questions, less of *how* a people may struggle towards an end, than through what *devices.** Discussion and debate do provide what may loosely be called a technique, but discussion yields fruitful agreement in almost direct proportion to the adequacy of institutions founded upon and sustained by extensive general agreement. The tools of democracy are designed to operate within a set of generally agreed upon regulative principles. A range of systematic sub-philosophies — conservative, liberal, labor, socialist — characterizes the polity of the day. It is important to note that no other political system has been so satisfactory in assuring adaptation to the changing will of its citi-

---

* In his book, *The Techniques of Democracy* (New York: Duell, Sloan and Pearce, 1942), Alfred M. Bingham notes (p. 14) that "the use of the term 'technique' in connection with democracy is relatively new." He refers to Ordway Tead's work on scientific management as a "technique of democracy." The "techniques" which Bingham treats range from the ballot and federalism to "freedom of the mind" and "religious faith," all of which (together with many other devices, agencies, or approaches) he terms "techniques." Another study, Duval Talmadge McCutchen, "Technique for Democracy" (unpublished Ph.D. dissertation, University of Pennsylvania, 1938), proposes, as a progressive democratic "technique," an "Agency for Economic Equity." The emphasis, once more, is upon instruments and devices. Techniques of action, especially action during conflict, are altogether neglected.

zens. The democratic State is, indeed, an admirable form of political organization. So long as such a State meets no serious challenge from without and can maintain the large area of basic agreement within, it leaves little to be desired. So long as the many devices provided within the system are permitted to operate, conflicts continue to be satisfactorily resolved. But when threatened by aggression or subversion, the means available to the Liberal Democrat are no different from those available in rival systems. When the prerogatives of the people have been usurped, the citizens of such a State ultimately fall back upon the traditional mode of action: violent force. The ultimate remedy for usurpation of power implied in Liberal Democratic thought is revolution.

When democratic procedures have broken down partially or within limited areas in the State, the use of protest through demonstration and the extraconstitutional measures of civil disobedience may serve to restore democratic processes to their proper functioning. These measures may suffice, especially if strong support is available to back the protest. Acts of civil disobedience in the civil rights movement in the United States have been carried out as part of a struggle in which a regional ethic differs from the overriding national ethic. This context has accounted both for the breadth and strength of participation in the movement, and for its high degree of success. To the extent that these measures were conducted within a framework of satyagraha they could be expected to restore constructive discussion and debate and to establish a climate favorable to the smooth functioning of democratic procedures.

The democratic State is distinguished by its accommodation and encouragement of voluntary association and its preference for persuasion over coercion. Even so, there is an element of violent force which lies at the very foundation of every state. This can be demonstrated through an analysis of law as essentially an organization of force.* Just as the juridical sys-

* The most rigorous analysis of the legal framework as the essence of

tem of every state gives the monopoly of force to the community, the exercise of that monopoly is the function of law. In the system of norms and sanctions which found and inform every state, violence is the operative force and coercion constitutes the ultimate process. It is the legal sanction of violent force applied by agents of the community against delinquent members that supports the political order whether in Liberal Democracy or in other forms of polity. In international intercourse the ultimate sanction is war, a method legitimized in the corpus of international law. The further development of democratic polity may well await the redefining of the legal sanction. °

Within the broader usage of discussion and debate lies the technique of compromise — an essential method in the resolving of differences. It is compromise through which the conflicting elements within a democratic society are intended to reconcile their interests. The politics of elections, the collective bargaining of industrial relations, the diplomacy of foreign affairs — all involve the use of compromise. If at any point Liberal Democracy approaches consideration of the dynamic quality for which we have been searching, it is in the technique of compromise.†

In an age when dogmatism and authoritarian tactics are painfully pushed in upon our consciousness, compromise does, indeed, have the appeal of a superior procedure. Compromise, like satyagraha, is a technique intended to achieve an adjust-

---

the state, and the law as an organizational force is that of Hans Kelsen, especially in his *General Theory of Law and State* (trans. by Anders Wedber [20th Century Legal Philosophy Series, Vol. I; Cambridge: Harvard University Press, 1946]).

° See my paper, "The Case for Redefining the Legal Sanction of the Democratic State," in: *Politics of Persuasion*, ed. K. P. Misra and Rajendra Avasthi (Bombay: P. C. Manaktala and Sons, 1967).

† For a compelling statement of the value of compromise, see T. V. Smith, *Discipline for Democracy* (Chapel Hill: The University of North Carolina, 1942), Chapter IV. See also R. M. MacIver, ed., *Integrity and Compromise: Problems of Public and Private Conscience* (New York: Harper & Brothers, 1957).

ment of conflicting interests. The arts of accommodation upon which Lord Morley has so eloquently discoursed are, indeed, to be nurtured in a democratic society. And where compromise is not a violation of principle, but adjustment to reality, conflict may be avoided by declining "to press our ideas up to their remotest logical issues, without reference to the conditions in which we are applying them."[38a] It is when barter is introduced into a situation to avoid explicit conflict and proceeds to distort conviction and principle, that one must look for a better technique.

Ideally, compromise proceeds in a manner which admits to sacrificing some portion of an initially held position in exchange for a similar sacrifice on the part of an opponent. Compromise differs from the direct action techniques of satyagraha in that—again, ideally—the satyagrahi is at no time prepared to sacrifice substantial elements within his carefully detailed position unless, of course, he may be persuaded that he is in error in so holding them. Compromise is an eminently satisfactory procedure for the settling of disputes which do not involve serious matters of principle or do not involve issues understood in terms of grave social injustice. The methods now familiar in democratic systems—of which forms of compromise are the most prominent—can be relied upon to resolve conflict of opinion and of interest as long as broad and general agreement on fundamentals is sustained.

A satyagrahi cannot exclude compromise from his early attempts at settlement of disputes. Satyagraha is an elaborate technique which embraces a range of activities. In the earlier stages of satyagraha where, for example, negotiation is attempted, the practice of "the arts of accommodation" may, indeed, play a limited role. At no time, however, does a proper satyagrahi make extravagant or unreal claims for purposes of bargaining. He may concede to the opponent minor points, as for example in questions of his convenience or of opinion on technical matters, in return for similar concessions. The final steps of satyagraha which call for aggressive action and which go beyond compromise are employed when the conflict is one of basic truth-challenging.

Certain of the more recent "satyagraha" campaigns in India have appeared to enter later stages of satyagraha (or, more accurately, duragraha) at a point where compromise would surely have been more appropriate. To use the direct action techniques of satyagraha where the practical arts of compromise could settle the dispute without effecting a grave injustice is a tactical error against which every satyagrahi need be forewarned. Compromise, like non-cooperation and civil disobedience, is one of the tools which may be used in the promotion of a satyagraha campaign. To go beyond compromise into later stages of direct action may be to introduce an atmosphere of self-righteousness, stiff-necked opposition hardly appropriate to the conditions of a minor dispute. There is a time and place for compromise and to know that time and place is one of the skills which every leader of satyagraha should master.

When compromise breaks down into barter, its distance from satyagraha is pronounced. In operation, bargaining techniques, sometimes dignified by the name of compromise, easily become those of uncertain levelling, of obscuring of fundamental issues, and of uneasy resolution. Original claims of astute opponents are not expected to be fully honest claims. They are calculated with full recognition of bargaining margins. As these claims are reduced during the procedure, calculation turns to consideration of what the opponent can stand to lose, how far he is likely to be pressed, at what point he may be made to capitulate, whether he will modify his fundamental demands or what are guessed to be his fundamental demands. Meanwhile claims are scaled down to approach the real demand which had been embroidered for purposes of the bargaining. Beyond this, a point of the fundamental demand may have to be conceded for what appears to be a reciprocal concession on the part of the opponent. As the adjustment approaches a conclusion, each side loses substantial segments of its original claim. No objective observer is likely to know, if indeed the bargainers themselves clearly know, how close the final adjustment is to either of the original genuine claims. The conclusion is usually one which is tolerable, but not fully gratifying to either side.

It will be noted that the initial attitude of the satyagrahi — his statement of position and claims — is necessarily different from the bargaining approach, for at no time is there to be an effort to exaggerate claims. In the operation of the Gandhian dialectic there is in no sense an effort to buy agreement by sacrificing elements within the satyagraha position. On the other hand, there is every readiness to concede error and to agree with an opponent should the opponent demonstrate the superiority of his point in the light of the over-all situation.

Compromise is, then, a dynamic method relied upon within Liberal Democratic systems to adjust conflicting claims. When compromise breaks down into barter or when the issues involved in a conflict do not lend themselves to settlement through the simple arts of accommodation, the search for refinement in technique becomes crucial.

If refinement of technique is suggested by an evaluation of compromise, it is, as well, suggested by examination of the device of majority decisions. It is not necessary here to elaborate the faults which de Tocqueville found to constitute the tyranny of the majority. The weaknesses of the majority-rule principle have long troubled serious theorists of the Liberal Democratic tradition. Satyagraha, in its over-all approach to the question of conflict, may point the direction of certain refinement. Indeed, the Western tradition is not devoid of efforts to devise a better instrument for resolving clash of interests. The Quaker method of decision through the "sense of the meeting" is, in its implications, reminiscent of aspects of satyagraha. This method has been adopted from time to time as a substitute for majority vote-taking in reaching decisions within the councils of United States government committees.* The

* For a stimulating discussion of the use of "sense of the meeting"

method has been consciously adopted to overcome "unfortunate results developing from the great reliance on the reaching of decisions by majority rule."

> The introduction of a resolution for a yea-and-nay vote is conceived as a kind of contest between opposing forces each going into battle armed with fully formed conclusions which it then attempts to put over on the other side. If a group cannot force acceptance of the whole program, then it proceeds by a process of barter, to swap point for point often without regard to the right or wrong of the individual points.

> The outcome of the vote, then, is a victory for one side and a defeat for the other, which leads to grudges. It is likely to represent no group decision based on the intrinsic merits of the case but a sort of ledger sheet showing the result of bargaining negotiations. And it imposes on the minority a course of action in which they do not concur and which they may positively resent.[39]

By the Quaker method, resolutions are not directly introduced, but "queries" are put to elicit opinions from members of the group. The attitude with which each member approaches the problem at hand, and the manner in which the group resolves conflict of opinion is constructive and aimed at the widest possible agreement. Quakers claim for this procedure that it allows for the most complete form of democracy inasmuch as all decisions are reached by a process that considers the opinion of every person. Each member of the group considers contrary viewpoints as if they were his own. The Quaker phrase for this process is "getting under the weight" of the other man's doubts. When differences have been resolved by open discussion, the chairman announces the "sense of the meeting" and this stands as the group's decision unless a member then challenges the statement. In that event, the meeting

---

methods see Morris Llewellyn Cooke, "The Quaker Way Wins New Adherents," *New York Times Magazine*, June 17, 1951, pp. 21 ff.

is suspended, possible further research is arranged for, and the meeting is called for a later date at which time the process is again set in motion.

The Quaker method has served to resolve conflicts of opinion of the most serious nature in committees and commissions dealing with keenly controversial issues.* Morris Llewellyn Cooke, Chairman of the President's Water Resources Policy Commission, who has had direct experience with the Quaker method in the course of the proceedings of the Commission has this to say about the possible future adoption of the method:

> If the executives of organizations dealing with public affairs, from the municipal level up through the councils of the United Nations, will test this technique they will find that important decisions can be airived at with less partisanship, more harmony and with great faith in the results achieved. . . .[40]

Similarities between the Quaker method of decision-making and satyagraha as a technique for conducting conflict are immediately apparent. In both cases the effort is to arrive at a mutually satisfactory solution in terms of the total situation and not in terms of victory for one side. The attitude is constructive and creative — the dynamic character of a "meeting of minds" is in both processes elementary. Satyagraha, as we have seen, goes beyond the Quaker method of decision-making and operates in realms of social action. Nevertheless, the Quaker way approaches the sort of dynamic process, the creative resolution, which is for the most part lacking in Western social and political systems.

Liberal Democratic theory emphasizes devices, machinery, instruments; it slights concern for action techniques. The Liberal Democratic state is designed to operate within a social situation where extensive, fundamental agreement already ob-

---

* Cooke, *op. cit.*, pp. 27 and 42, cites instances of the use of the "sense of the meeting" method by the following organizations: Acheson-

tains. Within this situation the most prominent device for regulative action is majority decision. The premier technique for adjusting conflicting interests is the unrefined method of compromise. Should the representative, majority system be subverted, the ultimate remedy lies with violent revolution.

Unmodified satyagraha as it operated in the Indian experiment should not, of course, be thought of as a direct remedy for weaknesses to be found within Liberal Democratic systems. An analysis of satyagraha as a technique of action does, however, point up areas where refinement or introduction of new techniques may be indicated if Liberal Democracy is to gain the strength it needs to resist encroachments of rival systems. In the daily business of democratic government and social life within a Liberal Democracy, the familiar devices and rudimentary techniques have proved themselves adequate. Any Liberal Democrat can agree with T. V. Smith that the "fertility of discussion" is "superior to the sterility of domination as a social method."[41] And, further, the "politics of compromise" may, indeed, breed a tolerance which Smith considers the "*sine qua non* of the pluralistic values which democracy enshrines."[42] Were the system never to be challenged, were the area of agreement wide enough and sufficiently secure, the familiar processes would surely suffice. The all-embracing method of satyagraha, as we have seen, employs widely these well-tried means — until they no longer serve to solve the problem. It is when conflict persists that satyagraha supplies the processes whereby constructive solutions may yet be achieved. Satyagraha points directly to a new method of revolution: it was as a revolutionary technique that satya-

---

Lilienthal atomic energy commission; Joint Committee on the Organization of the Congress (La Follette-Monroney Committee), 1948-49; Senate Republican Conference under chairmanship of Senator Millikan; International Monetary Fund which has a by-law reading "The Chairman will ordinarily ascertain the sense of the meeting in lieu of a formal vote"; Committee on Economic Development; the First National Conference on Aging meeting in August 1950 in Washington under the auspices of the Federal Security Agency with a group numbering 816.

graha developed on the historic scene of Indian national politics against the British Imperial rule. It also points the direction in which techniques of adjustment of persisting conflict could be developed within a Liberal Democratic State. Of perhaps greater importance, the operative principles of satyagraha suggest a point of departure from which techniques for conducting large-scale conflict on the international level might be devised. The Gandhian "experiments with truth" have not yet been completed.

The Operation of Satyagraha against a Totalitarian Regime

Discussion of the success of satyagraha in India evokes the question, "Yes, but could the technique work within a totalitarian regime?" We do not have any direct empirical evidence upon which to base an answer to this question. Certain of the steps required in an ideal satyagraha campaign would be impossible under circumstances obtaining in monolithic authoritarian States. Such, for instance, is the step of widespread publicity and propaganda conducted without secrecy. Yet, certain points may be reasonably supposed with regard to the success of satyagraha even under totalitarian conditions.

Every political regime rests upon the cooperation of individuals within the society in the performance of their respective functions. Large-scale disobedience is disruptive and, if it is sufficiently widespread, it makes the position of those in control untenable. This is the basis of the theory of general strike, just as it is of civil disobedience. The problem centers upon the extent to which this non-cooperation can be attained. For ideal satyagraha, it depends upon the degree to which the people could be educated in the tactics and the strategy which we have described above as a dialectical process.

Gandhi believed that satyagraha, if properly applied, would always meet with a high degree of success. He appears, also, to have believed that it could have been used in such concrete cases as the opposition of Jews in Germany to the Nazis. It can certainly be agreed that had the Jews offered satyagraha against the Nazi regime their losses could scarcely have been greater. They should then have mobilized world opinion behind them much more rapidly than they did. It appears quite likely that the use of a constructive technique of active resistance would have achieved more than either sporadic efforts at violence or an over-all reaction of non-resistance.

In further speculation on the possibilities of satyagraha for success within a totalitarian system, it appears that this may depend to a substantial extent upon the prior knowledge and/or experience of members of that society with satyagraha. It is doubtful that any totalitarian system, however effective in its policing, could prevent word-of-mouth propagation of an idea, or even of an understanding of a technique, if there had been some previous understanding of its meaning and its effectiveness. For example, had the Jews of Germany been schooled in the art of satyagraha, an organized effort of satyagraha might have got underway. The chances for success are certainly as great as are the chances for violent revolution under the modern police-state system.* Satyagraha may, in fact, be the only possibility open to an oppressed people in this age of highly technical means of oppression.[43] Reflection upon this likelihood suggests the utility

---

* An example of passive resistance (but certainly not satyagraha) was reported during the 1956 uprising in Hungary. On 4 December thousands of Hungarian women staged a mass march to the tomb of Hungary's Unknown Soldier in Heroes Square, Budapest. They sang Hungary's old national anthem and recited Alexander Petofi's poem to freedom. Soviet soldiers posted around the heroes' memorial tried to prevent the crowd from approaching it, whereupon the women cried: "We have no weapons, only flowers! Are you afraid of flowers?" The soldiers gave way and the women heaped the monument with wreaths. During this demonstration one woman is reported to have angrily protested to a Soviet officer, who thereupon attempted to arrest her. Other women hastened to her side and pushed the Russian away. At this incident several shots were fired, one of the women was struck in the leg and carried away by others in the crowd. (*New York Times*, 5 December 1956.)

of developing techniques akin to satyagraha, as well as education in their use.

There is no longer validity to the proposition that satyagraha can be successful only in the Indian milieu which supported and gave rise to it. Its use in a modified form among the Pathans of the Frontier is historical evidence that it is not dependent upon a specific philosophical or cultural background. Doubtless the technique would necessarily undergo modifications and development in its adaptation to other social circumstances and cultural experiences.

A Note on the Function of Suffering in Satyagraha

It is perhaps the element of suffering in satyagraha which remains most obscure to the Western mind. *Tapasya* in the Indian ethos connotes certain value in suffering—that of purification. Suffering is not valued for its own sake, but is held to promote non-attachment from the insistent claims of the body, to emphasize the spirit as superior to the material and the physical. The self-suffering of satyagraha serves yet another function. It is effective to the extent to which it demonstrates sincerity and cuts through the rationalized defenses of the opponent. Willingness to make the sacrifice of life is the ultimate in non-cooperation, just as it is the ultimate price to be paid in violent conflict. The considered willingness to suffer—or to endure—in the satyagraha approach is the step beyond the appeal to reason which, though reason persists throughout, dominates the earlier steps of satyagraha. Suffering operates in the satyagraha strategy as a tactic for cutting through the rational defenses which the opponent may have built in opposing the initial efforts of rational persuasion through the clear statement and the argument of the satyagrahi position. This process may be referred to as catharsis.* It achieves shift in focus, an alteration of the field of

* See Naomi Mitchison, *The Moral Basis of Politics* (London: Constable and Co., [1938]), Chapter III and also pp. 286-288 for a treatment of a similar appeal in political action.

vision. Mitchison[44] describes the role of tragedy, from the Greek drama to the social and political myth, as effecting this type of shifting of emphasis for one who witnesses it—of "enlarging or altering his field so that he becomes aware of morality." It may be sufficiently pertinent to our discussion of the significance of satyagraha for political theory to add Mitchison's comment in the course of her treatment of tragedy:

> The same kind of thing [catharsis and conversion] . . . happens to those who are in some way devoted, but not in the end actually sacrificed: the priest, the ritual king, the political leader . . . even the writer. There is a hint here of a solution to our problem about the tendency of political parties to become immoral. It may be that leaders and led should always have this "tragic drama" relation between them: that no leader should be tolerable to the led unless he or she has made the act of acceptance, has experienced the change of focus . . . and is prepared if necessary to be the sacrifice. As it is, a certain number of leaders have done this, to some extent at least, but not all. . . . [the led] should insist on their leaders' personal preparedness for all risks, and should also insist on their being in a fairly constant state of catharsis—that is to say, of thinking and acting in the external field, because of moral reasons. . . . this would be a very efficient way of stopping oligarchical tendencies in political parties, and, in general, of keeping them alive.[46]

It is a similar function which the self-suffering of satyagraha serves. When appeal to reason through the persistent efforts of rational argument have failed to persuade the opponent, where the conflict challenges the basic truth-concepts of the satyagraha position, the further course of satyagraha, including suffering, acts as a shock treatment—a dramatization of the satyagrahi position. One should observe that in the usual mode of violent conflict, preparation for sacrifice is also implied. That the immediate objective of violent action is to inflict rather than to endure suffering does not detract from the preparation and, indeed, the realistic expectation of suffering. Moreover, the loss of life and injuries sustained by satyagrahis in conducting non-violent action campaigns is likely to be less than those sustained in violent combat. A comparison of campaigns of civil disobedience which remained non-violent with others in which satyagraha deteriorated into violence, indicates significantly greater incidence of injury and death in the latter cases.

Ends-Means as Convertible Terms

Coming once again to the implications of satyagraha for political theory, a final word may be said about the ends-means concept. If the dichotomy between ends and means is logically tenable, the most acute problem for social and political thought is their reconciliation on the field of action. "The travel-image," T. V. Smith observes in his provocative article, "Democracy and Humany Destiny,"[46]

> explains man's inveterate subserviency to the distinction between means and ends. Anything for the sake of something else, if the something else be both future and roseate. . . . How far this travel-image can lead men astray from both reason and benevolence is seen luridly in communism, though communism but exaggerates a tendency resident in every political 'ism.' The Marxist end—a classless society—is made so glorious that it always recedes, like a lovely mirage, to keep from being dissipated through any concrete approach. The utopianism of communism but warns us of a dangerous element in all our natures.

Nowhere is the problem of means and ends more serious than in the consideration of the conduct of conflict. Political thought has, on the whole, ignored the central problem of means—the development of a technique of action which, in the hands of individual members of a society, can be used for the constructive resolution of conflict. Where political theory has attended the problem, it has been satisfied to rely ultimately on the admittedly unsatisfactory means of violent force; or, as in the case of Marxist thought, it has attempted to bridge the gap by introducing a determinist philosophy which operates in an abstract realm to reconcile oppositional forces by effecting a predetermined, inevitable synthesis in which human individuals are inescapably acting as puppets pulled by the strings of their economic circumstance on their peculiar stage of advancing history. For Marxist thought—as for Fascist—violence has sufficed for a means in the hands of individuals. For the Liberal Democratic political thinker, on the other hand, as for certain other political theorists, violence has not been enough—but his efforts have been only to mitigate, and not to supplant, violent force. The fault has been largely that of false analysis. Device can never succeed as surrogate for technique. The engineer must be flanked by the scientist on the one hand, and the construction worker on the other. To build the tools of democratic control is one necessary step. But to what purpose? The dynamics of a creative technique which takes not its end to be preservation of a static way-of-life, or triumph of a stable system, but which proceeds as a means which assumes the proportion of an end in itself, a means which is at once constructive and creative and which embraces changing ends: this is the need which Liberal Democratic theory has yet to fulfill.

In the realm of political philosophy, as on the field of action, the dynamic technique of satyagraha suggests a reexamination of the means-ends relationship. Satyagraha, claiming to be more than means, to be, indeed, end-creating, introduces a dynamic element with challenging implications for political method. If the dichotomy of ends and means is yet meaningful, satyagraha confronts the cry of Spengler that man needs above all a noble end, with the inerrant proposition that what political man needs is not a noble end, but constructive, creative means.

From among the great thinkers within the Liberal Democratic tradition have, indeed, come suggestions which could well point the way towards the development of a philosophy of conflict consonant with the "ends-in-view" of Liberal Democracy — were they to be pressed further and carried into yet other dimensions. Such for example, is the contribution of John Dewey, whose discourse on social inquiry has implications far beyond logic and bears directly upon the development of a technique of action in conflict situations. Dewey has argued that

> Only recognition in both theory and practice that ends to be attained (ends-in-view) are of the nature of hypotheses and that hypotheses have to be formed and tested in strict correlativity with existential conditions as means, can alter current habits of dealing with social issues.[47]

The treatment of "ends-in-view" as hypotheses and as "procedural means" was, for Dewey, essential to any social scientific enquiry. Such a treatment is also essential to the formulation of a constructive philosophy of conflict. Dewey has further pointed up the fallacy in accepting ends as fixed and has emphasized the dangers of basing human action upon "ends-in-themselves." It is within human action, he suggests, that "ends arise and function."[48] But, whereas Dewey has called attention to the need for considering means and ends as "two ways of regarding the same actuality" and has insisted that ends be developed with the fullest consideration of existential circumstance, he has stopped short of that step which could lead to a yet more rewarding approach to a philosophy of action. The ends-means relationship, viewed from this other perspective requires a shift in focus. It is only when means themselves are understood to be—and designed to be — more than instrumental, to be, in fine, *creative* that the next step will be taken in the evolvement of a constructive philosophy of conflict.

The search for constructive, creative means has been

pressed forward in fields of enquiry peripheral to the study of politics. The political philosopher who would pursue the search for an adequate technique of action can view the Gandhian philosophy of conflict as little more than a point of departure. He must bring to bear upon this central problem the findings of his colleagues regarding conflict on very different levels of human experience. The complexities of modern society, the advances in techniques of human organization, the intensifying pressures created by the human mind and spirit which continue to press beyond the known to ever-extending frontiers of the unknown — these complexities, advances, and pressures demand that the search be carried into yet other dimensions. Inevitable conflict and the threat of uncontrolled violence are conditions of the human circumstance. Man grows increasingly concerned over the dangers which freight his ventures into violence. But it is not enough that he should take unreasoned flight from violence. The Gandhian experiments suggest that if man is to free himself from fear and threat alike, he pause in his flight from violence to set himself the task of its conquest.

NOTES

CHAPTER I

1. For a scholarly review of the elements involved in civil disobedience see David Spitz, "Democracy and the Problem of Civil Disobedience," *The American Political Science Review*, June 1954, pp. 386-403.

2. For a discussion of Sarvodaya and the Bhoodan movement see Margaret W. Fisher and Joan V. Bondurant, *Indian Approaches to a Socialist Society* (Berkeley: Indian Press Digests, 1956).

3. They are: the autobiography, *The Story of My Experiments with Truth*, translated from the original in Gujarati by Mahadev Desai (Ahmedabad: Navajivan, 1940); *Satyagraha in South Africa*, translated from the Gujarati by Valji Govindji Desai (Madras: S. Ganesan, 1938); *Hind Swaraj or Indian Home Rule* (Ahmedabad: Navajivan, 1938); *Key to Health*, translated by Sushila Nayyar (Ahmedabad: Navajivan, 1948).

4. *E.g.*, *Non-Violence in Peace & War* (Ahmedabad: Navajivan, 1942), a collection of articles treating the subject non-violence; and *Delhi Diary: Prayer Speeches from 10-9-'47 to 30-1-'48* (Ahmedabad: Navajivan [1948]), a chronological collection of Gandhi's prayer speeches from September 1947 to January 1948.

5. *Indian Opinion* (Phoenix, Natal); *Young India* (Ahmedabad); *Harijan* (Ahmedabad).

6. Gandhi, *Satyagraha in South Africa*, p. 172.

7. See prayer speeches recorded in Gandhi, *Delhi Diary: Prayer Speeches from 10-9-'47 to 30-1-'48, passim.*

8. I have taken these definitions, only slightly modified, from Theodore Paullin, *Introduction to Non-Violence* (Philadelphia: The Pacifist Research Bureau, 1944), p. 6.

9. *Loc.cit.*

10. *Cf.* Krishnalal Shridharani, *War Without Violence: A Study of Gandhi's Method and Its Accomplishments* (New York: Harcourt, Brace, 1939), p. 292.

11. Clarence Marsh Case, *Non-Violent Coercion: A Study in Methods of Social Pressure* (London: George Allen & Unwin, 1923), pp. 404-405.

12. *Cf.* Webster's definition.

13. Case, *op.cit.*, p. 3.

CHAPTER II

1. On 9 January 1920. For the exchange between Lord Hunter and Gandhi, and Sir Chimanlal Setalwad and Gandhi during this examina-

tion, see D. G. Tendulkar, *Mahatma*, Vol. I (Bombay: Jhaveri and Tendulkar, 1952), pp. 340-343.

2. M. K. Gandhi, *Speeches and Writings of Mahatma Gandhi* (4th ed.; Madras: Natesan [n.d.]), p. 506.

3. Jag Parvesh Chander, ed., *Teachings of Mahatma Gandhi* (Lahore: The Indian Printing Works, 1945), p. 494.

4. Gandhi, *Young India*, November 17, 1921. Also Tendulkar, *op.cit.*, Vol. II, p. 98.

5. Tendulkar, *op.cit.*, Vol. II, p. 249.

6. *Ibid.*, p. 312.

7. *Ibid.*, Vol. III, p. 176.

8. N. K. Bose, *Studies in Gandhism* (2nd ed., Calcutta: Indian Associated Publishing Co., 1947), p. 269.

9. M. K. Gandhi, *An Autobiography or The Story of My Experiments with Truth*, translated from the original in Gujarati by Mahadev Desai (Ahmedabad: Navajivan, 1940), p. 4.

10. From a letter to P. G. Mathew, 9 July 1932, as quoted in *Harijan*, 27 March, 1949, p. 26.

11. April 3, 1924 as quoted in Chander, *op.cit.*, p. 266.

12. Tendulkar, *op.cit.*, Vol. I, p. 342. This text also appears in *Young India, 1919-1922* (Madras: S. Ganesan, 1922), pp. 33-36.

13. Translated from Gujarati in *Harijan*, July 18, 1948. The passage in Hindi occurs in Gandhi, *Satyagraha Ashram ka Itihas*, translated from the original in Gujarati into Hindi by Ramnarayan Choudhuri (Ahmedabad: Navajivan, 1948), p. 13.

14. *Young India*, December 25, 1925, as quoted in Chander, *op.cit.*, pp. 559-560.

15. See Louis Renou, "Gandhi and Indian Civilization" in Kshitis Roy, ed., *Gandhi Memorial Peace Number* (Santiniketan [India]: The Visva-Bharati Quarterly, 1949), pp. 230-238.

16. *Indian Thought and Its Development*, Mrs. Charles E. B. Russell, tr. (London: Hodder and Stoughton, 1936), p. 79.

17. M. K. Gandhi, *From Yeravda Mandir: Ashram Observances*, translated from the original Gujarati by Valji Govindji Desai (3rd ed., Ahmedabad: Navajivan, 1945), p. 7.

18. *Young India*, January 19, 1921, as quoted in Chander, *op.cit.*, p. 412.

19. Gandhi, *From Yeravda Mandir: Ashram Observances*, p. 8.

20. *Ibid.*, p. 19.

21. From an address to the YMCA, Madras, February 16, 1916, as quoted in Chander, *op.cit.*, pp. 405-406.

22. *Young India*, August 11, 1920, as quoted in Chander, *op.cit.*, pp. 409-410.

23. *Young India*, July 9, 1925, as quoted in Chander, *op.cit.*, p. 352.

24. *Young India*, June 12, 1922, as quoted in Chander, *op.cit.*, p. 352.

25. M. K. Gandhi, *Non-Violence in Peace & War* (2nd ed., Ahmedabad: Navajivan, 1944), p. 49.

26. M. K. Gandhi, *Satyagraha in South Africa*, translated from the Gujarati by Valji Govindji Desai (Madras: S. Ganesan, 1928), p. 175.

27. *Loc.cit.*

28. *Ibid.*, p. 179.

29. *Young India*, August 11, 1920, as quoted in Chander, *op.cit.*, p. 408.

30. *Young India*, October 31, 1929.

31. *Harijan*, July 20, 1935, as quoted in Chander, *op.cit.*, pp. 417-418.

32. *Harijan*, September 1, 1940, as quoted in Chander, *op.cit.*, p. 422.

33. Gandhi, *Non-Violence in Peace & War*, p. 360.

34. Eric Fromm, *Escape from Freedom* (New York, Toronto: Rinehart, 1941), p. 268.

35. From Gandhi's address to the All-India Congress Committee, following the adoption of the famous "Quit India" Resolution, 8 August 1942. Tendulkar, *op.cit.*, Vol. VI, p. 199.

36. *Harijan*, February 1, 1942, as quoted in Chander, *op.cit.*, p. 321.

37. Gandhi, *Non-Violence in Peace & War*, pp. 390-391.

38. Ludwig Feuerbach, *The Essence of Christianity*, Marion Evans, tr. (London: John Chapman, 1854), p. 157.

39. From an address to the YMCA, Madras, February 16, 1916, quoted in Chander, *op.cit.*, pp. 405-406.

40. M. K. Gandhi, *Delhi Diary: Prayer Speeches from 10-9-'47 to 30-1-'48* (Ahmedabad: Navajivan, 1948), p. 58.

41. *Harijan*, January 28, 1939, as quoted in Chander, *op.cit.*, p. 320.

CHAPTER III

1. *Harijan*, March 11, 1939, as quoted by N. K. Bose, *Studies in Gandhism* (2nd ed., Calcutta: Indian Associated Publishing Co., 1947), p. 159.

2. *Harijan*, July 26, 1942.

3. *Harijan*, October 13, 1940, as quoted by N. K. Bose, *op.cit.*, p. 157.

4. These rules have been adapted and elaborated from N. K. Bose, *op.cit.*, p. 175.

5. These points are paraphrased from D. G. Tendulkar's account, *Mahatma*, Vol. III (Bombay: Jhaveri and Tendulkar, 1952), p. 17.

6. A similar set of progressive steps have been listed in Krishnalal Shridharani's classic work *War Without Violence* (New York: Harcourt, Brace, 1939). See pp. 5-42.

7. For a description of this movement, see *Indian Press Digests*, Vol. II, No. 7, Margaret W. Fisher and Joan V. Bondurant, eds. (Berkeley: Institute of East Asiatic Studies of the University of California, 1955), pp. 64-80.

8. The data used in this outline have been abstracted from the following sources: C. F. Andrews, *Mahatma Gandhi's Ideas* (New York: Macmillan, 1930). Andrews was present during this struggle and therefore writes as an eye witness. R. R. Diwakar, *Satyagraha: Its Technique and History* (Bombay: Hind Kitabs, 1946), p. 115; Richard B. Gregg, *The Power of Non-Violence* (rev. ed., London: George Routledge and Sons, Ltd., 1938): Files of *Young India* during the period of the movement; Correspondence exchanged between the author and the following: The Hon. R. R. Diwakar, Richard R. Keithahn, and Pyarelal (Nayyar).

9. See Gandhi, *Young India 1924-26* (New York: The Viking Press, 1927), for a description of the road as public.

10. *Ibid.*, p. 857.

11. The data for this outline have been abstracted from the following sources: Mahadev Desai, *The Story of Bardoli: Being a History of the Bardoli Satyagraha of 1928 and Its Sequel* (Ahmedabad: Navajivan, 1929). This intimate record of the Bardoli campaign is credited by Indian authorities with primary authenticity. Mahadev Desai acted as one of three representatives for the peasants at the time of the Broomfield Committee enquiry which followed the satyagraha. The appendix to this work includes the following documents which supply further critical data: Notification of the Government of Bombay (May 21, 1928) to the occupants of land in Bardoli *taluka* and Valod *mahal*; The reply of Sir Leslie Wilson to K. M. Munshi (May 29, 1928); Speech of the Governor of Bombay in the Legislative Council (July 23, 1928). Gregg, *op.cit.*; G. N. Dhawan, *The Political Philosophy of Mahatma Gandhi* (Bombay: The Popular Book Depot, 1946); Diwakar, *op.cit.*, B. Pattabhi Sitaramayya, *The History of the Indian National Congress: (1885-1935)* (Madras: Working Committee of the Congress, 1935); *The Indian Year Book, 1929*, Sir Stanley Reed, S. T. Sheppard, eds. (Bombay: Bennett, Coleman, 1929); *The Indian Quarterly Register*, Nripendra Nath Mitra, ed. (Calcutta: Annual Register Office, 1930?), Vol. II, July-December, 1928, Vol. I, January-June, 1929; *Jawaharlal Nehru: An Autobiography* (London: John Lane, The Bodley Head, reprint with add. chapter, 1942). See also, *Times of India* for the period March to August 1928 for pro-government and anti-satyagraha opinion on the Bardoli dispute.

12. Data for this outline have been abstracted from the following sources: M. K. Gandhi, *An Autobiography or The Story of My Experiments with Truth*, translated from the original in Gujarati by Mahadev Desai (Ahmedabad: Navajivan, 1940); Mahadev Haribhai Desai, *A Righteous Struggle: A Chronicle of the Ahmedabad Textile Labourers' Fight for Justice*, translated from Gujarati by Somnath P. Dave, edited by Bharatan Kumarappa (Ahmedabad: Navajivan, 1951). Appended to this work are full texts of: (a) the statement on behalf of the workers, (b) the statement on behalf of the mill-owners, (c) the arbitrator's decision, (d) Gandhi's explanation regarding the struggle and his fast,

(e) leaflets circulated during the movement. Diwakar, *op.cit.*; *Indian Labour Gazette*, Government of India, Ministry of Labour, Labour Bureau, Vol. VIII, No. 9, March 1951 (New Delhi: 1951); R. N. Bose, *Gandhian Technique and Tradition in Industrial Relations* (Calcutta: All India Institute of Social Welfare and Business Management, 1956).

13. P. 348.

14. Dhawan, *op.cit.*, pp. 239-240.

15. The data for this outline were abstracted from the following sources: Andrews, *op.cit.*; N. K. Bose, *Studies in Gandhism*; Winston S. Churchill, *India: Speeches and an Introduction* (London: Thornton Butterworth, 1931); *Congress Presidential Addresses from the Silver to the Golden Jubilee: Full Text of the Presidential Addresses from 1911 to 1934* (Madras: Natesan Second Series, 1934); Sir John Cumming, ed., *Political India, 1832-1932, A Co-operative Survey of a Century* (London: Humphrey Milford, 1932); Diwakar, *op.cit.*; Gandhi, *An Autobiography or The Story of My Experiments with Truth*; *India in 1919: A Report Prepared for Presentation to Parliament in Accordance with the Requirements of the 26th Section of the Government of India Act* by L. F. Rushbrook Williams (Calcutta: Home Department, Government of India, 1920); Nehru, *An Autobiography*; *Young India, 1919-1922*, Vols. I and II (Madras: S. Ganesan, 1922); Sitaramayya, *op.cit.*

16. *Congress Presidential Addresses*, p. 432.

17. *Ibid.*, p. 433.

18. The data for this outline were abstracted from the following sources: Robert Bernays, *"Naked Faquir"* (New York: H. Holt, 1932); Glorney Bolton, *The Tragedy of Gandhi* (London: Allen & Unwin, 1934); *Congress Presidential Addresses*; Sir Reginald Coupland, *The Indian Problem: Report on the Constitutional Problem in India* (New York, etc.: Oxford University Press, 1944); Cumming, *op.cit.*; Diwakar, *op.cit.*; Negley Farson, "Indian Hate Lyric" in Eugene Lyons, ed., *We Cover the World*, by fifteen foreign correspondents (New York: Harcourt, Brace, 1937); Gregg, *op.cit.*; *India in 1930-31: A Statement Prepared for Presentation to Parliament in Accordance with the Requirements of the 26th Section of the Government of India Act* (5 and 6 Geo. V, Chap. 61) (Calcutta: Government of India Central Publishing Branch, 1932); Alan Campbell Johnson, *Viscount Halifax, A Biography* (London: Robert Hale, 1941); Webb Miller, *I Found No Peace: The Journal of a Foreign Correspondent* (New York: The Literary Guild, 1936); *The Indian Annual Register*, Nripendra Nath Mitra, ed. (Calcutta: Annual Register Office, 1930 and 1931), Vols. I and II, 1930, Vols. I and II, 1931; Nehru, *An Autobiography*; *The New York Times*, for this period; Sitaramayya, *op.cit.*; G. C. Sondhi, ed., *To the Gates of Liberty: Congress Commemoration Volume* (Calcutta: Swadesh Bharati, 1948); *Young India*, for this period; Correspondence between the author and R. R. Diwakar, Pyarelal (Nayyar), and R. R. Keithahn.

19. Nehru, *An Autobiography*, p. 209.
20. In a letter to the author, 17 October 1951.

CHAPTER IV

1. Vincent Sheean records that Gandhi mentioned this to him during his last interview. Sheean's article, "Gandhiji's Last Discourse," *Bombay Chronicle Weekly*, February 22, 1948, p. 6.
2. In an address to a missionary conference in Madras. M. K. Gandhi, *Speeches and Writings of Mahatma Gandhi* (4th ed., Madras: Natesan, n.d.), p. 337.
3. Jawaharlal Nehru, *The Discovery of India* (New York: John Day, 1946), pp. 73-74.
4. See Hari Mohan Bhattacharyya, *The Principles of Philosophy* (Calcutta: University of Calcutta, 1944), p. 147.
5. Sushil Kumar Maitra, *The Ethics of the Hindus* (Calcutta: University of Calcutta, 1925), pp. 7-10.
6. *Ibid.*, p. 8.
7. Gandhi in *Young India*, May 7, 1925.
8. Gandhi in *Harijan*, May 8, 1937.
9. Gandhi in *Young India*, December 6, 1928.
10. Maitra, *op.cit.*, p. 11.
11. Gandhi, *Modern Review*, October 1916, quoted in *Speeches and Writings of Mahatma Gandhi*, p. 345.
12. Gandhi in *Young India*, August 11, 1920.
13. Nehru, *The Discovery of India*, p. 100.
14. *Harijan*, July 6, 1940.
15. S. Radhakrishnan, *Indian Philosophy* (London: George Allen & Unwin, Indian edition, 1940), Vol. I, p. 107.
16. *Ibid.*, pp. 215-216.
17. *Ibid.*, p. 244.
18. Gandhi in *Young India*, October 18, 1928.
19. Translation of the original in Gujarati by Mahadev Desai (Ahmedabad: Navajivan, 1946), cited hereafter as Gandhi-Desai.
20. *Ibid.*, p. 129.
21. *Ibid.*, p. 123.
22. See *ibid.*, pp. 123-124.
23. In his article, "Gandhiji's Last Discourse."
24. Gandhi-Desai, *op.cit.*, p. 130.
25. *The Forum*, LXXXV (May, 1931), p. 287.
26. *Jawaharlal Nehru: An Autobiography* (London: John Lane The Bodley Head, reprint with add. chapter, 1942), p. 72.
27. C. F. Andrews, *Mahatma Gandhi's Ideas* (New York: Macmillan, 1930), p. 61.
28. *Young India*, September 29, 1920.
28a. Tendulkar, *op.cit.*, Vol. II, p. 312.

29. Louis Renou, "Gandhi and Indian Civilization," *Gandhi Memorial Peace Number*, ed. Kshitis Roy (Santiniketan: Visva-Bharati Quarterly, 1949), p. 231.

30. Max Weber, *The Theory of Social and Economic Organization*, A. M. Henderson, tr., Talcott Parsons, ed. (New York: Oxford University Press, 1947), pp. 358-359.

31. *Ibid.*, pp. 359-360.

32. *Young India*, May 25, 1921.

33. *Ibid.*, September 11, 1924.

34. *Ibid.*, March 17, 1927.

35. *Harijan*, March 2, 1940.

36. *Ibid.*, March 30, 1940.

37. Weber, *op.cit.*, p. 361.

38. The Congress was founded in 1885.

39. *Young India*, June 25, 1925.

40. *Ibid.*, October 3, 1929.

41. Weber, *op.cit.*, p. 328.

42. See S. N. Agarwal, *Gandhian Constitution for Free India*, forward by Mahatma Gandhi (Allahabad: Kitabistan, 1946).

43. See Subhas C. Bose, *The Indian Struggle, 1920-1934* (London: Wishart & Co., 1935), p. 327.

44. See pp. 53-64 of Chapter III above for an outline of the Bardoli satyagraha campaign.

45. See p. 86 of Chapter III above.

46. Pp. 72-73.

47. *Loc.cit.*

48. Arun Chandra Das Gupta, *Non-Violence The Invincible Power, Its Primordiality, Practicability and Precedents* (2nd ed., Calcutta: Khadi Pratisthan, 1946), pp. 53-54.

49. *Young India*, March 5, 1925, in the article "God and Congress."

50. Andrews, *op.cit.*, pp. 62-63.

51. Quoted in *ibid.*, pp. 73-74.

52. Satya Parkash, ed., *Hindu Rashtravad: An Exposition of the Ideology and Immediate Programme of Hindu Rashtra as Outlined by Swatantrayaveer V. D. Savarkar* (Rohtak: published by Dr. Satya Parkash, 1945), p. 146.

53. Syama Prasad Mookerjee, then leader of the Hindu Mahasabha, quoted on the jacket of Parkash, *op.cit.*

54. Parkash, *op.cit.*, p. 177.

55. See *ibid.*, *passim*, especially pp. 203-206.

56. *Gandhi-Jinnah Talks: Text of Correspondence and Other Relevant Matter, July-October, 1944* (New Delhi: Hindustan Times, 1944).

57. William Crooke, *The Tribes and Castes of the North-Western Provinces and Oudh* (Calcutta: Office of the Superintendent of Government Printing, 1896), Vol. IV, pp. 167-168.

58. See *The Geographical Review*, Vol. XVI, April 1926, for a description of the land of the Pathans at a time when the non-violent movement against the British was underway.

59. G. FitzGerald-Lee, "Tribes of the Tirah," *Eastern World*, Vol. III, March 1949.

60. Louis Fischer, *The Life of Mahatma Gandhi* (London: Jonathan Cape, 1941), p. 370.

61. Pyarelal, *A Pilgrimage of Peace: Gandhi and Frontier Gandhi Among N. W. F. Pathans* (Ahmedabad: Navajivan, 1950), p. 118.

62. The translation of the pledge here given is that of Wilfred Cantwell Smith, *Modern Islam in India: A Social Analysis* (Lahore: Minerva Book Shop, 1943), pp. 258-259, from a leaflet, issued by the movement, which Professor Smith notes as being in his possession, p. 357.

63. Pyarelal, *op.cit.*, p. 37.

64. *Loc.cit.*

65. "The Struggle with Congress," *Roundtable*, Vol. XXII, March 1932, p. 328; Lt.-Colonel The Hon. C. B. Birdwood, *A Continent Experiments* (London, New York, etc.: Skeffington & Sons, 1945?), p. 134; *India in 1931-32: A Statement Prepared for Presentation to Parliament in Accordance with the Requirements of the 26th Section of the Government of India Act* (5 and 6 Geo. V, Chap. 61) (Calcutta: Government of India Central Publications Branch, 1933), p. 22.

66. Smith, *op.cit.*, p. 255.

67. The Quran xlii:39. See *The Koran* (translated into English from the original Arabic by George Sale, London: Frederick Warne, n.d.), p. 472.

68. Smith, *op.cit.*, p. 259.

69. Halidé Edib, *Inside India* (London: Allen & Unwin, 1937), p. 334.

70. Two former residents of the Northwest Frontier Province, one a member of the Khudai Khidmatgar, supplied information relating to the use of symbols and slogans.

71. *India in 1930-31: A Statement Prepared for Presentation to Parliament in Accordance with the Requirements of the 26th Section of the Government of India Act* (5 and 6 Geo. V, Chap. 61) (Calcutta: Government of India Central Publication Branch, 1932), p. 129.

72. *Ibid.*, p. 125.

73. "The Unrest on the Indian Frontier," *Roundtable*, Vol. XXI, March 1931, p. 351.

74. "The Struggle with Congress," *Roundtable*, Vol. XXII, March 1932, p. 328.

75. See also G. C. Sondhi, ed., *To the Gates of Liberty: Congress Commemoration Volume* (Calcutta: Swadesh Bharati Ltd., 1948), p. 211.

76. J. Coatman, *Years of Destiny: India 1926-1932* (London: Jonathan Cape, 1932), p. 284.

77. See also B. Pattabhi Sitaramayya, *The History of the Indian National Congress: 1885-1935* (Madras: The Working Committee of the Congress, 1935), pp. 691-697.

78. Coatman, *op.cit.*, p. 283.

79. Quoted by Robert Bernays from his own diary, *"Naked Faquir"* (New York: H. Holt 1932), p. 317.

80. See *The Legislative Assembly Debates* (Official Report), Vol. IV, 1930 (Simla: Government of India Press, 1931), No. 6, p. 237.

81. See the correspondence between Gandhi and Lord Willingdon, the Viceroy, regarding such ordinances. M. K. Gandhi, *India's Case for Swaraj: Being Select Speeches, Writings, Interviews, et cetera of Mahatma Gandhi in England and India: September 1931 to January 1932*, Waman P. Kabadi, ed. (Bombay: Yeshanand & Co., 1932), pp. 25ff.

82. Quoted by Pyarelal, *op.cit.*, p. 41.

83. Pyarelal, *op.cit.*, p. 123.

84. *Ibid.*, p. 139.

85. Edib, *op.cit.*, p. 334.

86. *Ibid.*, p. 336.

87. R. Coupland, *The Indian Problem: Report on the Constitutional Problem in India* (New York, London, etc.: Oxford University Press, 1944), Part II, p. 122.

88. Pyarelal, *op.cit.*, pp. 117-118.

89. Edib, *op.cit.*, p. 338.

CHAPTER V

1. On 19 January 1946 at Sodepur, near Calcutta.

2. Jawaharlal Nehru, *Towards a New Revolution*, Youth Congress Series, No. 2, New Delhi, pp. 5-6, 13-14.

3. *Harijan*, February 11, 1939.

4. This statement of the four criteria of conservatism, only slightly modified, has been adapted from George Sabine, *A History of Political Theory* (New York: Henry Holt, 1947), p. 617.

5. Roberto Michels, "Conservatism," *Encyclopaedia of Social Sciences*, Vol. IV, pp. 230-232.

6. For a detailed account of a national political structure built on Panchayats see S. N. Agarwal, *The Gandhian Plan of Economic Development for India* (Bombay: Padma, 1944), and S. N. Agarwal, *Gandhian Constitution for Free India*, with a foreword by Mahatma Gandhi (Allahabad: Kitabistan, 1946).

7. See Gandhi's prayer speech of October 7, 1947, in M. K. Gandhi, *Delhi Diary: Prayer Speeches from 10-9-'47 to 30-1-'48* (Ahmedabad: Navajivan, 1948), p. 71.

8. For a brief review of these characteristics, see Radha Kumud Mookerji, *Nationalism in Hindu Culture* (London, Los Angeles: Theosophical Publishing House, 1921).

9. *Harijan*, July 26, 1942.

10. For an analysis of the traditional system see Henry Sumner Maine, *Village-Communities in the East and West* (London: J. Murray, 1871), p. 216.

11. For an outline of a Panchayat federative system on Gandhian lines see: Agarwal, *The Gandhian Plan of Economic Development for India*, p. 103.

12. *Young India*, September 19, 1929. See also Gandhi's *Delhi Diary: Prayer Speeches from 10-9-'47 to 30-1-'48*, p. 71, for a similar statement on Rama Raj made shortly before his assassination.

13. See *Young India*, July 19, 1924; *Young India*, November 27, 1924; *Young India*, October 1, 1931; M. K. Gandhi, *An Autobiography or The Story of My Experiments with Truth*, translated from the original in Gujarati by Mahadev Desai (2nd ed., Ahmedabad: Navajivan, 1940), pp. 404-405.

14. M. K. Gandhi, *From Yeravada Mandir*, translated from the original Gujarati by Valji Govindji Desai (3rd ed., Ahmedabad: Navajivan, 1932), Chapter XI.

15. *Young India*, March 5, 1925.

16. *Harijan*, February 10, 1934.

17. *Young India*, August 28, 1924.

18. *Ibid.*, January 9, 1930.

19. *Ibid.*, October 20, 1927.

20. *Ibid.*, May 28, 1931.

21. *Harijan*, April 23, 1938.

22. M. K. Gandhi, *Constructive Programme: Its Meaning and Place* (2nd ed., new and enl., Ahmedabad: Navajivan, 1945), pp. 20-21.

23. *Harijan*, August 18, 1940.

24. See N. K. Bose, "An Interview with Mahatma Gandhi," *Modern Review*, Vol. LVIII, October, 1935. See also S. N. Agarwal's *The Gandhian Plan of Economic Development for India* for one view of the organizational result of Gandhian principles applied to the zamindari.

25. N. K. Bose, "An Interview with Mahatma Gandhi."

26. Quoted by G. N. Dhawan, *The Political Philosophy of Mahatma Gandhi* (Bombay: The Popular Book Depot, 1946), from *Young India*, Vol. II, p. 81.

27. *Young India*, November 15, 1928.

28. Gandhi, *An Autobiography or The Story of My Experiments with Truth*, p. 365.

29. See especially Benjamin Evans Lippincott, *Victorian Critics of Democracy* (Minneapolis: University of Minnesota Press, 1938), p. 59, note.

30. Tolstoy adopted the term "bread-labor" from the peasant writer Timofei Mikhailovich Bondarev whose work he introduced and elaborated.

31. *Loc.cit.*

32. Gandhi, *From Yeravada Mandir*, p. 50.

33. Quoted by Dhawan, *op.cit.*, p. 282, from *Young India*, Vol. II, pp. 435-436.

34. Dhawan, *op.cit.*, p. 282.

35. *Harijan*, June 22, 1935.

36. *Ibid.*, June 25, 1938.

37. Lippincott, *op.cit.*, p. 56.

38. *Ibid.*, p. 91.

39. *Young India*, March 26, 1931.

40. *Loc.cit.*

41. Edmund Burke, *Reflections on the Revolution in France* (Philadelphia: Young, Dobson, Carey, and Rice, 1792), pp. 100-101.

42. Edmund Burke, *An Appeal from the New to the Old Whigs, The Works of . . . Edmund Burke* (London: Thomas M'Lean, 1823), Vol. VI, p. 204.

43. *Mahadev Desai, With Gandhi in Ceylon: A Journal of the Tour,* with authorized version of all important speeches (Madras: Ganesan, 1928), p. 105.

44. *Young India*, February 9, 1921.

45. *Ibid.*, March 3, 1928.

46. *Harijan*, May 27, 1939.

47. *Ibid.*, February 1, 1942.

48. For pertinent comment on the philosophy of T. H. Green, see Sabine, *op.cit.*, p. 674 ff.

49. M. K. Gandhi, *Speeches and Writings of Mahatma Gandhi* (4th ed., Madras: Natesan, n.d.), p. 388.

50. See Sabine, *op.cit.*, p. 677.

51. *Young India*, August 13, 1925.

52. *The Metaphysical Theory of the State: A Criticism* (London: Allen & Unwin, 1918), p. 43.

53. Sir S. Radhakrishnan, *The Heart of Hindusthan* (5th ed., Madras: Natesan, 1945), pp. 17-18.

54. *Young India*, November 10, 1921.

55. *Ibid.*, September 13, 1919.

56. *Ibid.*, October 22, 1919.

57. See Karl Popper, *The Open Society and Its Enemies* (London: Routledge & Kegan Paul, 1949), Vol. II, p. 78.

58. Burke, *Reflections on the Revolution in France*, p. 53.

59. *Young India*, December 27, 1930.

60. Quoted from *Young India* by Jag Parvesh Chander, p. 72.

61. *Harijan*, February 13, 1937.

62. From his statement issued 4 November 1932 from Yeravada Prison, as it appears in *The Indian Social Reformer*, 12 November 1932, p. 165.

63. *Young India*, December 8, 1920.

64. N. K. Bose, "An Interview with Mahatma Gandhi."

65. *Harijan*, September 28, 1934.

66. *Young India*, September 22, 1927.

67. *Ibid.*, September 29, 1921.

68. *Ibid.*, September 8, 1920.

69. *Ibid.*, November 3, 1920.

70. *Ibid.*, April 24, 1924, and July 30, 1931.

71. *Young India*, Vol. II, p. 1029, as quoted in Dhawan, *op.cit.*, p. 295.

72. Dhawan, *op.cit.*

73. *Ibid.*, p. 3.

74. In *Harijan*, January 13, 1940, quoted by N. K. Bose, *Studies in Gandhism* (2nd ed., Calcutta: Indian Associated Publishing Co., 1947), p. 69.

75. Quoted in N. K. Bose, *Studies in Gandhism*, p. 69.

76. *Harijan*, February 1, 1942.

77. N. K. Bose, "An Interview with Mahatma Gandhi."

78. *Harijan*, May 27, 1939.

79. *La Capacité politique des classes ouvrières*, p. 124, as quoted by Henri de Lubac, *The Un-Marxian Socialist: A Study of Proudhon*, R. E. Scantlebury, tr. (New York: Sheed & Ward, 1948), pp. 214-215.

80. de Lubac, *op.cit.*, p. 215.

81. Proudhon's *La Capacité politique des classes ouvrières*, as quoted in de Lubac, *op.cit.*, p. 215.

82. Proudhon, *op.cit.*, p. 200, as quoted by de Lubac, *op.cit.*, p. 216.

83. William Godwin, *An Enquiry Concerning Political Justice and Its Influence on General Virtue and Happiness*, ed. by Raymond A. Preston (New York: Knopf, 1926), Vol. I, p. 120.

84. *Ibid.*, p. 129.

85. See F. E. L. Priestley, ed., *Enquiry Concerning Political Justice and Its Influence on Morals and Happiness by William Godwin*, critical introduction and notes (Toronto: University of Toronto, 1946), Vol. III, p. 49.

86. L. N. Tolstoi, *My Religion* (New York: T. Y. Crowell, 1885), p. 124.

87. Godwin, *op.cit.*, p. 100.

88. *Ibid.*, p. 105.

89. Priestley, *op.cit.*, p. 62.

90. See Gandhi, *Constructive Programme: Its Meaning and Place*, *passim*.

91. Eunice Minette Schuster, *Native American Anarchism: A Study of Left-Wing American Individualism*, Smith College Studies in History, Vol. XVII, Nos. 1-4 (Northampton, Massachusetts: Dept. of History of Smith College, 1932), p. 121.

92. S. Saklatvala and M. K. Gandhi, *Is India Different? The Class Struggle in India: Correspondence on the Indian Labour Movement*

and Modern Conditions (London: Communist Party of Great Britain, 1927), p. 23.

93. *Harijan*, November, 1934.

94. *Ibid.*, August 18, 1940.

95. Dhawan, *op.cit.*, p. 185.

96. Agarwal, *The Gandhian Plan of Economic Development for India*, p. 33.

97. Dhawan, *op.cit.*, p. 285.

98. *Loc.cit.*

99. *Harijan*, January 11, 1936.

100. *Young India*, August 18, 1920.

101. *Ibid.*, July 2, 1931.

102. Robert Ludlow, "The Gandhian Revolution," *The Catholic Worker* (New York), February, 1950.

103. Max Stirner, *The Ego and His Own*, tr. from the German by Steven T. Byington (London: A. C. Fifield; New York: E. C. Walker, 1912), p. 152.

104. Godwin, *op.cit.*, p. 96.

105. Robert Ludlow, *loc.cit.*

CHAPTER VI

1. Krishnalal Shridharani first used this phraseology. See *War Without Violence: A Study of Gandhi's Method and Its Accomplishments* (New York: Harcourt, Brace, 1939), p. 316.

2. Sidney Hook, *From Hegel to Marx: Studies in the Intellectual Development of Karl Marx* (London: Victor Gollancz Ltd., 1936), p. 72.

3. *Loc.cit.*

4. Cf. Karl Popper, *The Open Society and Its Enemies* (London: Routledge & Kegan Paul, 1949). Popper writes, Vol. II, p. 78: "Marx is responsible for the devastating influence of the historicist method of thought within the ranks of those who wish to advance the cause of the open society. . . . Marxism is a purely historical theory, a theory which aims at predicting the future course of economic and power-political developments and especially of revolutions."

5. Hook, *op.cit.*, p. 67.

6. Cf. Karl Mannheim, *Ideology and Utopia: An Introduction to the Sociology of Knowledge* (New York: Harcourt, Brace, 1949). Mannheim writes, p. 252: ". . . the divergent participants may also be approached with the intention of using each theoretical point of contact as an occasion for removing misunderstandings by ascertaining the source of the differences. This will bring out the varying presuppositions which are implied in the two respective perspectives as consequences of the two different social situations. In such cases, the sociologist of knowledge does not face his antagonist in the usual manner, according to which the other's arguments are dealt with directly. He seeks rather

to understand him by defining the total perspective and seeing it as a function of a certain social position." Mannheim is, of course, not concerned with activism, but his suggestion for the sociologist of knowledge is, on the intellectual level, parallel to the approach of the satyagrahi in a situation of conflict.

7. Ludwig Feuerbach, *The Essence of Christianity*, Marion Evans, tr. (London: John Chapman, 1854), p. 157.

8. Peter H. Odegard, "Needed: New Symbols of Peace," *Peace or War? A Conference*, H. S. Quigley, ed. (Minneapolis: University of Minnesota Press, 1937), p. 25.

9. George H. Sabine, *A History of Political Theory* (New York: Henry Holt, 1947), p. 617.

10. Edmund Burke, *An Appeal from the New to the Old Whigs, The Works of . . . Edmund Burke* (Boston: Wells and Lilly, 1826), Vol. III, p. 433.

11. *Ibid.*, p. 347.

12. John Emerich Edward Dalberg-Acton, First Baron Acton, *Essays on Freedom and Power*, selected and with introduction by Gertrude Himmelfarb (Boston: The Beacon Press, 1948), p. 193.

13. Edmund Burke, *Reflections on the Revolution in France, The Works of . . . Edmund Burke* (Boston: Wells and Lilly, 1826), Vol. III, p. 64.

14. Burke, *An Appeal from the New to the Old Whigs*, p. 402.

15. William Godwin, *An Enquiry Concerning Political Justice and Its Influence on General Virtue and Happiness*, edited by Raymond Preston (New York: Alfred Knopf, 1926), Vol. II, p. 66.

16. J. de Maistre, "Essai sur le Principe Générateur," *Oeuvres* (Paris: Migne, 1862), p. 116.

17. Burke, *Reflections on the Revolution in France*, p. 51.

18. *Ibid.*, p. 117.

19. *Ibid.*, p. 38.

20. *Ibid.*, p. 51.

21. *Ibid.*, p. 69.

22. See Thomas Stearns Eliot, *Notes toward the Definition of Culture* (New York: Harcourt, Brace, 1949).

23. ". . . il ferait du bourreau tous les éloges . . . 'C'est un etre sublime, nous dirait-il; c'est la pierre angulaire de la société; puisque le crime est venu habiter votre terre, et qu'il ne peut etre arreté que par le chatiment, otez du monde l'exécuteur, et tout ordre disparait avec lui. . . . Je suis donc persuadé que l'opinion l'environne de tout l'honneur dont il a besoin, et qui lui est du à si juste titre.'" Joseph de Maistre, *Les Soirées de Saint-Pétersburg* (Paris: Jean Gillequin, n.d.), p. 111.

24. William Archibald Dunning, *A History of Political Theories from Rousseau to Spencer* (New York: Macmillan, 1930), p. 175.

25. Burke, *Reflections on the Revolution in France*, p. 180.

26. Burke, *An Appeal from the New to the Old Whigs*, p. 438.

27. *Ibid.*, p. 372.

28. Burke, *Reflections on the Revolution in France*, p. 39.

29. Burke, *An Appeal from the New to the Old Whigs*, p. 366.

30. Burke, *Reflections on the Revolution in France*, pp. 47-48.

31. Dunning, *op.cit.*, p. 155.

32. Georg Wilhelm Friedrich Hegel, *Philosophy of Right*, translated by S. W. Dyde, *Hegel's Philosophy of Right* (London: G. Bell, 1896), p. 240.

33. *Ibid.*, p. 240.

34. *Loc.cit.*

35. "a) The power to fix and establish the universal. This is legislation. b) The power, which brings particular spheres and individual cases under the universal. This is the function of government. c) The function of the prince, as the subjectivity with which rests the final decision. In this function the other two are brought into an individual unity. It is at once the culmination and beginning of the whole. This is constitutional monarchy." *Ibid.*, p. 278.

"We have already regarded subjectivity as existing in the monarch, and in that capacity occupying the pinnacle of the state." *Ibid.*, p. 328.

36. Sabine, *op.cit.*, p. 641.

37. Hegel, *op.cit.*, p. 281.

38. A. D. Lindsay, *The Modern Democratic State* (London, New York [etc.]: Oxford University Press, 1943), Vol. I, p. 12.

38a. John Morley, *On Compromise* (London: Chapman and Hall, 1877), p. 184.

39. Morris Llewellyn Cooke, "The Quaker Way Wins New Adherents," *New York Times Magazine*, June 17, 1951, pp. 21ff.

40. *Ibid.*, p. 42.

41. *Ibid.*, p. 115.

42. *Ibid.*, p. 130.

43. See Aldous Leonard Huxley, *Ends and Means: An Inquiry into the Nature of Ideals and into the Methods Employed for Their Idealization* (London: Chatto and Windus, 1938), *passim*, for a stimulating discussion of this proposition.

44. Naomi Mitchison, *The Moral Basis of Politics* (London: Constable and Co., 1938), pp. 286-288.

45. *Ibid.*, p. 288.

46. T. V. Smith, "Democracy and Human Destiny," *Human Destiny*, Vol. I, 1951, p. 27ff.

47. John Dewey, *Logic, The Theory of Inquiry* (New York: Henry Holt and Company, 1949), p. 497.

48. See John Dewey, *Human Nature and Conduct* (New York: Henry Holt and Company, 1938), pp. 223-237.

BIBLIOGRAPHY OF WORKS CITED

BOOKS

ACTON, JOHN FRIEDRICH EDWARD DALBERG-. *Essays on Freedom and Power.* Selected and with introduction by Gertrude Himmelfarb. Boston: The Beacon Press, 1948.

AGARWAL, SHRIMAN NARAYAN. *Gandhian Constitution for Free India.* Foreword by Mahatma Gandhi. Allahabad: Kitabistan, 1946. 136 pp.

————. *The Gandhian Plan of Economic Development for India.* Foreword by Mahatma Gandhi. Bombay: Padma Publications, 1944. 115 pp.

AMEER ALI, SYED. *The Spirit of Islam or The Life and Teachings of Mohammed.* Calcutta: Lahiri, 1902. 419 pp.

ANDREWS, CHARLES FREER. *Mahatma Gandhi's Ideas.* New York: Macmillan, 1930. 348 pp.

BEER, SAMUEL. *The City of Reason.* Cambridge: Harvard University Press, 1949. 227 pp.

BERNAYS, ROBERT. *"Naked Faquir".* New York: Henry Holt, 1932. 335 pp.

BHATTACHARYYA, HARI MOHAN. *The Principles of Philosophy.* Calcutta: University of Calcutta, 1944. 428 pp.

BINGHAM, ALFRED MITCHELL. *The Technique of Democracy.* New York: Duell, Sloan and Pearce, 1942. 314 pp.

BIRDWOOD, C. B. *A Continent Experiments.* London and New York: Skeffington and Son, 1945. 252 pp.

BOLTON, GLORNEY. *The Tragedy of Ghandi.* London: Allen and Unwin, 1934. 326 pp.

BOSE, NIRMAL KUMAR. *Studies in Gandhism.* 2nd ed. Calcutta: India Associated Publishing Co., 1947. 354 pp.

BOSE, R. N. *Gandhian Technique and Tradition in Industrial Relations.* Calcutta: All India Institute of Social Welfare and Business Management, 1956. 228 pp.

BOSE, SUBHAS CHANDRA. *The Indian Struggle: 1920-1934.* London: Wishart, 1935. 353 pp.

BURKE, EDMUND. *Reflections on the Revolution in France.* Philadelphia: Young, Dobson, Carey, and Rice, 1792. 256 pp.

————. *The Works of The Right Honourable Edmund Burke.* Vol. III. Boston: Wells and Lilly, 1826.

————. *The Works of the Right Honourable Edmund Burke.* Vol. VI. London: Thomas M'Lean, 1823.

CASE, CLARENCE MARSH. *Non-Violent Coercion: A Study in Methods of Social Pressure.* London: Allen and Unwin, 1923. 414 pp.

CHURCHILL, WINSTON S. *India: Speeches and an Introduction.* London: Thornton Butterworth, 1931. 141 pp.

COATMAN, JOHN. *Years of Destiny: India. 1926-1932.* With a foreword by Lord Irwin of Kirby. London: Jonathan Cape, 1932. 384 pp.

COUPLAND, REGINALD. *The Indian Problem: Report on the Constitutional Problem in India. . . .* New York and London: Oxford University Press, 1944. 3 vols. in 1.

CROOKE, WILLIAM. *The Tribes and Castes of the North-Western Provinces and Oudh.* Calcutta: Office of the Superintendent of Government Printing, 1896. Vol. IV.

CUMMING, JOHN, ed. *Political India. 1832-1932: A Co-operative Survey of a Century.* London: Oxford University Press, 1932. 324 pp.

DAS GUPTA, ARUN CHANDRA. *Non-Violence the Invincible Power, Its Primordiality, Practicability and Precedents.* 2nd ed. Calcutta: Khadi Pratisthan, 1946. 130 pp.

DESAI, MAHADEV HARIBHAI. *The Gospel of Selfless Action or The Gita According to Gandhi.* Translation of the original in Gujarati with an additional introduction and commentary by Mahadev Desai. Ahmedabad: Navajivan, 1946. 390 + iv pp.

———. *A Righteous Struggle: A Chronicle of the Ahmedabad Textile Labourers' Fight for Justice.* Translated from Gujarati by Somnath P. Dave, edited by Bharatan Kumarappa. Ahmedabad: Navajivan, 1951. 97 pp.

———. *The Story of Bardoli: Being a History of the Bardoli Satyagraha of 1928 and Its Sequel.* Ahmedabad: Navajivan, 1929. 355 pp.

———. *With Gandhiji in Ceylon: A Journal of the Tour.* With authorized version of all important speeches. Madras: Ganesan, 1928. 159 pp.

DEWEY, JOHN. *Human Nature and Conduct, An Introduction to Social Psychology.* New York: Henry Holt and Company, 1938, 336 pp.

———. *Logic, The Theory of Inquiry.* New York: Henry Holt and Company, 1949. 546 pp.

DHAWAN, G. N. *The Political Philosophy of Mahatma Gandhi.* With a foreword by S. Radhakrishnan. Bombay: The Popular Book Depot, 1946. 329 pp.

DIWAKAR, R. R. *Satyagraha: Its Technique and History.* Foreword by Rajendra Prasad. Bombay: Hind Kitabs, 1946. 197 pp.

DUNNING, WILLIAM ARCHIBALD. *A History of Political Theories from Rousseau to Spencer.* New York: Macmillan, 1930. 446 pp.

EDIB, HALIDÉ. *Inside India.* London: Allen and Unwin, 1937. 368 pp.

ELIOT, THOMAS STEARNS. *Notes Towards the Definition of Culture.* 1st American ed. New York: Harcourt, Brace, 1949. 128 pp.

FEUERBACH, LUDWIG. *The Essence of Christianity.* Translated by Marion Evans. London: John Chapman, 1854. 340 pp.

FISCHER, LOUIS. *The Life of Mahatma Gandhi.* London: Jonathan Cape, 1951. 584 pp.

FISHER, MARGARET W. AND JOAN V. BONDURANT. *Indian Approaches to a Socialist Society.* Indian Press Digests Monograph No. 2. Berkeley (Institute of International Studies): University of California, 1956. 105 pp.

FROMM, ERICH. *Escape from Freedom.* New York and Toronto: Rinehart, 1941. 299 pp.

GANDHI, MOHANDAS KARAMCHAND. *An Autobiography or The Story of My Experiments with Truth.* Translated from the original in Gujarati by Mahadev Desai. 2nd ed. Ahmedabad: Navajivan, 1940. 405 pp.

————. *Constructive Programme: Its Meaning and Place.* Ahmedabad: Navajivan, 1941. 28 pp.

————. *Delhi Diary: Prayer Speeches from 10-9-'47 to 30-1-'48.* Ahmedabad: Navajivan, 1948. 392 pp.

————. *From Yeravda Mandir: Ashram Observances.* Translated from the original Gujarati by Valji Govindji Desai. 3rd ed. Ahmedabad: Navajivan, 1945. 67 pp.

————. *Hind Swaraj or Indian Home Rule.* Rev. ed. Ahmedabad: Navajivan, 1939. 68 pp.

————. *India's Case for Swaraj: Being Select Speeches, Writings, Interviews et cetera of Mahatma Gandhi in England and India. September 1931 to January 1932.* 2nd ed., edited by Waman P. Kabodi. Bombay: Yeshanand, 1932. 416 pp.

————. *Key to Health.* Translated by Sushila Nayyar. Ahmedabad: Navajivan, 1948. 83 pp.

————. *Non-Violence in Peace and War.* Ahmedabad: Navajivan, 1942. 551 pp.

————. *Satyagraha Ashram ka Itihas.* (In Hindi.) Translated from the original in Gujarati by Ramnarayan Chaudhuri. Ahmedabad: Navajivan, 1948.

————. *Satyagraha in South Africa.* Translated from the Gujarati by Valji Govindji Desai. Madras: Ganesan, 1948. 511 pp.

————. *Speeches and Writings of Mahatma Gandhi.* 4th ed. Madras: Natesan, n.d. 1072 pp.

————. *Teachings of Mahatma Gandhi.* Edited by Jag Parvesh Chander. Lahore: The Indian Printing Works, 1945. 620 pp.

GHOSHAL, U. N. *A History of Hindu Political Theories: from the Earliest Times to the End of the Seventeenth Century A.D.* London, Bombay (etc.): Humphrey Milford, Oxford University Press, 1927. 243 pp.

GODWIN, WILLIAM. *An Enquiry Concerning Political Justice, and Its Influence on General Virtue and Happiness.* Edited and abridged by Raymond A. Preston. New York: A. A. Knopf, 1926. 2 vols.

GREGG, RICHARD B. *The Power of Non-Violence.* Rev. ed. London: George Routledge, 1938. 295 pp.

HEGEL, GEORG WILHELM FRIEDRICH. *Philosophy of Right.* Translated by S. W. Dyde, *Hegel's Philosophy of Right.* London: G. Bell, 1896. 365 pp.

HOBHOUSE, LEONARD TRELAWNEY. *The Metaphysical Theory of the State: A Criticism.* London: Allen and Unwin, 1918. 156 pp.

HOOK, SIDNEY. *From Hegel to Marx: Studies in the Intellectual Development of Karl Marx.* London: Victor Gollancz, 1936. 335 pp.

HUXLEY, ALDOUS LEONARD. *Ends and Means: An Inquiry into the Nature of Ideals and into the Methods Employed for Their Idealization.* London: Chatto & Windus, 1938. 335 pp.

JOHNSON, ALAN CAMPBELL. *Viscount Halifax, a Biography.* London: Robert Hale, 1941. 575 pp.

KOESTLER, ARTHUR. *Darkness at Noon.* New York: Macmillan, 1941. 267 pp.

LASSALLE, FERDINAND. *Franz von Sickingen.* Berlin: Weltgeist-Bucher, n.d. 188 pp.

LINDSAY, A. D. *The Modern Democratic State.* Vol. I. London, New York, Toronto: Oxford University Press, 1943. 286 pp.

LIPPINCOTT, BENJAMIN EVANS. *Victorian Critics of Democracy: Carlyle, Ruskin, Arnold, Stephen, Maine, Lecky.* London: H. Milford, Oxford University Press; Minneapolis: University of Minnesota Press, 1938. 276 pp.

LUBAC, HENRI DE. *The Un-Marxian Socialist: A Study of Proudhon.* Translated by R. E. Scantlebury. New York: Sheed & Ward, 1948. 304 pp.

LYONS, EUGENE, ed. *We Cover the World.* By Fifteen Foreign Correspondents. New York: Harcourt, Brace, 1937. 441 pp.

McCUTCHEN, DAVID TALMADGE. "Technique for Democracy." Unpublished Ph.D. dissertation, University of Pennsylvania, 1938. 95 pp.

MacIVER, R. M., ed. *Integrity and Compromise: Problems of Public and Private Conscience.* New York: Harper & Brothers, 1957. 150 pp.

MAINE, HENRY SUMNER. *Village-Communities in the East and West.* London: J. Murray, 1871. 216 pp.

MAITRA, SUSHIL KUMAR. *The Ethics of the Hindus.* Calcutta: University Press, 1925. 331 pp.

MAISTRE, JOSEPH MARIE, comte de. *Oeuvres.* Paris: J. P. Migne, 1862. 642 pp.

———. *Les Soirées de Saint-Pétersbourg, extraits.* Paris: J. Gillequin, 1910. 215 pp.

MANNHEIM, KARL. *Ideology and Utopia: An Introduction to the Sociology of Knowledge.* New York: Harcourt, Brace, 1936. 318 pp.

MILLER, WEBB. *I Found No Peace: The Journal of a Foreign Correspondent.* New York: The Literary Guild, 1936. 325 pp.

MITCHISON, NAOMI. *The Moral Basis of Politics*. London: Constable, 1938. 366 pp.

MOOKERJI, RADHA KUMUD. *Nationalism in Hindu Culture*. London, Los Angeles (etc.): Theosophical Publishing House, 1921. 104 pp.

MORLEY, LORD JOHN. *On Compromise*. London: Chapman and Hall, 1877. 227 pp.

NEHRU, JAWAHARLAL. *The Discovery of India*. New York: John Day, 1946. 581 pp.

————. *Jawaharlal Nehru: An Autobiography, with Musings on Recent Events in India*. New ed. containing an additional chapter. London: John Lane The Bodley Head, 1942. 616 pp.

————. *Towards a New Revolution*. New Delhi: Indian National Congress, 1956. 21 pp.

PARK, RICHARD L. and IRENE TINKER, eds. *Leadership and Political Institutions in India*. Princeton: Princeton University Press, 1959.

PAULLIN, THEODORE. *Introduction to Non-Violence*. Non-Violent Action in Tension Areas Series III, No. 1. Philadelphia: The Pacifist Research Bureau, 1944. 58 pp.

POPPER, KARL R. *The Open Society and Its Enemies*. London: Routledge and Kegan Paul, 1949. 2 vols.

PRIESTLEY, F. E. L., ed. *Enquiry Concerning Political Justice and Its Influence on Morals and Happiness by William Godwin*. Critical introduction and notes. Toronto: University of Toronto Press, 1946. 3 vols.

PYARELAL. *A Pilgrimage for Peace: Gandhi and Frontier Gandhi Among N.W.F. Pathans*. Ahmedabad: Navajivan, 1950. 206 pp.

QUIGLEY, HAROLD S., ed. *Peace or War? A Conference*. Minneapolis: University of Minnesota Press, 1937. 205 pp.

RADHAKRISHNAN, S. *The Heart of Hindusthan*. 5th ed. Madras: Natesan, 1945. 125 pp.

————. *Indian Philosophy*. London: Allen and Unwin, 1940. 2 vols.

————. *Mahatma Gandhi: Essays and Reflections on His Life and Work*. Presented to him on his Seventieth Birthday, October 2nd, 1939. 2nd enl. ed. London: Allen and Unwin, 1949. 557 pp.

————., ed. *The Principal Upanisads*. With Introduction, Text, Translation and Notes. London: Allen & Unwin, 1953. 938 pp.

ROY, KSHITIS, ed. *Gandhi Memorial Peace Number*. Santiniketan (India): The Visva-Bharati Quarterly, 1949. 337 pp.

SABINE, GEORGE H. *A History of Political Theory*. New York: Henry Holt, 1947. 775 pp.

SAKLATVALA, SHAPURJI and M. K. GANDHI. *Is India Different? The Class Struggle in India: Correspondence on the Indian Labour Movement and Modern Conditions*. London: Communist Party of Great Britain, 1927. 35 pp.

SALE, GEORGE. *The Koran*. Translated into English from the original Arabic. London: Frederick Warne and Co., Ltd., n.d. 596 pp.

SAVARKAR, V. D. *Hindu Rashtravad: Being an Exposition of the Ideology and Immediate Programme of Hindu Rashtra.* Collected and edited by Satya Parkash. 218 pp.

SCHUSTER, E. M. *Native American Anarchism: A Study of Left-Wing American Individualism.* Smith College Studies in History, Vol. XVII, No. 1-4. Northampton, Massachusetts: Department of History of Smith College, 1932. 197 pp.

SCHWEITZER, ALBERT. *Indian Thought and Its Development.* Translated by Mrs. Charles E. B. Russell. London: Hodder and Stoughton, 1936. 265 pp.

SHRIDHARANI, KRISHNALAL. *War Without Violence: A Study of Gandhi's Method and Its Accomplishments.* New York: Harcourt, Brace, 1939. 323 pp.

SITARAMAYYA, BHOGARJU PATTABHI. *The History of the Indian National Congress: (1885-1935).* Madras: Working Committee of the Congress, 1935. 1038 pp.

SMITH, THOMAS VERNON. *Discipline for Democracy.* Chapel Hill: The University of North Carolina Press, 1942. 137 pp.

SMITH, WILFRED CANTWELL. *Modern Islam in India: A Social Analysis.* Lahore: Minerva Book Shop, 1943. 343 pp.

SONDHI, G. C., ed. *To the Gates of Liberty: Congress Commemoration Volume.* Calcutta: Swadesh Bharati, 1948. 416 pp.

STIRNER, MAX. *The Ego and His Own.* Translated from the German by Steven T. Byington. London: A. C. Fifield; New York: E. C. Walker, 1912. 506 pp.

TENDULKAR, D. G. *Mahatma.* Bombay: Jhaveri and Tendulkar, 1952. 8 vols.

TOLSTOI, L. N. *My Religion.* Translated from the French by Huntington Smith. New York: Y. T. Crowell, 1885. 274 pp.

WEBER, MAX. *The Theory of Social and Economic Organization.* Translated by A. M. Henderson, edited by Talcott Parsons. New York: Oxford University Press, 1947. 436 pp.

DOCUMENTS

Congress Presidential Addresses. Full Text of the Presidential Addresses (of the Indian National Congress) from 1911 to 1934. 2nd ser. Madras: G. A. Natesan, 1934.

Gandhi-Jinnah Talks: Text of Correspondence and Other Relevant Matter, July-October, 1944. New Delhi: Hindustan Times, 1944.

Indian Labour Gazette. Government of India, Ministry of Labour, Labour Bureau. Vol. VIII, No. 9, March 1951.

India in 1919. A report prepared for presentation to Parliament in accordance with the requirements of the 26th Section of the Government of India Act by L. F. Rushbrook Williams. Calcutta: Home Department, Government of India, 1920.

BIBLIOGRAPHY

India in 1928-29. A statement prepared for presentation to Parliament in accordance with the requirements of the 26th Section of the Government of India Act (5 & 6 Geo. V, Ch. 61). Calcutta: Government of India Central Publications Branch, 1930.

India in 1930-31. A statement prepared for presentation to Parliament in accordance with the requirements of the 26th Section of the Government of India Act (5 & 6 Geo. V, Ch. 61). Calcutta: Government of India Central Publications Branch, 1932.

India in 1931-32. A statement prepared for presentation to Parliament in accordance with the requirements of the 26th Section of the Government of India Act (5 & 6 Geo. V, Ch. 61). Calcutta: Government of India Central Publications Branch, 1933.

The Legislative Assembly Debates (Official Report). Vol. IV, 1930. Simla: Government of India Press, 1931.

REFERENCE WORKS

The Indian Annual Register: An Annual Digest of Public Affairs of India, January-June 1930. Edited by NRIPENDRA NATH MITRA. Vol. I. Calcutta: The Annual Register Office, 1930.

The Indian Annual Register: An Annual Digest of Public Affairs of India, July-December 1930. Edited by NRIPENDRA NATH MITRA. Vol. II. Calcutta: The Annual Register Office, 1930.

The Indian Annual Register: An Annual Digest of Public Affairs of India, January-June 1931. Edited by NRIPENDRA NATH MITRA. Vol. I. Calcutta: The Annual Register Office, 1931.

The Indian Annual Register: An Annual Digest of Public Affairs of India, July-December 1931. Edited by NRIPENDRA NATH MITRA. Vol. II. Calcutta: The Annual Register Office, 1931.

The Indian Year Book 1929. Edited by STANLEY REED and S. T. SHEPPARD. Bombay: Bennett, Coleman and Co., 1929.

Indian Press Digests. Edited by MARGARET W. FISHER and JOAN V. BONDURANT. Vol. II, No. 7. Berkeley: Institute of East Asiatic Studies of the University of California, 1955.

The Indian Quarterly Register: Being a Quarterly Journal of Indian Public Affairs in Matters Political, Social and Economic, etc., July-December 1928. Edited by NRIPENDRA NATH MITRA. Vol. II. Calcutta: The Annual Register Office, 1928.

The Indian Quarterly Register: Being a Quarterly Journal of Indian Public Affairs in Matters Political, Social and Economic, etc., January-June 1929. Edited by NRIPENDRA NATH MITRA. Vol. I. Calcutta: The Annual Register Office, 1929.

The Roots, Verb-Forms, and Primary Derivatives of the Sanskrit Language. By WILLIAM DWIGHT WHITNEY. Leipzig: Breitkopf and Hartel; London: Trübner and Co., 1885.

BIBLIOGRAPHY

Sanskrit-English Dictionary, Etymologically and Philologically Arranged. By MONIER MONIER-WILLIAMS. New edition enlarged and improved. Oxford: Clarendon Press, 1899.

ARTICLES

BONDURANT, JOAN V. "The Case for Redefining the Legal Sanction of the Democratic State," *Politics of Persuasion,* ed. K. P. Misra and Rajendra Avasthi. Bombay: P. C. Manaktala and Sons, 1967.

————. "Satyagraha vs. Duragraha: The Limits of Symbolic Violence," *Gandhi: His Relevance for Our Time,* ed. G. Romachandran and T. K. Mahadevan. Bombay: Bharatiya Vidya Bhavan, 1964, pp. 67-81.

BONDURANT, JOAN V. AND MARGARET W. FISHER. "The Concept of Change in Hindu, Socialist, and Neo-Gandhian Thought," *South Asia Politics and Religion,* ed. Donald E. Smith. Princeton, N. J.: The Princeton University Press, 1966, pp. 235-248.

————. "Ethics in Action: Contrasting Approaches to Social and Political Problems in Modern India," *Australian Journal of Politics and History* (special number, *Modern India,* ed. Gordon Greenwood), XII, 2 (August 1966), 177-193.

BOSE, N. K. "An Interview with Mahatma Gandhi," *The Modern Review* (Calcutta), LVIII, October 1935.

BRAILSFORD, H. N. "Why India Follows Gandhi," *The Forum,* LXXXV, May 1931.

COOKE, MORRIS LLEWELLYN. "The Quaker Way Wins New Adherents," *The New York Times Magazine,* June 17, 1951.

GANDHI, M. K. "Statement on Caste Restrictions," *Indian Social Reformer,* November 12, 1932.

HOPKINS, WASHBURN. "On the Hindu Custom of Dying to Redress a Grievance," *Journal of the American Oriental Society,* Vol. XXI, July-December 1900.

LEE, G. FITZ-GERALD. "Tribes of the Tirah," *The Eastern World,* III, March 1949.

LUDLOW, ROBERT. "The Gandhian Revolution," *The Catholic Worker,* February 1950.

MICHELS, ROBERTO. "Conservatism," *Encyclopaedia of the Social Sciences,* IV, 1935.

"The North-West Frontier of India," Geographical Record, *The Geographical Review,* XVI, 1926.

SHEEAN, VINCENT. "Gandhiji's Last Discourse," *The Bombay Chronicle Weekly,* February 22, 1948.

SMITH, T. V. "Democracy and Human Destiny," *Human Destiny,* I, 1951.

SPITZ, DAVID. "Democracy and the Problem of Civil Disobedience," *The American Political Science Review,* June 1954.

"The Struggle with Congress," *The Roundtable,* XXII, March 1932.

"The Unrest on the Indian Frontier," *The Roundtable,* XXI, March 1931.

BIBLIOGRAPHY

NEWSPAPERS

Harijan (Ahmedabad), 1932-1951.

The New York Times, April 1930-July 1930.

Times of India (Bombay), March 1928-August 1928.

Young India (Ahmedabad), 1919-1932.

Compilations: *Young India, 1919-1922.* Madras: S. Ganesan, 1922. Vols. I-II.

> *Young India, 1924-1926.* New York: The Viking Press, 1927.

GLOSSARY

ahimsa	non-injury
aparigraha	non-possession
asteya	non-stealing
ashram	a retreat for research and study; an institution on monastic lines, but not necessarily of religious application
bania	of the class of traders and money-lenders
brahmacharya	celibacy; chastity
charkha	spinning wheel
dharma	duty; right course of conduct or action; religion
dharna (dhurna, dharana)	a form of sit-down strike
duragraha	stubborn persistence
goonda	ruffian
harijan	untouchable; literally, people of God
hartal	closing of shops and suspension of work, often as a sign of mourning
himsa	violence; injury
hizrat	voluntary exile; mass emigration
jirga	tribal council
karma	the doctrine of existence conditioned by the sum of good and evil action
khaddar, khadi	hand-spun and hand-woven cloth
lathi	a five-foot club tipped with metal

mahal	subdivision of a taluka
moksha	liberation from earthly bondage; salvation
panchayat	originally a committee or council of five members, now a small local council
parda (purdah)	the veil; institution of seclusion of women
patel	village headman
Quran	Koran, the holy book of Islam
sabha	assembly; society
sanatani	a strict follower of ancient Vedic religion; orthodox
satya	truth
satyagraha	truth-force, or, the technique developed by Gandhi for social and political change, based on truth, non-violence, and self-suffering
satyagrahi	one who practices satyagraha
savarna	orthodox
swadeshi	belonging to or made in one's own country
swaraj	self-rule; independence
talati	subordinate officer in charge of the collection of revenue of a village
taluka	a major administrative subdivision of a district
tapasya, tapas	religious penance; austerity; sacrifice
varna	caste, color
varnashrama	four-fold division of Hindu society
vethia	village peon

yoga	Hindu system of contemplation for effecting union of the human soul with the Supreme Being
yogi	one who practices yoga
zamindar	landholder

INDEX

aboriginals, 54

action; and the Gandhian dialectic, 189-196; philosophy of, 210; purposive, 195 and note; technique of, 4, 144, 188, 213, 230-231, 232-233

agape, 24

Agarwal, S. N., 126, 182

aggression, 96, 101

agitation, 40

agreement, 33-34, 161-164

ahimsa; defined, 23-24; function of in truth-seeking, 20; Gandhian conceptual innovations, 24-26, 111-113; Ghaffar Khan and, 139; independent of religion, 112; leads to social service, 32; as means, 25; in practice, 26; success of, 113; in traditional Hinduism, 111; truth inseparable from, 23

Ahmedabad labor satyagraha; outline of action, 65-71; summary analysis, 71-73

Ameer Ali, Syed, 142 note

anarchism; failure of, 186; and Gandhi, 172-188; and non-violence, 174; and violence, 173, 177, 185-187

Andrews, C. F., 120, 129

Antigone, 3

aparigraha, 12, 106, 154

arbitration; at Ahmedabad, 69, 70, 72-73; and satyagraha, 72-73

aristocracy; agency of reform, 208; agency of social virtue, 167; T. S. Eliot on, 204

Arjuna, 116

asteya, 106

atheism, 152, 193

authoritarian idealism; described, 211-213; in de Maistre, 205; and means, 211-214; post-Hegelian, 214

Bakunin, Mikhail; his anarchism, 178; contrast to Gandhi, 173; on labor non-cooperation, 186; his tactical failure, 187

banias, 60

Banker, Shankarlal, 66

Bardoli peasant satyagraha; outline of action, 53-61; summary analysis, 61-64

Beer, Samuel, 195 note

being, 17 and note, 19

Bentham, Jeremy, 216

Berkman, Alexander, 177

Bhagavad Gita, 112, 116-118

Bhave, Acharya Vinoba, *see* Vinoba

bhoodan yajna, 6-7

Bible, 121

de Bonald, Louis G. A., 203

Bosanquet, Bernard, 163 note

Bose, N. K., 18, 174

Bose, Subhas Chandra, 126

boycott; in the Bardoli campaign, 56, 58; as non-violent coercion, 10, 40; in the Salt satyagraha, 101

Brahma, 16

brahmacharya, 12

Brailsford, H. N., 120

bread-labor, 156-157

Broomfield Committee, 60

Burke, Edmund; conservative position summarized, 208; on the constitution, 203; on constitutional "a priorism," 202; on landed aristocracy, 167; on law, 163, 202; on liberty, 201, 211; on natural aristocracy, 204; on progress, 159-160; on reform, 206-208; on society, 159; on subversion, 208-211; on truth, 164

capital, 157-158

Carlyle, Thomas, 13, 170

Case, C. M., 10, 11

caste system; described, 160, 168; Gandhi on, 168-169